Use and Impact of Information and Communication
Technologies in Developing Countries' Small Businesses

T0200323

DEVELOPMENT ECONOMICS AND POLICY

Series edited by Franz Heidhues and Joachim von Braun

Vol. 27

PETER LANG

Frankfurt am Main · Berlin · Bern · Bruxelles · New York · Oxford · Wien

Use and Impact of Information and Communication Technologies in Developing Countries' Small Businesses

Evidence from Indian Small Scale Industry

Dietrich Müller-Falcke

PETER LANG

Europäischer Verlag der Wissenschaften

Die Deutsche Bibliothek - CIP-Einheitsaufnahme

Müller-Falcke, Dietrich:
Use and impact of information and communication technologies
in developing countries' small businesses : evidence from Indian
Small Scale Industry / Dietrich Müller-Falcke. - Frankfurt am
Main ; Berlin ; Bern ; Bruxelles ; New York ; Oxford ; Wien :
Lang, 2002
(Development economics and policy ; Vol. 27)
Zugl.: Göttingen, Univ., Diss., 2001
ISBN 3-631-39320-2

D 7
ISSN 0948-1338
ISBN 3-631-39320-2
US-ISBN 0-8204-5959-3

© Peter Lang GmbH
Europäischer Verlag der Wissenschaften
Frankfurt am Main 2002
All rights reserved.

Printed in Germany 1 2 3 4 6 7

www.peterlang.de

FOREWORD

The role of information in economic development has long been neglected. The idea that, through its influence on individual incentives and institutions, the specific set-up of information systems in developing countries is adverse to sustained economic development has been developed by Joseph Stiglitz, who was awarded the Nobel Price for Economics in 2001 for his work, including information economics.

High costs of acquiring, processing and disseminating information lead to a lack of transparency and consequently to severe constraints in the functioning of markets. Moreover, with the transformation towards an information society in the so-called "industrialised countries" there is the fear of a widening gap for developing countries that further diminishes their development prospects, since they cannot keep pace with the rapid development of information and communication technologies (ICT). Being concerned by the growing "digital divide" on the one hand, but as well recognising the immense potential inherent to ICT on the other a wide range of international activities and programmes has been started covering this issue. The World Bank, with the 1998/99 World Development Report "Knowledge for Development", as well as the UNDP, with the 2001 Human Development Report "Making Technologies Work for Human Development", have stressed the potential of ICT for developing countries. High level bodies such as the G8's "DOT Force" are looking for ways to seize the "digital opportunities" potentially offered by ICT. Due to the pervasive nature of ICT opportunities may exist to enhance the efficiency of markets, to improve governance, to enhance global integration and to foster democracy.

The current publication by Dietrich Müller-Falcke is part of a sequence of timely studies undertaken at the Center for Development Research (ZEF Bonn) on the impact of ICTs for development. The author concentrates on ICT in small enterprises. Small enterprises in developing countries are normally considered operating on a low technological level. Müller-Falcke, however, describes a surprisingly high penetration of ICT among the surveyed Indian Small Scale Industry, indicating a high innovative potential of small enterprises. Telephones, fax machines, cellular phones and e-mail have become a daily tool for many small entrepreneurs – at least in an urban context. The econometric analysis of adoption determinants, developed by the author, reveals that the introduction of ICT is mainly driven by the apparent advantages these technologies offer for enterprises' operations and perspectives. The additional analysis of the impact of ICT suggests a positive effect on enterprises' growth and proves a strong positive perception of the technologies.

This study enhances the understanding of technological innovation in small enterprises and raises awareness of the potentials, which ICTs offer for this important business section of developing countries' economies. Properly applied ICT can ease resource constraints faced by small entrepreneurs and expand markets. The results of the study call as well for a redesign of institutions in order to enable a rapid expansion of telecommunication networks and the spread of modern ICT to still unserved areas in order to enable small businesses participation in a global economy.

Prof. Dr. Joachim von Braun

Center for Development Research (ZEF)

University of Bonn

Prof. Dr. Franz Heidhues

Center for Tropical Agriculture

University of Hohenheim

ACKNOWLEDGEMENTS

This work would not have been possible without substantial support of various people and organisations. First of all, I would like to thank my advisor Prof. Dr. Wolfgang König who guided me throughout this dissertation and provided decisive impulses to carry on with this work. Moreover, I thank my second advisor Prof. Dr. Joachim von Braun for the opportunity to work in the stimulating atmosphere of the Center for Development Research (ZEF) and for his advise on the dissertation.

The field research in India was conducted in collaboration with Velammal College of Management and Computer Studies, Chennai. I would like to thank Dr. S.N. Soundararajan who made this co-operation possible. Moreover, I thank the students from Velammal College's Management Department for their enthusiasm and the good interviewing work. The survey would not have been possible without the active support of the Ambattur Industrial Estate Manufacturers' Association (AIEMA). Namely, I would like to thank K.P. Gopal, C.L.S Rosario and especially K. Srikanth for their interest in the study and help they provided. I am also obliged to all entrepreneurs, who invested their time participating in the survey. Special thanks go to Dr. Kaushalesh Lal from the Institute of Economic Growth, New Delhi, for providing valuable insights into technology use by Indian enterprises.

I profited a lot in preparing this dissertation from comments and discussions with a number of friends and colleagues, especially from ZEF. I would like to thank in particular Dr. Arjun S. Bedi, Dr. Maximo Torero and Dr. Susanna Wolf for their profound comments on method and content at various stages of this work. Moreover, I thank Matthias Blum, Angela Hullmann, Maria Iskandarani, Jörg Oelschläger, Gi-Soon Song and in particular Romeo Bertolini for fruitful discussions and shared insights.

Finally, I want to thank Anna for her support and patience, which has been of invaluable importance at all stages of this work.

TABLE OF CONTENTS

ABBREVIATIONS

AIAI	All Indian Associations of Industries
AIEMA	Ambattur Industrial Estate Manufacturers' Association
B2B	Business to Business
CAD/CAM	Computer Added Design / Computer Added Manufacturing
CEO	Chief Executive Officer
CII	Confederation of Indian Industry
CNC	Computer Numerically Control
COAI	Cellular Operators Association of India
CPP	Calling Party Pays
DoT	Department of Telecommunication
EDI	Electronic Data Interchange
ERNET	Education and Research Network
FASII	Federation of Associations of Small Industries of India
FNF	Friedrich Naumann Foundation
FTP	File Transfer Protocol
GNP	Gross National Product
GSM	Global System Mobile
ICT	Information and Communication Technology
IDC	International Data Corporation
ILO	International Labor Organisation
ISDN	Integrated Services Digital Network
ISP	Internet Service Provider
IT	Information Technology
ITU	International Telecommunication Union
MAIT	Manufacturers Association of Information Technology
MBA	Master of Business Administration
Mbps	Megabits per Second
MHz	Megahertz
MIS	Management Information System
MLE	Maximum Likelihood Estimator
NASSCOM	National Association of Software & Service Companies

NCAER	National Council of Applied Economic Research
NGO	Non-governmental Organisation
NTP 1999	New Telecom Policy 1999
NTP 1994	National Telecom Policy 1994
OLS	Ordinary Least Squares
PC	Personal Computer
PCA	Principal Component Analysis
PCO	Public Call Office
PPP	Purchasing Power Parity
R&D	Research and Development
Rs.	Indian Rupees
SIDCO	Small Industries Development Corporation
SISI	Small Industries Service Institutes
SME	Small and Medium-sized Enterprise
SMS	Short Message Service
SSI	Small Scale Industry
STRATOS	Strategic Orientation of Small and Medium Enterprises
TRAI	Telecom Regulatory Authority of India
U.S.	United States of America
US$	US-Dollar
WTO	World Trade Organisation
WWW	World Wide Web

LIST OF TABLES

LIST OF ANNEX TABLES

LIST OF FIGURES

1. INTRODUCTION

1.1. Problem setting

For some time information and knowledge have been considered important issues for developing countries. Stiglitz (1988) shows in his 'information-theoretic' approach to economic development, how the cost of information is influencing institutions and development perspectives. Information systems in developing countries often function in a way that makes the acquisition and distribution of information difficult and costly. Especially entrepreneurship and innovation are constrained by these information problems (Leibenstein 1968; Stiglitz 1988). Contrary, in the developed world information is considered a prime source of competitiveness (Porter / Millar 1985).

The information problem of developing countries gained prominence through the 1984 International Telecommunication Union's (ITU) special report *"The Missing Link"*, the so-called Maitland Report. The main issue it addressed was the deficiency of developing countries' telecommunication infrastructure that was assumed to seriously constrain development prospects (Mansell 1999). The following focus on regulatory issues and changes in technologies, i.e. the rise of mobile communications and the Internet, along with a dramatic decline of prices for transmitting information, led to a widened agenda (Forge 1995). In the second half of the 1990s the importance of knowledge and the establishment of effective knowledge systems in developing countries became the prime topic (World Bank 1998). Nowadays, attention has shifted to the major task to enable developing countries to participate in and reap some of the supposed benefits of the "Global Information Society" (G8 2000).

The major tools to acquire, store, process and disseminate information and to generate knowledge from information are modern information and communication technologies (ICTs). In the discussion outlined above, almost every international organisation stresses the importance of ICTs for sustainable economic development. The World Bank (1998:9), for example states in the World Development Report 1998/99 *"Knowledge for Development"*:

> *"This new technology greatly facilitates the acquisition and absorption of knowledge, offering developing countries unprecedented opportunities to enhance educational systems, improve policy formation and execution, and widen the range of opportunities for business and the poor."*

The potential ICTs have to enhance business development in developing countries is often stressed, as in the World Bank quote above. ICTs play a key role in globalisation (Avgerou 1998). Firstly, they have an enabling role for globalisation through their property to reduce time and space barriers. Secondly, ICTs are major determinants of competitiveness in the global economy, for enterprises as well as for countries (e.g. Hanna 1994; Hanna et al. 1996). Thus, ICTs may enable developing country businesses to participate in global markets but at the same time they also expose them to global competition (Mansell 1999).

Besides the globally operating enterprises, small businesses in developing countries are expected to benefit from access to ICTs, too. Players in small and remote markets can reduce information costs significantly, they have the potential to widen their markets and to become less dependent on middlemen for their businesses (Barten / Bear 1999). Evidence of these proposed effects is, however, still scarce. There is hardly any formal empirical research that accounts for ICT use in developing countries' small businesses. Most available evidence is, so far, of anecdotal nature or does not appear to be representative.[1]

1.2. Research questions and motivation

The aim of this work is to close the described gap by providing empirical evidence of ICT use and benefits derived from its use in small businesses located in a developing country. To shoulder this task three different questions have to be addressed:

1. To what extent are different ICTs already used by small enterprises and how does this use relate to the businesses' environment?

Since evidence on ICT use by small businesses in developing countries is scarce and ICTs markets are changing fast taking the stock of what is there is the first priority.

2. Why have ICTs been adopted by small businesses and what factors determine their use?

Since not all enterprises adopt new technologies at the same time there have to be specific factors that determine the time of adoption. To identify these factors will help to provide measures to enhance technology use.

3. Is there any measurable impact on business performance derived from ICT use?

In the discussion outlined above positive impacts of ICTs on business performance has been suggested. These possible effects are open to empirical verification. It still remains to be proven to what extent ICTs really change operations for developing countries' small businesses.

These questions will be answered by examining the adoption and use of ICTs in Indian small manufacturing enterprises. 295 businesses, located in an Industrial estate in the city of Chennai (formerly Madras) and belonging to the Indian Small Scale Industry (SSI) sector, were interviewed for this purpose.

1.3. Study structure

The study is structured according to the three research questions. However, at first, in Chapter 2 the characteristics of ICTs and the mechanisms how ICTs are expected to influence economic growth and business development are examined in more detail (Section 2.1). Furthermore, the peculiarities of small-scale enterprises and the specific problems they face in developing countries are discussed (Section 2.2).

The question about the actual evidence of use is addressed in Chapter 3. Section 3.1 describes the conditions faced by the surveyed enterprises, i.e. the development and problems of the Indian SSI sector as well as of Indian telecommunication and informa-

---

[1]   The World Bank is providing a few stories of successful ICT use by small businesses in the World Development Report 1998/99 (World Bank 1998:61). Other evidence of successful activities, such as for example e-commerce by small-scale producers, is often outcome of heavily subsidised donor-funded projects and therefore are not representative (e.g. projects by VITA.org).

tion technology (IT) markets. Special emphasis is given to the situation in the direct environment of the sampled enterprises. Section 3.2 introduces the survey process in detail. Section 3.3 provides an overview over general characteristics of the participating enterprises. Finally in Section 3.4 evidence of ICT usage is presented and linked to the basic enterprise characteristics presented in Section 3.3.

Chapter 4 is concerned with determinants of adoption and use in the surveyed enterprises, i.e. covering question two. Theories of technology adoption and diffusion are reviewed in Section 4.2 and checked for their appropriateness for the purpose of analysis. Empirical evidence of ICT adoption in small-scale enterprise is reviewed in Section 4.3. This section covers as well the scarce evidence from developing countries. Departing from this review, a model of technology adoption determinants is developed in Section 4.4. This general model is specified and applied for the survey data in Section 4.5. Three different aspects with this model are tested, firstly, identifying determinants of adoption, secondly, identifying determinants for the time of adoption, and, thirdly, identifying determinants of the intensity of use. The findings are discussed in Section 4.6.

The question of impact of ICT use is discussed in Chapter 5. Section 5.1 outlines the problems that occur when measuring impacts of ICTs in general and specifically in small-scale enterprises. Some relatively unproblematic measures are proposed. Testing for the impact of ICTs on these measures in the sampled enterprises is undertaken in Section 5.2. Perceived effects, anecdotes about effects and statistical tests are presented. The entire argument is summed up and policy conclusions are finally drawn in Chapter 6.

2. SMALL-SCALE ENTERPRISES AND INFORMATION AND COMMUNICATION TECHNOLOGIES (ICTS) IN DEVELOPING COUNTRIES

2.1. The impact of ICTs on business development

2.1.1. Definition and specificity of ICTs

Information and communication technologies (ICTs) are defined as "electronic means of capturing, processing, storing and communicating information" (Heeks 1999:3). They "enable the handling of information and facilitate different forms of communication among human actors, between human beings and electronic systems, and among electronic systems" (Hamelink 1997). The common feature of all ICTs is their electronic character and the "digitisation" of information, i.e. the reduction of information to ones and zeros.[2] ICTs comprise different components, i.e. networks, services and terminal equipment (Figure 2-1):

Figure 2-1: Components of information and communication technologies

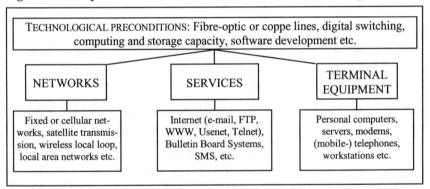

Source: Seibel / Müller-Falcke / Bertolini (1999:6).

In this work the information gathering, processing and communicating properties of ICTs are examined. Therefore, the focus is on communication technologies, i.e. fixed line telephony, cellular phones and pagers, and the Internet and its services. The use of information technologies in production and the wide literature on the impact of information technologies in production is consequently considered only in this context. However, the term ICT will be applied throughout this work for the technologies mentioned above.

The handling of information, and the technologies available for this task, is embedded in information systems made up of people and processes, which are set in a wider environment of institutions. This systemic view of information and information technologies is visualised in Heeks (1999) (Figure 2-2):

---

[2] In fixed-line telecommunication transmission can still be analogue but the trend to digital switches and transmission technologies is also strong in developing countries.

Figure 2-2: Systemic view of information and communication technologies

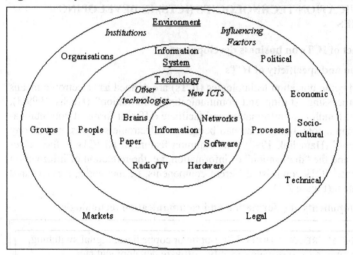

Source: Heeks (1999:4).

ICTs have a couple of inherent properties that influence their impact and use in the handling of information, i.e. decoupling, the generation of content-related, as well as network externalities and pervasiveness (Bedi 1999:6-7). Decoupling means that ICTs have the ability to separate information from its physical repository. Large volumes of information can be transmitted immediately without the physical movement of infor-mation storage, i.e. individuals or objects (Bedi 1999:6). This property allows for con-tent-related externalities. Access to information becomes non-rivalrous if it is possible to transfer it at low cost without any movement of the information source.[3]

Another specific feature of ICTs is the existence of network externalities, i.e. with each additional user the utility of a network increases for the present users. These ex-ternalities are direct network effects, generated on the demand side of communication networks. On the supply side indirect network effects are generated if the expansion of the network leads to economies of scale in provision and lowers the price of using the network (Schoder 2000:182-183). Network externalities constitute an advantage of large networks over small ones. A network has to reach a "critical mass" in order to become sustainable (Weiber 1992). Existing networks therefore have a decisive advan-tage over contenders planning to set-up a similar network. Network development be-comes path dependent as issues such as compatibility and standards gain greater im-portance in network development.[4]

---

[3]   Content-related externalities, however, occur only in the transmission of information. To interpret
       and apply information specific knowledge is needed. If this knowledge is tacit, i.e. it is embedded
       in the information source, information cannot be used effectively and the role of content-related
       externalities diminishes.

[4]   A detailed account on the economics of information networks is given by Antonelli (1992).

The last property to discuss is the pervasive nature of ICTs. ICTs are not restricted to specific sectors of the economy. They can be applied and used for a wide range of purposes and tasks in business, private and public environments in each of which they can be tailored for specific needs (Bedi 1999:6). These general purpose technologies will generate economic benefits beyond the actual investment because they will facilitate complementary technical and organisational innovations (Avgerou 1998:17; Brynjolfsson / Hitt 2000:24). Owing to these properties ICTs are assigned a positive influence on the whole economy, as well as on the functioning of organisations.

2.1.2. ICTs and economic development

Countering the neo-classical assumption of frictionless markets, Stiglitz (1988) presents an information-theoretic approach to economic development. He stresses the costliness of information and changes in behaviour of individuals in the presence of imperfect information. In this thinking institutions are endogenous since they adapt to information costs. However, in the presence of imperfect information the economy will not be in a Pareto-efficient state even if rationality of individuals and the adaptability of institutions is assumed. Thus, information and the handling of information by individuals will have a decisive influence on the development of the economy.

In the previous section it has been shown how ICTs influence the gathering, storing, processing and dissemination of information. Therefore, the application of ICTs can be expected to have an influence on the behaviour of individuals and institutions, i.e. influencing the functioning of markets, institutions and organisations (Bedi 1999). The two former mechanisms are described briefly in this section, which the latter is covered in more detail in the next section.

ICTs' main impact on markets is generated through their property of lowering the costs of gathering, storing, processing and transmitting information, i.e. lowering transaction costs. Norton (1992) shows in a simple supply-demand model that lowering transaction costs decreases the gap between the net price realised by the seller and the net price realised by the buyer of a good, leading to an increase in the equilibrium quantity and bringing markets closer to Pareto-optimal levels. Applying ICTs, therefore, has the potential to enhance existing market activities and to establish new markets, for they lower the threshold for the emergence of markets (Bedi 1999). Overall allocative efficiency is raised.

Decreases in transaction costs through ICTs can be significant. This is shown, for example, by Bayes et al. (1999) for the implementation of mobile phones in Bangladesh villages. Introducing telephone services to previously unserved villages raises consumer surplus in two ways. Firstly by saving the cost and travelling time required to gather market related information, and secondly by achieving higher product prices and lower factor prices through faster and more precise information. Referring to examples like this, the World Bank (1998:60-61) sees ICTs as a powerful instrument to mitigate information deficiencies on prices, market opportunities, best practices and financial systems.

The application of ICTs will not only change market outcomes but may also change the institutions that govern markets (Bedi 1999). Changes in the transaction cost structure will change incentives by changing consumer and producer surpluses. The position of middlemen is believed to weaken when producer and final consumer are better informed about the other side of the market. Outside the economic realm ICTs are expected to empower people and foster participation by providing access to a greater variety of information sources (World Bank 1998:61). Thus the set of institutional choices increases by providing easier accessible information on alternatives.

Special attention is often given to the potential for improved governance and delivery of government services through ICTs. The World Bank's Global Information and Communication Technologies Department (2000), for example, sees opportunities for greater access in decision-making and enhanced opportunities to give voice by marginalized groups through the help of non-governmental organisations (NGOs). Moreover, ICTs can reduce administration costs and the cost of service provision and can open government to more transparency and accountability.

All these aspects indicate the potential stimulating effect of ICTs on economic activity and efficiency, and hence their potential to lead to increased economic growth.[5] Empirical evidence to some extent supports this claim.[6] However, it seems that a certain threshold in telecommunication infrastructure has to be reached before significant growth effects can be generated, i.e. substantial investments are required (Bedi 1999).[7] Furthermore, applications for enhancing administration, such as those described in the previous section, are to a large extent outside the reality for poor developing countries. Avgerou (1998) argues that ICTs can also only unfold their potential when institutions are adapted to the pressure for readjusting in a favourable way through changing incentives and relative costs. She concludes that in developing countries "efforts to spread information and communication technologies are necessary in order to participate in the emerging global economy, but not adequate to create economic growth" (Avgerou 1998:24). Mansell (1999:41) identifies "improved awareness in the public and business sectors, better education and improved literacy rates, user involvement in designing and implementing new services and applications, policies for improved public access to networks, and a readiness on the part of governments and other stakeholders to assume responsibility for selecting and giving priority to a wide range of policy and practical initiatives" as requirements for successful ICT use, restating the pervasive and cross-cutting character of ICTs and the genuine importance of information and information management as such.

2.1.3. ICT infrastructure in developing countries

ICT infrastructure in developing countries is much less developed than in high income countries. Especially with regard to the Internet a wide gap has been created. A variety

---

[5] The recent so-called endogenous theories of economic growth, too, stress the importance of knowledge and human capital for the generation of growth (Maußner / Klump 1996).

[6] In a cross-country study on 47 countries in the period between 1957 and 1977 Norton (1992) finds a strong relation between telecommunication infrastructure and economic growth.

[7] This claim is reaffirmed through a study by Wang (1999) on ICT and economic growth in Taiwan who finds that IT investments in the economy only lead to economic growth if they are supported by a "robust information infrastructure that supports IT adoption and application." (p. 235)

Table 2-1: Selected telecommunication and Internet indicators by country group

Country group	Income	Fixed line telephony					Cellular telephony			Fax	Internet		PC
	GNP per capita measured at PPP in US$ (1999)	Main telephone lines per 100 inhabitants (1999)	Compound average annual growth rate (1995-99)	Waiting time in years (1999)	Faults per 100 mainlines per year (1999)	Ratio of largest city teledensity to rest of country (1999)	Cellular subscribers per 100 inhabitants (1999)	Compound average annual growth rate (1995-99)	Cellular subscribers as percentage of telephone subscribers (1999)	Fax machines per 100 inhabitants (1998)	Internet hosts per 10,000 inhabitants (1999)	Internet users per 100 inhabitants (1999)	PCs per 100 inhabitants (1999)
Low income	1.790	4,32	22,1	0,3	141,8	2,56	1,38	86,9	24,2	0,03	0,39	0,38	0,71
Lower middle income	3.960	11,99	6,7	3,2	31,9	2,73	2,28	64,0	16,0	0,08	4,28	0,79	2,57
Upper middle income	8.320	19,95	7,6	0,7	19,8	1,73	13,40	83,4	40,2	0,35	36,97	4,62	5,80
High income	24.430	58,50	2,6	-	10,6	1,17	37,79	44,9	39,2	5,99	775,65	20,88	34,80
World	6.490	15,16	5,7	0,6	24,8	2,73	8,22	52,6	35,2	1,04	120,46	3,98	6,84

Sources: ITU (2001 and 1999a), World Bank (2000) and own calculations

of initiatives and organisations have expressed concerns about this "digital divide", most notable the Group of Eight in the "Okinawa Charter on Global Information Society" (G8 2000). The "digital divide" is manifested in regulatory deficiencies in developing countries, in imbalances in the infrastructure development, in deficiencies in human capital and in the lack of appropriate applications. In this section the infrastructure aspect and the influence of regulation is briefly described in order to gain insight into the technological options available for businesses in developing countries.

In 1999 high income countries had on average 13.5 times more telephone mainlines per inhabitant, 27.4 times more cellular phones per inhabitant and more than 55 times more Internet users per inhabitant than low income countries (see Table 2-1). This difference is reinforced by a severe rural-urban gap in infrastructure procurement in many developing countries. In many cases significant parts of the country are unserved by mainline and cellular telephone networks. In low income countries teledensity in the largest city is on average 156 percent higher than in other parts of the country, compared to a 17 percent gap in high income countries. However, telecommunication networks in low-income countries are growing much faster on average than in high income countries, narrowing the gap. In particular the global distribution of cellular phones is changing in favour of developing countries (Wellenius et al. 2000). The Internet too is spreading rapidly in developing countries. At the end of 2000 already 83 million of the estimates 315 million Internet users world-wide were located in developing countries (ITU 2001a).

But it is not only the quantity of telecommunication networks that lags behind the industrialised countries but also the quality. Although many developing countries have recently managed to leapfrog stages in technological development by investing in modern switching and transmission technology, in 1999 it was still 13 times more likely for a mainline fault to occur in low income countries than in high income countries (see Table 2-1). This is especially alarming considering the fact that the extent and quality of the telecommunication network is a precondition for the development of the Internet. Canning (1999), for example, shows in a cross-country study that the quality of the network and the provision of Internet hosts are closely related. In addition to the low quality of access use of the Internet is relatively expensive in many low-income countries, constraining its use even further (Seibel et al. 1999:37-38).

A major factor determining the quantity and quality of telecommunication networks in developing countries is regulation. The peculiarities of ICTs that could lead to market failure in their provision were discussed in the previous section. Traditionally, fixed-line telecommunication has been a public monopoly in almost all countries. In many developing countries this proved disastrous, leading to underinvestment, low quality and long waiting lists. However, during the last decade a wave of de-regulation has begun. Different models and sequences of corporisation, privatisation and liberalisation have been applied with the aim of increasing efficiency and achieving the necessary investment for network expansion (Singh 2000). The most important problem in these attempts is how to regulate the market power of the incumbent monopolist and ensure new players' unconstrained entry to the markets. In order to achieve this situation a strong public institution, which can act autonomously from the vested interest of the incumbent monopolist, is needed. In developing countries this has rarely been the case. The example of India, which will be presented in the next chapter, shows the difficulty of establishing an autonomous regulatory regime when interests conflict. Evidence shows that best results, in terms of efficiency and expansion, are achieved if it is possible to ensure competition through adequate property rights and enforcement mechanisms. Singh (2000) concludes from a survey on privatisation and liberalisation in Asian countries that "introducing market competition is slow, messy and difficult to manage but, where present, it is better for growth than privatisation alone."[8] Prudent regulation, therefore, will be a precondition for narrowing the gap in ICT availability and usage between high and low income countries, and within low income countries.

2.1.4. ICTs and business performance

2.1.4.1. The impact of ICTs on organisations' productivity, flexibility and scale

The application of ICTs has an impact on organisations' operations because it changes the cost of handling information, and information is considered a prime factor to determine competitive advantages (Porter / Millar 1985). Through lowering information costs, ICTs enable the transmission of information to increase, and with this increase the quality of information available rises. The speed of communication and information exchange will be enhanced, uncertainty is reduced. Decision making will become improved and better-informed (Bedi 1999). The application of ICTs affects the competitive position of enterprises by changing industry structure, by giving companies new ways to outperform their rivals, and by creating new businesses. ICTs will channel these impacts through their potential to lower costs, enhance differentiation and change competitive scope (Porter / Millar 1985). In this section the influence of ICTs on enterprises' performance, i.e. productivity, flexibility and scale is briefly discussed.

An extensive discussion has evolved around the relationship between investment in ICTs and its effects on productivity. The ever increasing investment in ICTs has failed to show positive effects in aggregate output statistics, indeed productivity growth has slowed down since the early 1970s (Brynjolfsson / Yang 1996). Furthermore empirical studies on U.S. economy showed no or negative impacts of ICT investments until the early 1990. This "productivity paradox" has been explained in a variety of ways (Lefebvre / Lefebvre 1996:60-61). First, conventional measuring methods might have been wrong, not accounting, for product quality for example. Second, ICT adoption requires extensive learning and adjustments, thus their effect is subject to a time lag.[9] Third, ICT adoption only achieves the desired outcomes if it is managed well.[10]

---

[8] The regulation problem is most severe in mainline telephone service markets. For cellular telephony and Internet markets competition has often been achieved from the beginning, leaving these markets more liberalised (ITU 1999a:2). However even in cellular markets it can be shown that growth increases with the number of competitors in the market (Paltridge 2000).

[9] Brynjolfsson and Hitt (2000:33) indicate that evidence of productivity gains rises if longer periods are considered. Productivity increases if investment in IT is combined with organisational change.

[10] To develop the full positive potential of ICTs businesses have to change their strategic orientation. If these changes are not actively promoted by the management or resistance to them cannot be overcome, ICT investments fail to generate favourable results (Dos Santos / Sussman 2000).

Fourth, if not all enterprises benefit from the adoption, the enterprises that do not manage will fall back. The observed net-effect of ICT adoption on industry level will therefore be much lower than expected from evidence by success stories.[11]

Notwithstanding the problems of measuring productivity on the macro level, recent studies that focused on the firm level, showed positive productivity effects. For a data set of 300 large U.S. enterprises Brynjolfsson and Hitt (2000) report a "clear positive relationship but also a great deal of individual variation in firms' success with information technology". Other recent studies that did not concentrate on ICT investment but ICT use, found a relation between use and productivity (Brynjolfsson / Hitt 2000:31-32). These analyses, however, encounter severe problems in determining causality. For ICT investments Brynjolfsson and Hitt (1996) managed to show that attempts to control for causality lead to even higher returns of these investments. However, they still conclude that "there appears to be a fair amount of causality in both directions – certain organizational characteristics make information technology adoption more likely and vice versa." (Brynjolfsson / Hitt 2000:33). With the described evidence the "productivity paradox" seems to be solved. The statistical problems that still exist call for an examination of ICTs' influence on other areas, e.g. quality, flexibility, enterprise structure etc., that are not measured by productivity statistics (Bedi 1999:23; Brynjolfsson / Hitt 2000:45; Brynjolfsson / Yang 1996:192).

Flexibility is considered to be a source of competitive advantage. The capacity to adapt quickly to changing circumstances will give enterprises an edge over their slower adapting rivals. ICT are assigned the ability to enhance flexibility. First, ICTs enable the creation of more flexible links with trading partners through their property of speeding up information exchange. Second, ICTs enhance organisational flexibility when they are adapted to speed up internal processes, or when they allow enterprises to adapt their information systems to changing environments (Golden / Powell 2000:374).[12] Flexibility is considered a special advantage of small enterprises (see section 2.2.2.1 for details). Whether small enterprise will benefit depends, however, on their effectiveness in adopting and adapting ICTs in a way that enhances flexibility. ICTs will improve competitiveness of small enterprises through strengthening one of their core competencies - flexibility, but they can enhance competitiveness of large enterprises too by mitigating one of the weaknesses of large enterprises, i.e. the slow adaptation to changing conditions.

Considering the last argument, it becomes clear that ICTs have an influence on optimal business scale. Alcorta (1994) examines the scale effects for new, ICT-based production technologies, such as CNC machines, which are considered to increase flexibility in production. He stresses that scale is not uni-dimensional but can be measured on the product (batch size) level, on the plant (plant output) level and on the firm (total firm

---

[11] Brynjolfsson and Hitt (1995) show that, besides investment in information technologies, fixed firm characteristics play an important role in determining productivity. Slowly changing organisational practices will therefore affect the returns of ICT investments.

[12] As for productivity, positive effects of applying ICTs depend on the way they are embedded in the organisation. There is evidence that ICTs might also be a source of inflexibility when they change slower than the competitive environment of the enterprise (Golden / Powell 2000:375).

production) level. New flexible production technologies will only have negative scale effects at the product level because it becomes easier and less costly to produce different products with the same equipment. Enhanced flexibility will increase the ability to produce more with the same equipment leading to increased optimal scale at plant level. Since modern ICT-based equipment is in general capital intensive optimal scale in terms of employment on plant level might decrease. Owing to higher fixed costs on the firm level optimal scale tends to rise in the presence of economies of scale in marketing and distribution.

If office automation tools are considered similar results emerge. Hitt (1999) explores the impact of ICTs on firm boundaries, i.e. firm size. Analysing a data set of more than 500 large U.S.enterprises he finds that ICTs are associated with a decline in vertical integration as well as with an increase in diversification. The first result indicates that ICTs are especially beneficial in external co-ordination. Internal, often inherited, communication structures in large, vertically integrated enterprises are not that much affected. This result is in line with other studies which show that ICT and firm size are negatively related at the industry level (Hitt 1999:146). The second result indicates the increase in flexibility through ICTs which enhances possibilities of diversification. Therefore, again, scale effects are not clear-cut although there seems to be a tendency for a decrease in optimal scale with rising ICT investment.

However, most of the results presented in this section were derived from data by large U.S. enterprises. It is not sure whether these results hold for small-scale enterprises and enterprises in developing countries. Therefore, the next section briefly reviews some evidence from developing countries. The peculiarities of small-scale enterprises are discussed afterwards.

2.1.4.2. Evidence from developing countries

While most large-sample studies on the impact of ICTs on business performance have been done with U.S. data, there is only limited evidence on developing countries (Tam 1998). It has been shown that the diffusion of ICTs in developing countries is relatively low. Therefore, many entrepreneurs, especially from small-scale or micro enterprises, have to rely on informal information systems to a much larger extent than their high-income country colleagues (Heeks 1999:10). ICTs, where available, potentially enable enterprises to participate in local, national and global markets due to their properties of reducing information cost and increasing information quality (Mansell 1999:39). Reducing scale at the product level might offer opportunities for local production in places where previously aggregate demand from local sources and exports was insufficient (Alcorta 1994:765-766).

Based on the work of Brynjolfsson and Hitt, Tam (1998) investigates the impact of ICT investments on performance indicators, e.g. return on equity, return on asset and return of sales, for enterprises from Hong Kong, Singapore, Malaysia and Taiwan. As for other studies, results are mixed showing positive, negative or no correlation for different indicators and countries. Since he is using a rather simple lagged-OLS model Tam accounts these unsatisfactory results first to deficiencies in modelling and second to inaccuracy in the data sets. Furthermore he discusses the high probability that impact of ICTs on performance indicators are to a large extent determined by different institutions and societal factors. The study by Tam concentrated on so-called newly industrialised countries. The situation in low-income countries is marked by a poor physical infrastructure. Cane (1992) as well as Elliot (1995) stress the importance of adequate electricity supply and telecommunication infrastructure for the successful introduction of ICTs. If sufficient infrastructure is provided Cane (1992) sees potentials for the integration of developing country businesses in global production chains. Elliot (1995) is more sceptical, identifying three very basic factors as hindrances for more ICT-based businesses. Firstly, high prices for ICT solutions, which lower financial returns. Secondly, wage differentials between high-income and low-income countries, that call for more labour-intensive operations in the latter. Lastly, the lack of ICT systems suitable for a developing country context.

The scarce evidence discussed suggests that in principle impact of ICTs for business development will not be different in developing countries. However, since the decisive effect of computerisation will be on the cost of co-ordination rather than on the cost of production one can expect effects especially in the area of market development and reach (Blili and Raymond, 1993:442).

2.2. Issues of small -scale enterprise development

2.2.1. Defining small-scale enterprises

There is no unified definition of what constitutes small-scale enterprises.[13] The group of enterprises subsumed under this heading is very diverse, covering enterprises from manufacturing to services and enterprises of different size. Definitions depend as well on purposes and aims of the actual work (Hallberg 2000:1). Enterprise scale can be measured in various ways, e.g. in terms of employees, turnover, investments, number of business units, structure of management, which means that it is difficult to classify an enterprise by scale. Moreover, scale is relative, i.e. small-scale enterprises of one sector might be relatively large in others and small enterprises in one country might be considered large in other countries. Thus, a definition of small-scale enterprises depends on purpose and circumstances (König / Billand 1992:15; Mugler 1993:16).

Indicators for a definition can be quantitative or qualitative (König / Billand 1992; Mugler 1993:15). Easy to obtain and highly operative quantitative measures are sales and employment. These are also often used when small enterprises are defined for policy purposes.[14] The most common measure used is employment size. The lower limit for small-scale enterprises is in general set between five and ten employees, the upper limit between 20 and 100 (Hallberg 2000:1; Mugler 1993:26-28).[15] In developing countries the size distribution of enterprises is different from industrialised countries.

---

[13] In many cases literature refers to small and medium-scale enterprises (SMEs). Both categories are rarely distinguished. Therefore in this section the literature reviewed sometimes refers to both categories. However, when distinguishing these enterprises from large ones they are treated equally. Thus, it will be referred to small enterprises even if medium ones are included.

[14] The Indian definition of Small Scale Industry refers to the size of investment in plants and machinery, giving way to group enterprises of very different size under this category.

[15] Medium-scale enterprises will have a lower limit of between 20 and 100 and an upper limit of 100 to 500, thus their definition is even wider.

In general, with rising income more people are employed in larger enterprises (Hallberg 2000:3). Thus, the conventional definition of smallness in terms of employees will cover lower ranges in developing countries.

Quantitative measures, however, may not capture all the different characteristics of small-scale enterprises. Therefore, qualitative indicators can also prove to be useful. Table 2-2, for example, gives a guide for a distinction between SMEs and large enterprises based on qualitative measures.

Table 2-2: Application of qualitative indicators of enterprise size

Category	Small and medium-sized companies	Large companies
Management	Proprietor-entrepreneurship. Functions linked to personalities.	Manager-entrepreneurship. Division of labour by subject matters.
Personnel	Lack of university graduates. All around knowledge.	Dominance of university graduates. Specialisation.
Organisation	Highly personalised contacts.	Highly formalised communication.
Sales	Competitive position not defined and uncertain.	Strong competitive position.
Buyer's relationship	Unstable.	Based on long-term contracts.
Production	Labour intensive.	Capital intensive, economies of scale.
Research and development	Following the market, intuitive approach.	Institutionalised.
Finance	Role of family funds, self-financing.	Diversified ownership structure, access to anonymous capital market.

Source: König / Billand (1992:6).

These indicators, together with quantitative measures, give a reasonable idea of the difference between small-scale and large-scale enterprises. The most important qualitative criteria, seems to be the management and ownership of the enterprise, i.e. the decisive influence of an owner-manager (entrepreneur) in a small-scale enterprise. This strong position of the owner-manager leads to a different approach to gather, process and distribute information by the enterprise, which will be discussed in detail in the next section.

In developing countries small-scale enterprises are often equated with the so-called informal sector. This is, however, not the focus of this work. First, the concept of informality is relatively imprecise (Mead / Morrisson 1996) and, second, it has undergone changing interpretations since its introduction by Hart (1973) and the ILO (1972) in the 1970s.[16] Departing from De Soto's groundbreaking "The Other Path" (De Soto 1989) discussion on informality has recently focused on regulations, legality and the resulting constraints for enterprises (Müller-Falcke 1997). However, the notion of informality opens the view on the motivation of business activities. In the earlier understanding of informal activities these were considered marginal, with their main purpose being survival and subsistence. This view has changed significantly since then and informality can no longer be a category for this phenomenon. Recently micro-enterprises, as a category below small-scale enterprise, have been examined for their business prospects and motivations (e.g. Morrisson et al. 1994). In developing countries most micro-enterprises are family businesses or self-employed persons that have little chance and ability to become larger scale enterprises (Hallberg 2000:1).

A survey on technological innovation in small enterprises should abstract from these survivalist "micro" or "informal" businesses since their innovative capacity is limited. Small-scale enterprises, as understood in this work, therefore include only enterprises above subsistence level in which the personality of the entrepreneur still plays the major role.[17] The most basic features of small-scale in comparison to large-scale enterprises are discussed in the next section.

2.2.2. Specific features and problems of small-scale enterprise

2.2.2.1. Explaining the existence of small-scale enterprises

Economics has several approaches to explain the existence of small enterprises. Neoclassical economics sees firm size determined by economies of scale and scope, which are in turn influenced by production technologies. Size distribution is explained by the existence of minimum efficient scale that extent over a range of sizes, the existence of heterogeneous technologies, and differences in organisational input, e.g. entrepreneurial talent (You 1995:443-445). Another approach centres on the transaction cost argument fostered by Coase (1937) and Williamson (1985). In Coase's account firms exist if the costs of conducting external business transactions exceed internal governance costs for the same operations. The smaller external transaction costs are compared to internal governance cost the smaller the efficient enterprise size will be. According to Williamson (1985:52-61) there are three dimensions of transactions that influence transaction costs, asset specificity, uncertainty and frequency. Depending on the frequency of a transaction, asset specificity and uncertainty are of varying importance, leading to different organisational arrangements, so-called governance structures, that minimise transaction costs (1985:72-79). Changes in technologies will change transaction and governance costs and will therefore, change the efficient governance structure. The cost structure of a transaction will also be affected by the institutional environment, including the legal framework, the degree of trust between economic actors and cultural factors. In high-trust environments or agglomerations, for example, close co-operation between small enterprises might lead to "collective efficiency", a high competitive level of the co-operating group.[18]

---

[16] See Moser (1994) and Rakowski (1994) for a detailed discussion.

[17] A definition that is, for example, also used by Meier (1997:9).

[18] For the concept of collective efficiency see Schmitz (1995) or Pedersen (1994).

Flexibility is a basic characteristic of small enterprises that is referred to in industrial organisation literature (You 1995:452). But, flexibility might be embodied in technology enabling large firms to be flexible too.[19] In general it is assumed that small enterprises can rely on fast internal information flows, quick decision-making and closeness to customers, giving small enterprises that realise this potential, a competitive advantage. Consequently, if flexibility is an important source for competitiveness in a market, size distribution of firms should be relatively biased towards small enterprises.[20]

Evolutionary approaches are concerned with dynamics in enterprises' development. To a large extent they concentrate on innovative activities (which will be discussed in more detail in Section 4.2). In this approach the role of the entrepreneur is greatly emphasised. The control of an owner-manager is an important characteristic of a small-scale enterprise. Hence, the following section focuses on the role of the entrepreneur, and in particular on the consequences this has for communication and information processing in an entrepreneur-driven enterprise.

2.2.2.2. The role of the entrepreneur

The entrepreneur is a difficult figure in economic theory. So far, there is no unified, general accepted theory of entrepreneurial behaviour (Bull / Willard 1995:1). The term entrepreneur can be traced back to the 18th century when Cantillon described an entrepreneur as "someone who exercises business judgement in the face of uncertainty" (Bull / Willard 1995:3). Probably the most influential contribution to the understanding of entrepreneurship is given by Schumpeter who considered the entrepreneur as the driving force in the process of "creative destruction". The role of the entrepreneur in the Schumpeterian sense is to "carry out new combinations" which replace old routines. With this understanding Schumpeter does not restrict entrepreneurial behaviour to enterprises, but extends its applicablility to other organisations. His definition of entrepreneurship is functional. He splits off the function of the entrepreneur from the ownership of an enterprise. Not every owner is an entrepreneur, and managers may also be regarded as entrepreneurs.

This argument points to the fact that there are two uses of the term entrepreneur (Baumol 1995:18-19): First there is the "firm-organising entrepreneur", the one who creates, organises and operates new enterprises. Second there is the "innovating entrepreneur", the one who uses innovations in an economic way, not necessarily by creating new businesses or not. The latter type of entrepreneur is the Schumpeterian entrepreneur. The difficulties of fitting entrepreneurs into economic theory stem mostly from an understanding of the entrepreneur as an "innovating entrepreneur". The newness of

---

[19]   Acs and Audretsch (1990) claim however, that mean plant size is decreasing with the application of flexible production technology. Alcorta (1994) challenges this by stating that flexible production technologies reduce optimal production scale at the product level but probably raise optimal scale at the plant and firm level.

[20]   That flexibility is inherent to small-scale enterprises is not shared by all researchers. Levy and Powell (1998), for example, state that flexibility is less a property of small businesses but more of the small business sector as a whole, which is characterised by a relatively high degree of entries and exits. Small-scale enterprises have only a limited global flexibility because of a low variety of tactical responses to changes in the environment.

his or her actions makes it impossible to model this behaviour. Baumol (1995:22-23) suggests that one can only aim to discover attributes of the individual that makes him/her more likely to become an innovator, or to institutional arrangements that foster the emergence of entrepreneurial behaviour patterns. The "firm-organising entrepreneur", on the other hand, is subject to discussion in economics and business theory. The problems faced by founders of enterprises in establishing their operations and running new enterprises are widely researched and extensive models exist for this purpose (Baumol 1995:20).

For the purpose of this work, entrepreneurs will be understood in the sense of "firm-organising entrepreneurs" The adoption of a new technology will in general be no "innovative" behaviour *per se*. However, it is interesting to look at the process through which the decision-maker in the enterprise arrives at his decision. Thus, the concept of entrepreneurship that will be used has to be closely related to decision making. For this purpose the definition by Casson (1982:23) is useful. He considers an entrepreneur to be "someone who specialized in taking judgmental decisions about the coordination of scarce resources". This definition is very general and, like Schumpeter's definition, functional in nature. It is institution-free, i.e. an entrepreneur is not only found in enterprises but also in other organisations. Important is the relation of judgemental decision making to the entrepreneur. This means that an entrepreneur's choice of action depends on his or her perception of situations in which decisions are required. Owing to different access to information, a different interpretation of information, or simply different preferences decisions will differ under similar circumstances (Casson 1982:24). The emphasis on individual perception in the decision-making process supports Rogers (1995) account of the technology adoption process, which will be presented later. There is also the problem, that the entrepreneur has only limited cognitive resources to gather and process information, which will affect the performance of the enterprise the entrepreneur is running.

2.2.2.3. Information problem in small-scale enterprises

As mentioned in the previous section, neo-classical economic theory has difficulties in incorporating entrepreneurial behaviour. The functions an entrepreneur performs are performed by the Walrasian auctioneer (Casson 1997:4). The auctioneer performs this function for free. In the real world the entrepreneur needs to employ resources in order to arrive at decisions. Gathering and processing information in order to get to an informed decision is not costless and the personal resources of the entrepreneur, who is running a small-scale enterprise, are restricted.

Information, i.e. the ability to gather, select, process and evaluate information, is considered to have become even more important with the development of new ICTs that enhance the quality and quantity of information flows. Therefore, information becomes an important determinant in shaping competitive advantages or disadvantages (Porter / Millar 1985). It will add to the strategies and objectives of small firms and affect their relative competencies in competition, which is trapped between cost leadership and differentiation (Bamberger 1989). Information is needed in a variety of categories in an enterprise. Pleitner (1995) divides the information problem into two dimensions, content and technology. The former one is concerned with information content, which might be internal or external. Internal information comprises, on the one hand, information on management and on the other information on all other functional parts of the enterprise. External information is needed on supply markets, markets for sales and the general business environment. The technological dimension of information comprises the way information is handled, i.e. how it is gathered, selected, processed and evaluated. Thus, the task of information management in an enterprise is pervasive and requires a great deal of resources.

As mentioned above, in small enterprises this task lies, to a large extent, with the entrepreneur. Larger businesses are characterised by a sophisticated division of labour, i.e. they are capable of gathering, evaluating and processing a greater quantity, as well as more specific information. Whereas small enterprises are restricted by the cognitive abilities of the entrepreneur, whose "strategic position serves as a 'focal' point, around which all business activities are centralized" (Lybaert 1998:188). Scanning for information in small-scale enterprises will therefore often be of informal nature (Julien et. al 1999). Acknowledging that dealing with information incurs costs, it is even rational for the entrepreneur not to deal with all the information potentially available to conduct his business. This is the concept of bounded rationality, introduced by Simon in the 1950s (Simon 1987).[21] However, information is still important for business performance. Lybaert (1998) shows that for Belgian SMEs firms that use more information perform better, and are more optimistic about the future.

In general, the information base of a small enterprise is much smaller than the one of large enterprises, since the latter can rely on a sophisticated division of labour in information gathering and processing. Decisions in small-scale enterprises are thus taken rather intuitively and under more severe uncertainty, leading to more risks involved in business. This disadvantages small enterprises compared to larger businesses. However, small enterprises still have the advantage of smaller internal co-ordination costs, including the costs of monitoring and steering internal information flows. The entrepreneur has much more control of the operations within his enterprise than the CEO of a large business. Nevertheless, many small entrepreneurs lead their businesses intuitively, based on prior experience (Pleitner 1995).

Referring back to the transaction cost argument, it has been shown how the mix of internal and external information costs influences the optimal scale of enterprises. The governance structure will be chosen in a way that minimise the sum of internal co-transaction costs (mainly co-ordination costs) and external transaction costs. Internal information costs constitute, besides costs to set-up, maintain and change organisations, a major part of internal transaction costs. Internal information costs consist of cost of the decision process, cost of monitoring, cost of assessing the activities undertaken, management costs and information processing costs (Richter / Furubotn 1996:53). This problem is formalised in principal-agent models. External transaction costs occur in the initiation, negotiation and enforcement of contracts. Significant information costs occur _ex ante_ in the initiation phase in the form of search and informa-

---

[21] Studies on the behaviour of small entrepreneurs show that their decision-making process is intuitive and pragmatic rather than being based on formalised methods and models (e.g. Rice / Hamilton 1979).

tion costs and *ex post* in the enforcement phase as monitoring costs (Richter / Furubotn 1996:51). External information costs will be relatively more important in small-scale enterprises as internal information costs are relatively low. Internal information costs are of higher relative importance in large-scale enterprises. The specific internal and external information costs that occur in special markets and economic activities will, therefore, determine, to some extent, the optimal scale of enterprises operating in this environment (Rautenstrauch 1997:109-113).

Modern ICTs enhance the quantity and quality of information that can be transferred, stored and processed. Thereby the capability to screen the enterprises' environment for relevant information, as well as to co-ordinate internal information flows, is increased (see section 2.1.4.1). The latter aspect will be especially rewarding for large enterprises since costs of co-ordinating internal information flows rise disproportionately with increasing enterprise size. This offsets the potential relative gains that will occur through lowering the costs of generating external information. Due to these two counteracting effects it depends on the specific technologies, organisational characteristics, market conditions and the character of transactions (i.e. specificity, frequency and uncertainty) whether new ICTs will increase or reduce optimal scale.

2.2.2.4. Resource problem of small-scale enterprises

The previous sections showed the importance of the entrepreneur for small-scale business and the information problems related to this. However, it is not only in the field of information that small-scale enterprises face different prospects than large-scale enterprises. Due to their size small businesses are considered resource poor, which makes them more vulnerable to fluctuations in business and framework conditions (Welsh / White 1981:18).[22] This limited resource base restricts operations of small-scale enterprises in factor and product markets. Most of these restrictions are due to high fixed costs and a certain risk involved in participating in these markets.

In input markets small-scale enterprises have only restricted access to capital. As shown in Table 2-2 small-scale enterprises have no access to the anonymous capital market. Bank lending might also be difficult for several reasons. First, lending to small-scale enterprises is more risky since the probability of exit is larger. Second, lending to small-scale enterprises incurs relatively high costs per unit. Therefore, credit might only be available at higher rates or not at all for small-scale enterprises (Little 1987:231-232; Tybout 1998:6). This problem is of importance especially in developing countries (Hallberg 2000:7). Thus, small-scale enterprises, and especially family firms, often rely on family resources to finance their operations (Casson 1999).

Labour use is also constrained in small-scale enterprises. Due to a lesser division of labour small-scale enterprises tend to employ generalists rather than specialists. If there is a scope for specialised functions, small-scale enterprises can only offer limited career paths (Thong 1999:188).

---

[22]   In the context of this section resources are discussed mainly in terms of financial potency. However, resources can include brand names, technological knowledge, skills, contacts etc., defining them as all "(tangible and intangible) assets which are tied semipermanently to the firm" (Wernerfelt 1984:172).

Owing to a lack of resources small-scale enterprises also face constraints in their output market. Developing new markets requires information about these market, and entering new markets is risky. As these costs are fixed a low financial and personell resource base will restrict market entry (Hallberg 2000:7). When operating in foreign markets in particular small-scale enterprises face higher transaction costs due to a lack of resources (e.g. for sales promotion or branding) which cannot be offset by lower coordination cost and higher flexibility (Schmidt 1996:12).

2.2.3. Small-scale enterprises in developing countries

The development of small-scale enterprises in developing countries is assigned much importance as the small-scale sector is, in general, much larger than in high-income countries. Businesses with less than 20 employees can employ up to 70 percent of the labour force (Hallberg 2000:3; Schneider-Barthold 1998:56). However, despite the importance of the small-scale sector in many developing countries the institutional framework is often unfavourable for them (Schneider-Barthold 1998:57). Tybout (1998:4) describes the situation as follows: "Typically, product markets are small, access to manufactured inputs is limited, human capital is scarce, infrastructure is poor, financial markets are thin, macro volatility is high, the legal system functions poorly, and corruption and property crimes are relatively common." This situation leads, for example, to start-up and closure rates up to three times higher than in industrialised countries (Mead / Liedholm 1998). Out of the start-ups a significant number of very small businesses are set-up to support the survival of the owner rather than to capture a profitable business opportunity. These businesses are the first to leave the market when better opportunities become visible elsewhere. Thus, they do not constitute a dynamic growing sector (Mead / Liedholm 1998).

Profit-oriented small-scale enterprises, too, face the constraints discussed by Tybout (1998). The small size of most developing countries' economies constrains the production of specialised goods which only have a small home market. With no domestic base the cost of entering foreign markets is even higher. Operating on international markets bears higher transaction costs per se. Moreover, small domestic markets make it necessary to import factors. In many countries small-scale enterprises still face restrictions to access foreign currencies due to unfavourable currency regimes and banking systems. In addition to these factors, inadequate physical infrastructure increases the cost of serving and using distant markets, leading to a lower market reach in product and in supply markets. Reliance on foreign markets and small domestic markets will make small-scale enterprises face more relative price volatility, increasing the risk of business and straining the limited enterprise resources.

Limitations in human capital will also constrain small enterprises in developing countries. Small-scale enterprises have, in general, difficulties in employing specialised labour. Low rates of secondary education and scarcity of technicians in developing countries make it difficult to absorb, adapt or develop new technologies. Wage rates in large enterprises tend to be higher, too, making it more difficult for small-scale enterprises to employ qualified personnel.[23]

Access to capital for small-scale enterprises is more constrained in developing countries than in high income countries. In developing countries, the banking system as yet does not specifically cater for small-scale business needs. Financial markets abstain from serving small enterprises because of high service per unit costs (Hallberg 2000:11). This lack of access to credit in particular constrains the growth of dynamic, potentially fast-growing enterprises.[24] Only specialised programmes and institutes will lessen this bias.

The most important constraint for the development of small-scale enterprises is a deficient institutional infrastructure. Governance problems, reaching from problems in the legal system over corruption to inappropriate laws and regulations, lead to higher transaction costs. In this way market access and efficient market use are constrained for businesses that have to work in these environments. Crime and corruption are major obstacles to business in developing countries (Brunetti et al. 1998). Inefficient (and often also corrupt) legal systems makes enforcement of property rights difficult or costly (Schneider-Barthold 1998:57). If entering relations with unknown business partners becomes risky small enterprises will retreat to personal relations, or to relations in an environment marked by social enforcement mechanisms. However, this will again lead to smaller potential markets for these enterprises (Müller-Falcke 1997). That laws and regulations might push businesses to operate illegally was most prominently shown by de Soto (1989) for the case of Peru. Other studies have also shown that the costs of registering and running a business are very high, and in some cases prohibitive, for small-scale enterprises (Lagos 1994).

The discussion of the framework conditions in developing countries shows that these conditions raise the costs of participating in domestic and foreign markets. These conditions also hold for large-scale enterprises. However, due to their poor resource base small-scale enterprises will, in general, be more severely affected. By inhibiting the operation and development of a major part of economic activities the overall economic growth potential is reduced.

2.3. Summing up: ICTs and small-scale enterprise development

In section 2.1 the characteristics of ICTs have been described in detail. It has been shown that ICTs have the potential to enhance market activities and create new markets, by stimulating economic activity. ICTs when used in enterprises, have the ability to increase productivity and flexibility, and to influence efficient scale of operation. These potentials also exist in developing countries, but are hindered by a deficient ICT infrastructure and institutional weaknesses.

---

[23]   Goedhuys (2000), for example, shows the wage differential between small and large enterprises in Côte d'Ivoire. She accounts for this by referring to different levels of complexity and different degrees of division of labour and quality of labour.

[24]   Goedhuys and Sleuwaegen (1999) report this from a survey in Burundi. Dynamic and young small enterprises feel most constrained by the lack of access to credit, followed by over-regulation and general market conditions.

The specificity of small-scale enterprises was described in section 2.2. Small-scale enterprises are characterised by small size, the dominant role of the entrepreneur, underdeveloped division of labour, limited ability to process information, and a restricted resource base. It was shown that, although small-scale enterprises are more important in developing countries, the institutional environment is often unfavourable further constraining their growth potential.

Blili and Raymond (1993) examine in detail how the specific characteristics of small-scale enterprises influence the impact of ICTs. They identify five specific areas. First, small-scale enterprises face a more uncertain environment which makes it more difficult to identify appropriate technological options. Furthermore this makes them more likely to become dependent on large customers and suppliers through demand for specific technological options. Second, small-scale enterprises do not have the resources to develop their own information systems. Therefore, they have to rely on third parties for these products, which increases risk because of a lack of control. Third, because of a lack of cognitive resources the time-horizon in small-scale enterprises is often short-term. Therefore, the implementation of ICT systems is often not a strategic decision but based on the entrepreneur's intuition. Fourth, the entrepreneur plays a dominant role in the enterprise. ICT introduction depends on his perception. Furthermore, diffusion of ICTs through small-scale enterprises is constrained by deficient training experience. Fifth, information systems in small enterprises in general are rather simple. Applications are usually subordinated to accounting rather than to enterprise planning, thus they are often under-utilised in small-scale enterprises. Blili and Raymond (1993:448) conclude that "despite the sophistication of technology and the investment required in both financial and human terms, it is already within the grasp of some innovative small firms. For these firms, it has become a strategic opportunity to be seized." Enterprises that are not proactive in applying ICTs are threatened to become more dominated by their (large) business partners that apply these technologies.

ICTs are considered to enhance flexibility, which is one of the core characteristics of small-scale enterprises. ICTs can help to strengthen this capacity. However, large, formerly slow-moving enterprises can also gain flexibility from the adoption of ICTs, rendering small-scale enterprises less competitive. Flexibility gains do not come automatically. This holds especially for small-scale enterprises (Levy / Powell 1998). ICTs as such can contribute to organisational flexibility because they are more flexible than previously used technologies. However, they age rapidly calling for continuous investment in order to maintain flexibility. In the presence of indivisibilities this is more difficult for small-scale enterprises that can only rely on limited financial resources.

The issue of scale effects, induced by ICTs, has been already discussed in section 2.1.4.1. The evidence is by no means clear. Considering the arguments reviewed in this section one can conclude that only by proactively adopting and using ICTs can small-scale enterprises gain a competitive edge. Otherwise they will be threatened to be left behind. This proactive and bold behaviour will be more difficult to achieve for small-scale enterprises operating in an adverse institutional environment, which, unfortunately, is the case in many developing countries.

3. PATTERNS OF ICT USE IN INDIAN SMALL SCALE INDUSTRY EN-TERPRISES

3.1. Background and framework conditions

In this section background and framework conditions for the examined enterprises are reviewed. Section 3.1.1 describes the development of the Indian Small Scale Industry sector and discusses the policies governing this sector. Special emphasis is given to technology and innovation (3.1.1.5). Section 3.1.2 describes the development of the Indian markets for telecommunication and information technologies concentrating especially on the messy regulation of the telecommunication markets (3.1.2.2) and the development of the Internet (3.1.2.3). In both sections, 3.1.1 and 3.1.2, special reference is made to the situation in Tamil Nadu and Chennai, where the enterprise survey took place. The specific framework conditions and situation at the survey site, Ambattur Industrial Estate in Chennai, are presented in section 3.1.3.

3.1.1. Small Scale Industry in India

3.1.1.1. The Indian definition of Small Scale Industry

In section 2.2 it was stated that small enterprises are normally defined by employment or turnover. Contrary to international custom India adopted a different definition of smallness, defining the Indian Small Scale Industry (SSI) sector by the original value of investment in plant and machinery. Only manufacturing enterprises below certain limits, set by law, can claim to be Small Scale (or any other related category) and are governed by the extensive regulation of the sector (see Table 3.1).

Table 3-1: Investment limits in plants and machinery for small industry sectors:

Sector	Rs.	US$ (appr.)[25]
Small Scale Industry	10,000,000	230,000
Ancillary Industrial Undertakings	*10,000,000*	*230,000*
Export Oriented Units	*30,000,000*	*690,000*
Tiny Enterprises	*2,500,000*	*58,000*

Source: Government of India (2000a).

The current limit for SSI enterprises has been in existence since April 1998. It was Rs. 30 million in the year before - up from Rs. 6 million in 1997. The limit was readjusted due to lobbying activities by SSI representatives who claimed that the increased limit covered rather large enterprises too. The existence of investment limits gives way to two peculiar phenomena. Firstly, SSI enterprises can be quite large if their capital intensity is low. Especially SSI enterprises in the leather and textiles sector would often not qualify as "small" in terms of employment and management structure. Secondly, in order to remain "small" and still get protection or escape regulation under medium and

---

[25]   US$ exchange rate set at the rate of Rs. 43.33 per 1 US$ which was the average annual rate in the financial year 1999/2000, the year in which the survey took place. The average annual exchange rate for 1998/99 was Rs. 42.07 (Government of India 2001).

large enterprise regimes, it is a common practice that SSI enterprises are split up into different units when they reach a certain size. Seen in total, Indian SSI definition and politics are often considered major constraints to enterprise growth (Bala Subrahmanya 1998; Katrak 1999; Little et al.1987; NCAER / FNF 1993).

The SSI sector covers a wide range of enterprises. Most notably is the division between "small" and "tiny" enterprises. The latter have their own regulations and promotion measures. The differentiation between "small" and "tiny" is accepted by the entrepreneurs. Associations, such as AIEMA for example, do not allow tiny enterprises as members because they consider their problems totally different from the ones of larger SSI. Tiny enterprises account for the vast majority of enterprises in the SSI sector. They generate also the majority of employment but only less than half of the output of the sector. A study by the National Council of Applied Economic Research (NCAER) and the Friedrich Naumann Foundation (FNF) (1993) elaborates on the differences between small and tiny enterprises, the former having a more formal and advanced character than the latter ones (see Table 3-2):

3.1.1.2. Indian Small Scale Industry politics

Since independence the Indian state has developed a highly sophisticated system of protection and regulation around the SSI sector with a large number of institutions and initiatives on central, state and district level. This system has seen attempts at simplification and reform after the general economic reforms had begun in 1991 (Bala Subrahmanya 1998). However, some of the sector's representatives still react rather reluctantly to any changes in the direction of liberalisation of the sector. Liberalisation is considered a threat, rather than a chance for more dynamic development.[26] Therefore, many reforms stopped half way, leaving the sector's potential dynamic still very much constrained by protection and regulation.

The origins of the SSI sector's regulation go back to the 1950s. Various Indian governments have acknowledged a need to protect and promote small businesses because they saw specific advantages generated from a vibrant and large small-scale sector (Gaur / Reddy 1995:41; Bala Subrahmanya 1998:35).[27] Until the 1991 economic reforms a vast scheme of promotion and protection policies evolved that to concentrated on the protection measures (NCAER / FNF 1993:162).

---

[26]   The most notable voice in this direction is the Federation of Associations of Small Industries of India (FASII) (Interview with Mr. Pandiaraj, Secretary of FASII, 18.03.1999). FASII is a relatively weak association although it is considered the SSI representative by many SSI enterprises. A more liberal stance is taken by the Confederation of Indian Industry (CII). CII has its origin in engineering and is claiming to have a strong SSI wing, which probably represents the upper and technologically more advanced part of the sector. Smaller SSI enterprises thus suspect CII to represent large enterprises' interests. Nevertheless, CII is very influential, being one of the major promoters of the Indian reform process in the 1990s (Pedersen 2000).

[27]   These expected advantages generated by the small-scale sector were: (1) Generation of employment opportunities with low investments. (2) Promotion of more equitable distribution of income. (3) Effective mobilisation of untapped capital and human skills. (4) Regional dispersal of manufacturing activities.

Table 3-2: Characteristics of tiny and non-tiny small scale enterprises

Characteristics	Tiny enterprises	Non-tiny enterprises
Number of workers	Roughly 10 or less full-time workers	Roughly more than 10 and up to 50 workers
Organisation	Almost wholly family owned proprietorship or partnership	Predominantly family owned proprietorship or partnership; but greater share of limited companies in higher investment slabs
Management	Little management specialisation	Some specialisation in management functions, particularly in bigger units
Technology and manufacturing process	Simple technology, mainly using manual processes of manufacturing	Less traditional and manual processes. Greater use of semi-automatic processes. In some units in higher investment categories use of automatic processes
Products	Products and services are simple; prices are low; cater for low income consumers	Range from simple to more complex and sophisticated, broad range and diversified
Markets	Generally serve local markets; some units undertake subcontracting jobs for export	Wider sales area (region, state, country, international)
Competition	Intense competition as a result of ease of entry and localised market area	Competition relatively less due to better access to concessions and facilities; entry barriers for large and medium enterprises to enter reserved products
Earnings	Return on capital employed and profits are generally low	Return on capital employed and profits are higher particularly in higher investment slabs
Employment and Wages	Lower in categories of employees	Relatively higher and increases with rise of investment slab
Utilisation of government promotional and extension services, facilities, subsidies	Very little	Limited use of extension and promotion measures, much greater benefit from facilities, subsidies and concessions

Source: NCAER / FNF (1993), p. 98.

The most peculiar of these policies were product reservation (i.e. specific products can only be produced by SSI enterprises) and the government purchasing scheme (i.e. the government sources some part of their purchases exclusively from SSI enterprises).[28] The impact of the reservation scheme in particular, has been widely reviewed. Katrak (1999) finds that reservation has increased the number of production units per item produced, but that these units had a lower level of capacity utilisation and did not perform better than others. He concludes that the policy has not generated any benefits, but has hindered the utilisation of economies of scale in production, thus causing a loss in overall welfare. Bala Subrahmanya (1998) argues that "with reference to growth, efficiency, innovativeness and technological progress" the SSI policy proved counter productive. The protection schemes inhibited growth of the most efficient SSI units as the higher costs incurred by large enterprises make it disadvantageous to do so. The emphasis on protection rather than promotion also discouraged investment in new technologies, leaving growth in the sector more quantitative than qualitative.

In course of the general economic reforms' begin after the 1991 balance of payments crisis, the policy environment of SSI also changed. Firstly, regulations from which SSI enterprises had been exempt were also cancelled for large units exposing SSI enterprises to more internal competition. Secondly, the "Small Sector Industrial Policy", announced in August 1991, brought changes in the direction of promotional and protection policies (Government of India 1991). The main move was away from subsidising credit towards enabling an adequate flow of credit (Bala Subrahmanya 1998:40). However, most old policies remained basically intact. The new policy measures were generally applauded as steps in the right direction for small industry promotion. Nevertheless the chance was missed to expose small enterprises to competition. The concept of central planning still persisted.

By the mid 90s there were new attempts to change the SSI policy even further. In 1997 the "Abid Hussain Committee Report", commissioned by the government, proposed a complete reorientation from protection towards promotion of small scale enterprises. Some of the measures were put in place by the then governing moderate left-wing "United Front" government. However, after the Hindu-nationalist BJP took over in

---

[28]   The policy to reserve specific products for production by SSI enterprises was introduced in 1967 and started with 47 products. At that time the argument for this policy was on infant-industry lines. In the late 70s the direction changed. It was argued, "whatever can be produced by small and village industries must only be so produced". Consequently the number of products went up to more than 800 in 1978, peaked at 847 in 1987 and has declined only slightly to 812 in 2000. By the mid 90s, about 21% of the SSI sector's total output was covered.

In the purchase reservation scheme the government has committed itself to purchasing a range of products only from SSI enterprises. This programme came into existence in 1956. By 1993 412 different products were part of the programme, in 2000 then were still more than 350. In addition the purchase scheme involves a price preference. If a product is also offered by a large enterprise the SSI product may be 15% more expensive and still be preferred. Purchases under the SSI scheme summed up to 11 to 12% of total government purchases by the mid 90s. SSI enterprises have to register with the Directorate General of Supplies and Disposals to get included.

1998 it reversed some policy changes due to pressure by SSI representatives (e.g. the investment limit was lowered again).[29]

The SSI policy is still resisting the general trend towards liberalisation of the Indian Economy, the SSI sector is still regarded as a vulnerable segment to be protected (and not as a source of entrepreneurship and dynamics). However, sustained external pressure from the WTO to open the Indian market puts pressure on all actors to adjust to competition.[30] In August 2000 the government has announced a new SSI policy package which includes - besides the usual measures such as new credit and promotion schemes - the foundation of another consultation group to advise on streamlining SSI regulation, repealing redundant ones (Government of India 2001).

As well as the central SSI policy there are additional SSI policy initiatives on the state level. Every Indian state carries out a range of promotion and subsidy schemes adding to the complexity of SSI regulation (Government of India 1995). The Tamil Nadu SSI policy, that is relevant for the enterprises examined in this work, concentrates on granting capital subsidies on own energy generation, subsidised credit for specific sectors and specific "backward" areas and a sales tax waiver. Furthermore it provides a single window clearance scheme for setting up small-scale units and runs a number of promotion agencies (Government of Tamil Nadu 2000).

3.1.1.3. Sectoral development of Indian Small Scale Industry

Notwithstanding the extensive regulations described, the Small Scale Industry sector has consistently generated relatively high growth rates. Particularly in the organised small business sector (as defined by the Indian state) SSI enterprises have been outperforming other segments (see Table 3-3). In the years since the reform began the SSI sector's growth rates have outpaced overall growth of the economy as well as growth of the industrial sector for almost all years. By the end of the financial year 1999/2000 provisional government figures estimated that 3,225,000 units produced Rs. 5,784,700 million of output (about US$ 133,500 million) while employing 17.85 million people (see Table 3-4). Real output has been growing faster than employment consistently since 1992/93, i.e. since liberalisation started. Labour productivity has risen by an average annual rate of 4.8 percent between 1992/93 and 1999/2000. However, the average size of SSI units has decreased from 6.5 employees in 1990/91 to 5.5 in 1999/2000.

These official figures are, however, misleading because official data is insufficiently adjusted for closures of companies. Using data from the 1987/88 census on the SSI sector, NCAER/FNF (1993:55) estimate that in 1990/91 and 1991/92 about one quarter of the enterprises included in the statistics are no longer in operation. Consequently

---

[29] The majority of SSI enterprises, though, was not satisfied with this roll-back. In the 13th Small Business Outlook Survey, conducted in July / August 1998 by CII, 63 percent of the small industry units reportedly did not to favour the decrease (CII 1998).

[30] Many SSI enterprises, being well-aware of potential challenges to come, try to assess and prepare for future changes. AIEMA, for example, commissioned a survey on the impact of liberalisation on its members (Besant Raj International 1999) and organised a high-level workshop on the topic in June 1999 under the heading "Gearing Up For Global Competition".

Table 3-3: Composition of output of the Small Scale sector (in percent)

Year	73/74	79/80	84/85	90/91	91/92
Traditional Industries	16,10	13,26	11,45	10,82	10,71
Khadi	0,44	0,27	0,26	0,18	0,14
Village Industries	0,90	1,04	1,17	0,96	1,10
Handlooms	6,20	5,19	4,45	2,95	2,08
Sericulture	0,46	0,39	0,49	0,43	0,51
Handicrafts	7,83	6,11	5,41	6,18	6,79
Coir	0,44	0,26	0,15	011	0,09
Modern Small Industries	67,50	74,20	88,05	89,18	89,29
Small Scale Industries	52,94	64,51	78,12	80,55	81,93
Powerlooms	14,56	9,69	9,93	8,63	7,36
Others	16,44	12,54	0,50	0,00	0,00

Source: NCAER / FNF (1993), p. 59.

Table 3-4: Development of the Small Scale Industry sector 1990/91 - 1999/2000

Year	Units		Production		Employment	
	1000	Annual growth rate	(Mio. Rs. at 90/91 prices)	Annual growth rate	1000	Annual growth rate
1990/91	1,948	6.9	1,553,400	9.5	12,580	5.2
1991/92	2,082	6.9	1,601,560	3.1	12,980	3.6
1992/93	2,235	7.9	1,691,250	5.6	13,406	3.3
1993/94	2,384	6.0	1,811,330	7.1	13,938	4.0
1994/95	2,571	8.0	1,994,270	10.1	14,656	5.2
1995/96	2,724	6.0	2,221,620	11.4	15,261	4.1
1996/97	2,854	4.9	2,473,110	11.3	16,000	4.8
1997/98	3,014	5.5	2,681,590	8.4	16,720	4.5
1998/99	3,121	3.6	2,888,070	7.7	17,158	2.6
1999/00*	3,225	3.3	3,125,760	8.2	17,850	4.0

* provisional figures
Sources: Government of India (2000a; 2001).

the share of the SSI sector is less than estimated. NCAER/FNF (1993:56) correct the share of net value added of the SSI sector for 1987/88 to 34.8 percent, down from 51.75 percent based on official numbers. Another reason for exaggerated growth rates is the inclusion of new companies in the sector due to a revision of the SSI definition (NCAER/FNF 1993; Ramaswamy 1994).

Tamil Nadu is one of the most industrialised states of India with the manufacturing sector accounting for about one third of the state's domestic product and ranking third in terms of manufacturing value added for all Indian states (Government of Tamil Nadu 1998; European Commission 1996:143). In 1994/95 Tamil Nadu accounted for 11.1 percent of gross value of output, 10.7 percent of net value added, 15.4 percent of employment and 15.6 percent of factories of the whole of India (Government of Tamil Nadu 1998). However, this relative strength comes from large scale industry. The importance of the SSI sector is relatively small, accounting for only 9.2 percent of all Indian units in 1996/97.

3.1.1.4. Perceived problems of Small Scale Industry development

Although the growth rates of the Small Scale Industry sector look impressive it is suspected that this growth is more quantitative than qualitative, i.e. the competitive position of SSI enterprises is threatened if they face competition (Bala Subrahmanya 1998). Indian SSI enterprises face problems in a wide range of areas that obstruct them doing their business. The comprehensive NCAER/FNF (1993) survey identifies finance, inputs (supplies and labour) and marketing as the most serious constraints to SSI performance. For small SSI enterprises in particular it is difficult to get access to working capital credits and term loans. By the time of the survey in 1992 many expanding SSI enterprises experienced shortages of raw materials due to foreign exchange scarcity – a problem that ceased with the opening of the Indian economy. Many enterprises also reported problems in recruiting skilled labour. According to NCAER/FNF (1993) one of the main problems in improving performance is marketing. With only limited resources and limited knowledge about marketing it is difficult, especially for smaller enterprises, to extent their markets. SSI products are also often considered to be of inferior quality. Thus, insufficient finance, management deficiencies, a low level of technology, together with the already described regulations, lead to the inadequate performance of many SSI enterprises.

The problem of lacking adequate finance is supported by a survey among carpenters and goldsmiths in Karnataka in the early 90s (Brouwer 1999). Moreover the artisans cited erratic power supply and pollution control measures as the most common problems, since these affect production and subsequently financial flows.

Another list of problems SSI enterprises face is compiled by the All Indian Associations of Industries (AIAI), an apex body of Indian industry. AIAI (1995) too stresses a lack of funds, deficient working capital as well as infrastructural bottlenecks. Internal obstacles, such as management deficiencies and marketing problems, are also raised. Bureaucratic procedures and adverse policies, such as the reservation policy, are cited as important factors in poor performance. All these problems lead to a low level of technology in SSI enterprises which constrains their long-term growth prospects.

The most comprehensive and continuous survey on the state of the SSI sector is carried out by CII. In its annual "Business Outlook of Small Industry", which covered over 400 enterprises in 1998, CII asked which factors constrain the growth of SSI enterprises (CII 1998). In July / August 1998 these were, in order of importance, outdated technology, delayed payments, lack of credit and finance, shortage of power and other infrastructural facilities, export difficulties, inadequate marketing facilities and shortage of raw materials. Comparing these results with the constraints given in the 1994 survey (CII 1994) reveals that technology in particular has been assigned a much more important role (rising from place seven to place one of the most important constraints). The issue of technology in SSI enterprises is therefore examined in detail in the next section.

3.1.1.5. Technology and innovation in Small Scale Industry enterprises

In the previous section it was repeatedly mentioned that the protective policy by the Indian government and the lack of available funds has discouraged SSI enterprises from upgrading technology. Nevertheless, results from recent small business surveys indicate that with retreating protection technology is considered more and more crucial by SSI enterprises and that technological deficiencies are more felt (CII 1998).

The general technology situation in SSI enterprises is very diverse. In the 1992 survey by NCAER & FNF 57 percent of the interviewed SSI enterprises were manually operated, 39 percent semi-automated and less than five percent automated. Technological progress was positively related to size and plans for technological upgrading (by more than 60 percent of the interviewed units) were reported to go hand in hand with expansion plans (NCAER / FNF 1993:141).[31] The large proportion of enterprises that planned to upgrade technology reflects a new dynamic thrust after the protection policy, that stifled technological progress, had been partly abolished. However, even after 1991, some authors still see deficiencies in technological progress due to the unavailability of appropriate technology and continued protection in some areas (Bala Subrahmanya 1998:44)

Owing to their limited resource base small enterprises usually cannot rely on in-house R&D for innovation. They must rely on institutional channels for technology upgrading (Mathur 1994). Within the promotion portfolio of Indian SSI policy this is taken care of. There are several institutions that are supposed to provide technological assistance and entrepreneurship training to SSI enterprises. Most prominent are the Small Industries Service Institutes (SISIs). There are 58 SISIs set up over the country. They provide technical support services, entrepreneur development programmes etc. and conduct modernisation and in-plant studies (Government of India 1995:11-12). However, their impact has been minimal because, reportedly, staff have only little exposure

---

[31] Technological upgrading might even be a necessary condition for sustained growth. Ramaswamy (1994a) studied technical efficiency in Indian SSI enterprises based on a panel of more than 1000 SSI enterprises compiled by the Reserve Bank of India. He found that intra-industry variation in technical efficiency are relatively low which, he concludes, indicates strong competitive pressure on the enterprises. Thus, only by shifting the production frontier through modernisation will their competitive position be improved.

to updated technical knowledge. Therefore the SISIs are only of little help for small entrepreneurs (NCAER / FNF 1993:211-213).

Nevertheless, it is believed that research and innovation by small enterprises – especially by reverse engineering – is significant, but it is not possible to get precise estimates of its scale (Alagh 1998; Kumar 1998).

Hardly any quantitative evidence on the use of ICTs in SSI enterprises is available. It is, nevertheless, assumed that manufacturing enterprises lag behind in the application of information technologies, especially in terms of intra-organisational diffusion. A survey by Dataquest, an Indian on-line journal, finds that in 80 percent of manufacturing SMEs less than 50 percent of employees used IT in early 2000, a figure that is much lower than in other sectors (Dataquest 2000).

3.1.2. India's markets for telecommunications and information technologies

3.1.2.1. Introduction

After reviewing the Indian Small Scale Industry sector we now turn to the Indian market for information and communication technologies. On the supply side, the development of India's markets for ICTs is influenced, on the one hand, by the general technological developments of ICTs, as described in chapter 2, and on the other, by the Indian government's regulation of these markets.[32] This section will concentrate on the latter aspect as this determines the speed at which national telecommunication markets can develop. An overview over Indian telecommunication markets and selected telecommunication indicators is given in Annex 1.

The regulation of the Indian telecoms market is marked by a series of changes in direction and a continuous power struggle between the different actors. The latter affects the efficient development of technologies, networks and services. In particular the former public monopolists, together with inward-looking and anti-market politicians, have countered attempts to liberalise and deregulate telecommunication markets, and have tried to block the entry of private players. This development is sketched in section 3.1.2.2. Regulation of IT and Internet markets has been more straightforward, moving towards unconstrained private sector participation, but the development of a functioning market has been hindered for some time, too. Regulation of the Internet sector is discussed in section 3.1.2.3. Section 3.1.2.4 gives a brief impression about the specific development in Chennai, i.e. in the area of the survey. The development of ICT markets sketched in this section provides the background against which individual actors decide on their use of particular technologies. This topic will be examined in more detail in chapter 4.

---

[32] The demand side is not the focus of this section. Determinants of the demand for telecommunication and information technologies by small enterprises are examined in chapter four in detail. The general demand for telephone usage in India was estimated by Das and Srinivasan (1999). They found that price elasticity of demand for long distance calls is higher than in developed countries whereas price elasticity for local calls are comparable to developed countries.

3.1.2.2. Liberalisation and regulation of fixed line telephony, cellular phone and paging networks

Pre-liberalisation development

Telephony was introduced in India in the late 19th century. Telephone networks were first run by private companies and were mainly set up for local communication while long-distance communication was covered by the telegraph system. During the 1940s telephone services were nationalised and run by the Department of Telecommunications (DoT). Up to the 1980s telecommunication was classified as a "luxury sector" and, as a consequence, by-passed in any development plans. Hand in hand with the development of a highly inefficient telecommunication bureaucracy, which did show not much interest in improving the state of telecommunication, official resistance to telecommunication development led to a very slow growth of telecommunication networks in India up to the 1990s. By beginning of the eighties India's teledensity was, with 0.31 mainlines per 100 inhabitants, even lower than Sub-Saharan Africa's (Singh 1999:115-138).

Pressure from core users (e.g. business, information industry and middle class) to extend telecommunication facilities mounted in the late 1970s and 1980s. Finally, by 1983 the policies towards telecommunication were changing. Telecommunication became a development priority and more public funds were allocated towards infrastructure development, in particular. In 1985 DoT was separated from Post and Telegraphs and became an independent department under the Ministry of Communications. The aim of this operation was to split up, and corporatise DoT, which was fiercely opposed by its staff. A partial success was achieved by spinning off operations in Delhi and Mumbai (formerly Bombay) into Mahanagar Telephone Nigam Ltd. (MTNL), and international traffic into Videsh Sanchar Nigam Ltd. (VSNL). A first regulatory body, the Telecommunications Commission was set up in 1989, but quickly deteriorated to become an advisory body of DoT, having been increasingly staffed with DoT cadres since 1990 (Singh 1999: 141-147). Nevertheless, from 1985 onwards the number of telephone lines and the quality of the network improved greatly. Especially the development of Public Call Offices (PCOs) in rural areas was promoted.[33] However, development and growth, especially of MTNL and VSNL, were constrained by a restrictive technology policy, which promoted domestic development of telecommunication hard- and software and heavily protected these markets against foreign competitors that could have offered state-of-the-art equipment (Singh 1999: 148-159).

Liberalisation of fixed line telephone services and regulation issues

Real liberalisation of the Indian telecommunications market started as the same time as the general liberalisation process in 1991 after the balance-of-payment crises. Liberalisation became necessary owing to the inability of public investment alone to secure growing demand for the expansion of networks and services. Moreover, internal and external pressure for liberalisation was mounting (Singh 1999:170-174). Operations of DoT were highly inefficient, rural expansion did not meet the growing demand, and

---

[33]   The number of mainlines increased from 3.17 Mio. in 1985 to 5.81 Mio. in 1991. In 1991 about 110.000 Public Pay Phone had been installed (ITU 1999).

efforts to adopt new communication technologies were insufficient.[34] In 1992 the opening up of value-added services began. Licences for mobile cellular and paging services were awarded in the following years. The National Telecom Policy of 1994 (NTP 1994) provided a first framework for opening up basic telephone services to foreign and private investors. This opening for competition was planned only on the local and state level. National and international telephony were to remain in the hands of DoT, MTNL and VSNL.

In 1995 a bidding process for basic telephony licences in 21 state and metro circles started. Eligible bidders were Indian registered companies with foreign minority participation and some experience in the sector (through their foreign partners). The process of awarding licences for basic telephone services in the circles proved to be rather bumpy and was marked by a tendency of DoT, which was both service provider and legislator, to obstruct the process.[35] The first round of bidding in August 1995 attracted 80 bids from 16 companies for 20 circles. However, only six licences were awarded after this round. In the subsequent rounds the number of bids and interested enterprises decreased substantially leaving, eight circles without any private interest after the third round in March 1996.[36] The bidding companies encountered a number of problems which, in the end, contributed to the failure to deliver a widespread private sector participation in the Indian telephone services (Dokeniya 1999).[37] By the end of 1998 licence agreements had only been signed for six out of the 21 circles.[38] For another

---

[34] In 1990 and 1991 the waiting list for telephones exceeded the annual number of new telephone lines by more than four times (Chowdary 1998). The inefficiency of DoT was indicated by its overstaffing, i.e. there were about 20 employees per phone, more than 10 times worse than that of comparable operators (Chowdary 1995).

[35] "The DOT as 'government', 'administrator' and 'regulator' has protected the DOT as 'operator', 'competitor' and 'service-provider'." (Dokeniya 1999)

[36] For a detailed description of the bidding process see Dokeniya (1999).

[37] First, the amount of the bid was the major criteria for awarding a licence. Other aspects, such as the investment plans and network extension to rural areas, that were stated as high priority objectives in NTP 1994, were of only minor importance. This method resulted in extremely high, and in some cases, unrealistic bids. For the second round DoT set minimum reserve prices for the remaining circles that were in many cases much higher than the highest bid in the first round. The formula behind these 'minimum reserve prices' was not revealed. Most serious bids were just above the reserve prices, indicating that these prices did not reflect the market value. Second, the tender stated that private operators were not allowed to charge higher tariffs than DoT. This gave DoT the possibility of squeezing their competitors margins because it could operate without the payment of any licence fee and had the possibility of cross-subsidising from the highly profitable national and international operations. Third, the new providers had to pay additional interconnection charges to DoT and had to bear the costs of equipment at DoT's switches. Fourth, the licences were assigned only to the awarded company. They were not transferable. This meant that banks did not accept the licence as a collateral and, consequently, new operators had only limited access to external funding to finance their investments.

[38] The circles for which a licence was awarded are Madhya Pradesh (Bharti Telenet), Andhra Pradesh (Tata Teleservices), Gujarat (Reliance Telecom), Punjab (Essar Comvision), Maharashtra (Hughes Ispat) and Rajastan (Shyam Telelink). The licence fees to be paid amounted to Rs. 300 billion (more than US$ 7 billion by that time) over 15 years.

seven circles letters of intent had been signed. The first provider started offering services only in mid 1998.[39]

Domestic industry, multinationals and international organisations, which saw the liberalisation process threatened, mounted pressure to establish an independent regulator (Singh 1999:179). In the beginning of 1997 the Telecom Regulatory Authority of India (TRAI) started its work.[40] After being established TRAI engaged itself in a continuous struggle with DoT and politicians on regulation issues. Major battles were fought up to the High Courts and the Supreme Court on interconnection and access charges as well as licensing procedures that still had remained in the hands of DoT (Chowdary 1998; Singh 1999). Since this power struggle paralysed the whole sector the government was forced to search for a another regulatory set-up. In an attempt to separate operations and licensing basic telephony was split off to a newly formed "Department of Telecommunication Services" in 2000.[41] This separation was, however, somewhat dubious since many officials still worked for both organisations after the split (Srivastava and Sinha 2001:23). Early in 2000 the government also redesigned TRAI, splitting off dispute settlement and arbitration to a new tribunal which can only be overruled by the Supreme Court, and making TRAI recommendations mandatory for all new licensees (Economic Times 2000). This move was supposed to strengthen TRAI but whether this would prove effective was still not clear by the end of 2000 (Singh 2000:899).

The most decisive political move occurred in late 1998 when a "Group of Telecommunications" was established at the Prime Minister's Office that drafted a New Telecom Policy (NTP 1999) coming into effect in April of the following year (Government of India 1999). NTP 1999 restated the importance of private sector involvement in the telecommunications sector but the privileged role of DoT remained still intact.[42] It also scheduled the opening for competition in the monopoly areas. National long distance services were to be opened from January 2000, a goal that, of course, has not been achieved. Only in August 2000 did the government announce the possibility for an unrestricted number of players to enter into long-distance telecommunications. International telephony remained in the hand of VSNL and is supposed to be opened only in March 2002.[43] Together with the prohibition of internet telephony, this

---

[39]   At June 1998 Bharti Telenet launched services in Madhya Pradesh under the brand of AirTel. By April 2000 it had 107,300 subscribers up from 22,000 a year earlier. Full network roll-out is expected to be in place by 2004 (CIT Publications Ltd. 2000a).

[40]   The constitution of TRAI proved problematic. The bill took several attempts to pass the parliament. As DoT was still trying to exercise notional power on the telecommunications sector it influenced the draft of the bill in a way that made TRAI relatively powerless. Thus, TRAI initially only obtained the power to settle disputes between service providers and to set prices, but had no jurisdiction over DoT.

[41]   In October 2000 the Department of Telecommunication Services was renamed into Bharat Sanchar Nigam Ltd. (BSNL).

[42]   For example, DoT/MNTL were allowed to enter as a third competitor into mobile phone circles. They will have to pay licence fees but the government will reimburse the full licence fee to DoT "as DoT is the national service provider having immense rural and social obligations".

[43]   The opening off international services has, however, been brought forward from March 2004 in 2000 (Government of India 2001:178).

indicates that there is a strong fear in the government of loosing considerable revenue from international traffic.

After eight years of liberalisation efforts in the Indian basic telephone market results are poor. By mid 2000 only about 164,000 out of the more than 27.5 Mio. mainlines belong to private operators. With 2.8 mainlines per 100 inhabitants India's teledensity improved but is still far below the numbers of other Asian countries. Furthermore, DoT constantly fails to reach the targets set for connection of villages to the telephone network. By October 2000 220,000 of India's more than 600,000 villages were still without a phone (Government of India 2001:178). Owing to the inconsistent regulation a number of large Western telecommunications companies left (or did not even dare to enter) the Indian market, leaving foreign investment to a few, mainly Asian operators such as Hutchison or Singtel (CIT Publications 2000; Mehta 2000).

Licensing and regulation of cellular phone services

The process of awarding licences to cellular telephone and paging service operators proved more successful but had its share of problems, too. The licensing was initiated in 1992. Bidding for licences to operate GSM cellular phone networks started in 1994 for two licences each in the four metropolitan cities. This bidding process was obscured by the Minister of Communications who awarded licences before the final ruling by DoT was made. This decision was challenged and, by court ruling, the DoT criteria were applied in 1994 (Singh 1999:184). Cellular services in the metropolitan areas started only in August 1995. The rest of the country was divided into 18 circles in which two operators each could get a licence for ten years.[44] This 1994 bidding process was constrained through changes by the Minister of Communication, a lack of transparency by DoT, and by unrealistically high bids submitted by the participating consortia (Singh 1999:185).[45] After the licences had been awarded DoT further hindered successful operations of private operations by setting high interconnection fees, an issues that later led to major battles with TRAI. By the end of 1998 eight cellular operators were working in the four metropolitan areas (Delhi, Bombay, Madras and Calcutta), and another 14 operators were working in 18 state circles, altogether there were about 1.07 million subscribers - about 500,000 in the metros and 507,000 in the circles (see Figure 3-1).

Owing to the delayed start of services, and because of the size of bids, which had overestimated the market potential for mobile phones, most operators had trouble paying their licences fees in 1998 and lobbied strongly for lowering these obligations. In NTP 1999, which came into operation in August 1999, this was taken care of. The major improvement for cellular service providers was the switch from licence fee pay-

---

[44] The circles were mapped according to state borders and were categorised into "A", "B" and "C" circles, depending on the assumed economic potential.

[45] These problems are best illustrated by the notorious case of Himachal Futuristic Corporation Ltd. (HFCL), a company with a turnover of Rs. 2 billion at that time, that put in bids for nine circles valuing Rs. 85.9 billion in total. In another act of favouritism, the Minister of Communications lowered the maximum number of circles that could be granted to any private bidder to three which made it possible to award licences to HFCL which is based in his home state (Dokeniya 1999:122; Singh 1999:188).

ment towards a revenue sharing scheme under which they are supposed to pay 15 percent of revenue as a fee (CIT Publications 2000a). Major problems concerning interconnection were also solved. What still remained in place was the "receiving party pays" system for call charges which is considered to be one of the main constraints for mobile telephony growth. By September 1999 TRAI ordered the introduction of the "calling party pays" (CPP) system. Consumer groups, that feared the rising costs of fixed line calls, and MTNL, which would loose revenue under the new order, went to court to prevent the introduction of CPP. They succeeded because the proposed change was not in the jurisdiction of TRAI and because it interfered with licensing terms.[46]

Figure 3-1: Cellular phone subscribers in India (1997-2000)

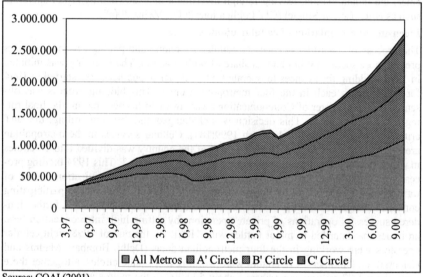

Source: COAI (2001).

The major stand-off between cellular companies and DoT happened when NTP 1999 was already under discussion and before it came into operation. In early 1999 the Ministry of Communications ordered the licensees to pay at least 20 percent of their outstanding fees before the switch of the licensing system. After the deadline ended only 20 percent of this amount was in and most companies could not provide guarantees for the remaining sums. By early May 1999 DoT terminated the interconnection facilities of three operators cutting off 100,000 cellular subscribers from the network. It was assumed that this measure had been taken to scare off foreign investors and to bring these operators under the control of DoT (CIT Publications 1999). As a concession to DoT NTP 1999 granted a third mobile licence for each circle to DoT/MTNL from 2001. Furthermore, it was scheduled to auction fourth licenses in 2001. These plans

---

[46]   This order was the final cause for the shake-up of TRAI (Srivastava / Sinha 2001).

have raised a great deal of resistance from private operators that fear further pressure on their already meagre or non-existing profits.[47]

Owing to the continuing problems experienced by operators during the first years of operation growth of the subscriber base stalled in 1998/99. After several issues had been solved by NTP 1999, general growth picked up significantly in the second half of 1999, with high growth rates experienced especially in smaller markets outside the metropolitan areas. By the end of 2000 more than 3.1 million subscribers were reached. The four metros accounted for nearly 1.2 million, but the fastest growth is outside the big cities (see Figure 3-1). During 2000 growth came, like in many other countries, to a large extent from pre-paid services, which already accounted for 40 percent of total users (CIT Publications 2000a). At the same time growth was taking off the industry was concentrating with big groups, such as Hutchison Whampoa (578,000 subscribers by the end of 2000), Bharti Industries (429,000), BPL Telecom (574,000) and Tata-Birla-AT&T, taking over smaller operators. The number of operators went down from 22 in 1997 to 15 by July 2000 indicating that the market is finally becoming more mature and organised (India Abroad News Service 2000).

Licensing of paging services

The bidding for licences for paging services also took place in 1994 with a similar procedure to the cellular phone bidding. Paging companies, however, could start their operations earlier than cellular phone operators. They witnessed rapid growth with more than 200,000 users one year after operations started. Paging operators worked in 27 cities soon after being allowed to do so and started service in the 18 state circles in 1998. High growth rates were achieved by heavily subsidising the pagers, sometimes giving them away for free with other consumer goods (Voice & Data 1998). By the end of fiscal year 1996/97 the subscriber base had gone up to 535,000. A year later the industry reported 833,000 subscribers – a poor result considering that it was expected to break the one million mark in that year (Voice & Data 1998).[48] By that time the industry had ceased subsidising pagers because, on the one hand, prices of pagers had gone down, and on the other companies faced serious financial constraints.[49] Paging companies faced licence fees of Rs. 100 per pager per annum which proved impossible to pay out of operating revenues alone (CIT Publications 1999). Thus, under NTP 1999 licence fees were linked to revenues. This made it possible to reduce the monthly rental charges of Rs. 300 for alpha-numeric and Rs. 175 for numeric pagers that have been constant for quite some time (Kumar 2000). Customs duty of pagers was also brought down from 25 to five percent, reducing the price of pagers by about Rs. 500. Yet, growth rates were decreasing with the spread and affordability of mobile phones, and by 1999 the number of subscribers even started to decline from its heights (CIT

---

[47] BSNL will start services during 2001 planning for a final roll-out of 1.5 million connections. MTNL has started operating in Mumbai and Delhi in early 2001 causing a fierce price war by undercutting the existing operators significantly.

[48] Independent estimates were even counting only 750,000 subscribers by March 1998 (Voice & Data 1998).

[49] The average price for a pager was Rs. 7,500 in 1995/96, Rs. 2,850 in 1996/97, Rs. 2,050 in 1997/98 and Rs. 2,200 in 1998/99 (Voice & Data 1998 and 1999).

Publications 1999). In the cities, especially paging companies were loosing customers. As early as 1998 the first paging service operators ceased services and surrendered their licences because they could not see their services becoming profitable (Economic Times 2000a). A few more followed in the next years. At the same time the industry was consolidating through mergers. By the end of March 2000 the subscriber base had already dropped to 600,000 leaving the market in a pitiful state (Voice & Data 2000).

3.1.2.3. The development of the Internet in India

The development of the Internet has some features similar to telecommunications. Liberalisation and regulation have not been without problems and there were attempts by public vested interest groups to obstruct private sector participation. However, these attempts have not been as successful as in the other telecommunications sectors. The internet has been developing rapidly during the last few years (see Table 3-5).

Table 3-5: The Growth of the Internet in India

Date	Internet connections	Internet users
15.08.1995	2,000	10,000
31.03.1996	50,000	250,000
31.03.1997	90,000	450,000
31.03.1998	140,000	700,000
31.03.1999	280,000	1,400,000
31.03.2000	900,000	2,800,000
31.12.2000	1,800,000	5,500,000

Source: NASSCOM (2001).

Use of the Internet started relatively early in India. In 1986/87 the United Nations funded the development of the Education and Research Network (ERNET) under the Department of Electronics. ERNET linked India's research and educational institutions. By the beginning of the 1990's India belonged to the top thirty Internet nations (Mehta 2000). However, the further development of ERNET was hindered largely by the DoT denying ERNET for example the use of additional bandwidth. In 1994 the government even tried to close ERNET, the sole Internet provider at that time. This move that was only prevented by furious lobbying from the users (Mehta 2000).

Commercial Internet services were started by VSNL in August 1995. It remained a monopoly until 1998. During this time e-mail providers complained about the high licences fees and lease line rates that had to be paid to VSNL, these seriously constrained the growth of e-mail in India (Singh 1999:193). VSNL tried to lobby against any opening of its market to private Internet Service Providers (ISPs). However, pressure mounted quickly from both businesses and IT activists. The newly elected Hindu-nationalist BJP government responded to this by setting up an "IT Taskforce" in May

1998.[50] Giving in to the pressure was also due to the rising importance of the domestic software industry which desperately needed access to Internet technologies. Additionally state and national governments aimed to make India a "Technology Superpower", which could, of course, only happen in a technology friendly environment.

By November 1998 private ISPs were finally allowed to operate.[51] A few of them began operating almost immediately, many followed. However, all international data traffic still had to be routed through the VSNL gateways. The first national ISP to enter the market a few weeks after liberalisation was Satyam Infoway, a daughter company of Satyam Computer Systems, one of India's largest software companies. Satyam managed to grab the largest share of the growing market. By the end of 1999 it already had over 100,000 subscribers, nearly 20 percent of the total market.[52] At that time, about one year after liberalisation, approximately 200 licences had been issued and nearly 50 ISPs had launched their services (Singhal 2000).

With the arrival of competition, access prices came under pressure at VSNL. A price war broke out in February 1999, when majority public owned MTNL entered the markets of Mumbai and Delhi and tried to undercut VSNL (Ganapati 1999).[53] During late 1999 the charging system changed and flatrates, i.e. unrestricted access at a fixed price, became popular (Varma 2000).[54]

The subscriber base expanded rapidly after liberalisation. By the time the ISP policy came into place VSNL had about 170,000 subscribers. Nine months later it had expanded by more than 80 percent to more than 310.000 subscribers (IDC India 1999). A year after private players had been allowed into the market it had risen to more than 500.000 and by the end of 2000 the subscriber base was approaching two million (see

[50] The taskforce combined government officials, politicians and business people from the IT industry (see: http://it-taskforce.nic.in/). In a few months it drafted a couple of action plans which supported the liberalisation and development of India IT markets. The relatively liberal approach to regulation was considered revolutionary by Indian standards (Bhasin and Srinivasan 1999).

[51] The licence conditions were as followed: There was no restriction in the number of licences issued. Foreign equity up to 49 percent was permitted. Licences were granted for fifteen years with no fees to be paid in the first five years and a token fee of Rs. 1 per year and subscriber in the years thereafter. Licences were awarded in three Categories: "A", covering all of India (requiring bank guarantees of Rs. 20 Mio.), "B", covering one of the eight biggest cities or a telecom circle (guarantee of Rs. 2 Mio.), and "C", covering any secondary switching area outside the eight largest cities (guarantee of Rs. 0.3 Mio.). ISPs were free to fix their tariffs and could set up their own transmission links but no international gateway. Offering Internet telephony was also not allowed (Government of India (1998)).

[52] Satyam Infoway even got listed on the NASDAQ in mid 1999 as the second Indian IT company.

[53] In late 1995 VSNL offered 250 hours of dial-up Internet connection for Rs. 25,000 (i.e. 100 Rs. per hour). By the end of 1998 rates had come down to Rs. 10,000 for 500 hours (Rs. 20 per hour). A year later, private ISPs were leading the field. Dishnet offered the 500 hour package for Rs. 5750 (Rs. 11.5 per hour) and VSNL at Rs. 7250 (Rs. 14.5 per hour). Soon after VSNL dropped its rate further to Rs. 5,500. 500 hours of access by ISDN were offered at Rs. 10,450 by VSNL at that time.

[54] At the beginning of 2000 MTNL, for example, offered a flatrate of Rs. 6000 per year. Half a year later flatrates were already offered by Satyam and DishnetDSL for Rs. 299 and Rs. 250 per month respectively.

Table 3-5). Yet the subscriber base does not account for all users. It is generally believed that for each subscriber at least an extra two people access the Internet via public places such as cyber cafés.[55]

With declining prices and rising visibility of the Internet the composition of the subscriber base changed quickly. Whereas in the early years growth was concentrated in large businesses and research, in later periods growth picked up in small businesses and later in the home segment. In July 1999, (which is also approximately the time of the survey), IDC India reported the following break-up of users with the home and small and medium organisation market being already constituting the most rapidly expanding market segments (see Table 3-6):

Table 3-6: Internet Subscriber Base by User Segment by 31.07.1999

Segment	Subscriber base	Share of total (percent)
Small & medium organisation	130,012	41.7
Large organisation	96,673	31.0
Education, research and government	24,528	7.9
Home	60,507	19.4
Total	311,720	100.0

Source: IDC India (1999).

The new private ISPs, with their rapidly growing customer base, continuously complaint about the lack of bandwidth provided by VSNL. They suspected that the incumbent was trying to dry their business and lobbied hard for the permission to set up their own international gateways. Only in Spring of 2000 did this become possible and subsequently the larger ISPs began to set up their own gateways, mainly through satellites.[56] By that time VSNL and other public agencies too were trying to increase bandwidth, so that the bandwidth scarcity is easing.

Local and localised internet content has been rising strongly since 1998. On the one hand there have been public efforts to enhance the spread of local and appropriate content and techniques. The Tamil Nadu state government, for example, launched an initiative to support Tamil in the Internet. The initiative included promotion of online content, support for a Tamil Internet Research Centre and support for the development of a standardised Tamil keyboard that was presented to the public in mid 1999 (Rao 1999; Senthil Nathan 1999). Not only public efforts enhance the use of local languages. Owing to the growing user base commercial websites have started offering their services in languages other than English.[57] Yet, English is still the most important

---

[55] Surveys of the Gartner Group and NASSCOM identify 60 percent of the Internet users in public places (Cyber Times 2000; NASSCOM 2001).

[56] The first private ISP to inaugurate its own satellite gateway was Bharti's MantraOnline on the 21.7.2000 in Delhi (8 Mbps downstream and 3 Mbps upstream).

[57] The first major portal offering local-language access was 1999 Satyam's "www.sify.com", one of largest portals in India. By the end of 2000 the portal covered Bengali, Hindi, Kannnada, Malayalam, Tamil and Telugu.

language. A study by the Gartner Group found that by mid 2000 only 11 percent of users had ever accessed a local language site and only one fourth of these did it on a regular basis (Cyber Times 2000). It is, however, expected that this figure will rise with a growing number of users and with growing local-language content.

Demand for locally relevant contents and local language contents comes from changing growth poles too. In the early phases subscriber and user growth concentrated in the urban elite, formal business and middle class. However, in 2000 the number of reports on internet usage in urban low-income areas as well as in smaller rural communities was rising. In these environments English language skills are not widespread. Nevertheless, basic connectivity in rural areas is still poor. Besides continuous announcements and pending plans to install at least one Public Call Office in each Indian village this has yet not been achieved yet and time targets are revised as they are continuously revised. By October 2000 there were still 220,000 villages without telecommunication facilities (Government of India 2001). Providing each village with Internet access is an even more challenging task. Bhasin and Srinivasan (1999) calculate infrastructure investments of Rs. 65 billion (about US$ 1.5 billion) and annual operation costs of Rs. 6.5 billion to achieve this aim.

Domestic software and hardware markets

The development of the Indian Internet industry cannot be separated from the development of domestic software and hardware industries and markets. As noted above, there are strong interconnections within the whole IT sector, with ISPs often being parts of larger telecommunications or IT conglomerates, as in the case of Satyam Infoways. The Indian software industry is an impressive success story with sustained growth rates of about 50 percent per year for the last decade.[58] During the financial year 1999/2000 it reached a turnover of US$ 5.7 billion of which US$ 4.0 billion were exports. The industry started by executing simple programming and data entry work for foreign companies, since then it has moved up the value-chain during recent years offering advanced services and products today.[59]

The diffusion of hardware in India can be illustrated with reference to Personal Computers (PCs). The use of PCs was for some time limited by high import barriers for foreign models and parts. As a consequence, a flourishing domestic industry came into existence (Dedrick and Kraemer 1993). However, management mistakes and lowered barriers led to a rising market share of international brands and to the disappearance of most domestic brands. Nevertheless, in 2000 the market leader in terms of sales was still the Indian company HCL.

The first PC was shipped to India in 1984. 16 years later about five million have been installed in the country with more than 1.4 million being shipped in 1999/2000 at an average price of about US$ 800[60] (MAIT 2000, Varma 2000a). Again, the growth rate

---

[58] For a detailed description of the origins of the success story see Heeks (1996). Information about the Indian Software industry's current state provides NASSCOM (2000).

[59] Some of the major players, such as Infosys, Satyam or Wipro, were even listed on the US high tech stock market NASDAQ during 1999 and 2000.

[60] Desktop PCs only, without keyboard, monitor etc.

for the "non-metro" PC market outpaces growth in the largest cities. The biggest share of sales in 1999-2000 went to the small business sector, with annual growth rates of about 50 percent. Sales to households too are growing rapidly, accounting already for about 20 percent of sales,. The PCs sold in India are technically up-to-date, but this is not so with peripherals. [61] In 1999/2000 almost 50 percent of printers were still dot-matrix printers and more than 75 percent of sold monitors had a size of 14''. However, more than 60 percent of PCs sold in 1999/2000 were net-enabled (MAIT 2000).

The review of the Internet and IT in India shows that India overall is a fast growing market for all these components. A closer inspection reveals different stages of development in different market segments. Whereas the markets for large establishments are maturing they are growing fast in the small scale business segment, the home segment and in non-metropolitan areas. This means that by the time the current survey had been undertaken in Chennai in mid 1999 growth of internet as well as IT components was at its heights in the small scale business sector.

3.1.2.4. Telecommunications and Internet in Tamil Nadu and Chennai

So far, the Indian telecommunications and IT markets have been discussed on an aggregate basis. This section will focus on the Chennai markets, in particular. The different situation in Tamil Nadu, and Chennai, was hinted at in the discussion of market regulation and in the development of ICTs. Firstly a regional imbalance exists in India. The South is in general technologically more developed than the North. Secondly urban areas enjoy a better ICT infrastructure with more potential customers being served at the same cost.

The South of India, i.e. the states Andhra Pradesh, Karnataka, Kerala, Tamil Nadu and Pondicherry, are considered the technological power houses of the country (Economic Times 2001). The success of Bangalore as a centre of the software industry is notorious. Recently though the importance of Andhra Pradesh has increased due to intense efforts by its Chief Minister Chandrababu Naidu to make it into an IT-State. However, it is Tamil Nadu and its capital Chennai, that have been outperforming the other states recently. By March 1999 there were already nearly 600 software units in the state. What makes Tamil Nadu and Chennai attractive to IT enterprises is a strong base in manufacturing, especially car manufacturing, and a highly skilled workforce (Economic Times 2000b).

Concerning Internet development Chennai has been one of the prime locations in India. Some important private ISPs, such as Satyam and Dishnet, set up their headquarters in Chennai. By the time of the survey in mid 1999 VSNL had about 35,000 subscribers in the city. At that time private ISPs, e.g. Satyam, just had only started their service but were expanding quickly. Cybercafés were mushrooming over the city in 1999. VSNL estimated that about two percent of all Internet connections were for public access places. Owing to the intense competition in the city, Internet access in Chennai is ranked the best in India (Cyber Times 2000a). Moreover, internet use is

---

[61]   By the second half of 1999/2000 almost two thirds of sold computers had a Pentium III or a 433 Mhz Celeron processor (MAIT 2000).

widespread in the whole Tamil Nadu. By end of September 2000 Tamil Nadu had more than 290,000 Internet subscribers (including the subscribers from Chennai) – nearly 20 percent of all subscribers in India.

Cellular Phone services were launched in Chennai in September 1995 by two operators.[62] These were RPG Cellular and Skycell.[63] By the time of the survey Chennai had the smallest cellular network of the four metros but the fastest growing subscriber base. During the first half of 1998 the subscriber base even declined (see Figure 3-2). By the end of June 1999 there were 36,200 customers in the two networks. The larger of the two operators was RPG cellular with 19,600 subscribers, it grew significantly during 1997/98 while the numbers of customers for its competitor Skycell declined. At the end of 1999 Bharti Telecom, which was heavily expanding in South India, attempted to take over Skycell by buying the shares of Crompton-Greaves and DSS – a deal that a year later still had to be finalised.[64] In 1999/2000 there were rumours about take-over bids for RPG from various sources (CIT Publications 2000a).[65] The uncertainty about Skycell's future was inhibiting its growth. By October 2000 the number of subscribers in Chennai had grown to 86,000 with RPG having 51,000 and Skycell only having 35,000 subscribers by that time (see Figure 3-2). By December 2000 the total subscriber base in Chennai was 96,224 and 201,522 in Tamil Nadu.

Paging companies were able to start their services in Chennai before mobile operators entered the market. Therefore, their subscriber base grew rapidly in the first year. Licensees are DSS Mobile Communications with the brand of MobiLink and EasyCall Services with the eponymous brand. These two companies, which also own licenses in other circles, rank first and second in the national market in terms of turnover and subscribers. By March 1998 Chennai had about 81,000 subscribers (Voice & Data 1998). A year later this dropped to 75,000 reflecting the general problem of paging operations in big cities (Voice & Data 1999). With mobile phones becoming more and more popular and affordable these figures are expected to drop further.

Summing up, Chennai offers, by Indian standards, a fine, up-to-date telecommunications and IT infrastructure. The population is well-aware of existing technologies and uses them widely. The city has a strong base in traditional industries which are expected to benefit from the growing IT sector in the city through the increasing pool of technology skills.

---

[62] Licenses for the four metro cities are awarded separately from the licenses of the states they belong to.

[63] By June 1999 RPG Cellular was owned by RPG Enterprises (51.7%), an Indian conglomerate, Cellfone (26.4%) and Vodaphone AirTouch (20%). Skycell belonged to the Indian electronics manufacturer Crompton Greaves (40.5%), BellSouth (24.5%), Millicom (24.5%) and DSS (10.5%) (CIT Publications 2000).

[64] Bharti Telecom is owned by Bharti Enterprises, an Indian conglomerate engaged in the manufacturing of telecommunications products, and by British Telecom and Telecom Italia.

[65] These movements reflect the concentration process that swept the Indian cellular market during 1999 and 2000. The Cellular Operators' Association of India expects that by 2001 only five to six operators will be left down from 21 in 1997 (India Abroad News 2000).

Figure 3-2: Cellular phone subscribers in Chennai (1997-2000)

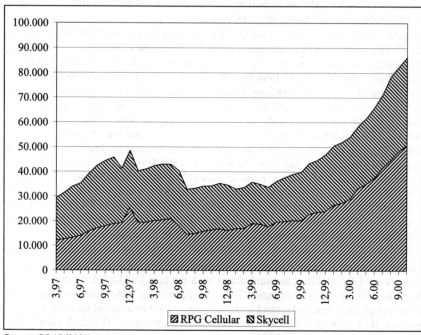

Source: COAI (2001).

3.1.3. Framework conditions in Ambattur Industrial Estate

All the enterprises that took part in the survey underlying this work are located at Ambattur Industrial Estate in Chennai. In the previous sections the general developments in the SSI sectors as well as in the Indian telecommunications and IT markets were discussed. Specific policies and market conditions for Chennai have also been described. This section will concentrate on location specific features connected to the Ambattur Industrial Estate, covering the history of the estate, business environment, general infrastructure situation, specific SSI agencies in the estate and the specific telecommunications situation.

Ambattur Industrial Estate is located about 15 kilometres West of Chennai city centre, covering about six square kilometres. It is connected to the urban rail system, has a large bus terminal and two major road passing through the estate. The Southern part of the estate (South of M.T.H. Road) was developed in 1963 by the Tamil Nadu Small Industries Development Corporation (SIDCO), the development of the Northern part started in 1969. In the first phase SIDCO built the infrastructure and the buildings. The latter were first rented out but later sold to the enterprises that had settled in the estate. SIDCO is still present in the estate running a site office and raw material depot. Official figures, and figures given by the estate association AIEMA count 2000 tiny, small, medium and large units in the estate which employ 200,000 people (AIEMA 1998). The annual turnover of the estate was estimated to be 20,000 million Rs. (approximately 460 million US$) in 1997/98 with exports accounting for 5,000 million Rs. (approximately 115 million US$).

The activities in the estate comprise automobile components, foundries, engineering products, garments, leather goods, rubber components, electrical equipment, tool rooms, machine tools, machine shops and service industries such as heat treatment and metal finishing (AIEMA 1998:7). Many of the smaller units are sub-contractors for large enterprises around Chennai. During the industrial recession in 1997 many enterprises were hit hard giving to comments that the estate is in decline.

One of the main actors in the estate is the estate's Small Scale Industry association Ambattur Industrial Estate Manufacturers' Association (AIEMA). By the time of the survey in May 1999 AIEMA had about 740 members. It refuses membership to tiny enterprises but its membership covers approximately 80 percent of all SSI enterprises in the state. Real coverage might be even higher since a number of entrepreneurs own more than one enterprise but join only with one of these. AIEMA is a comparatively strong association with a number of different activities, including renting out office space, running the "Technology Centre" that provides conference facilities, a canteen and training facilities, running a child day care centre, conducting seminars and organising a biennial engineering fair with more than 200 participating companies in 1998. The association is managed by a couple of dedicated entrepreneurs that developed a lot of thrust to promote the association. By 1998 a co-operation with a German chamber development project, the ZDH Partnership Programme, has been started that extended the scope of activities.

The main infrastructural problem in the estate is, as in most place in India, electricity. Power cuts occur quite regularly. Enterprises that have to rely heavily on electricity have their own generators. One of the long-term plans of AIEMA is to build a power station for the estate to become more independent from the public network. The telephone infrastructure has improved dramatically during the last years. In the early nineties waiting time too get a phone in Ambattur was more than a year. By the time of the survey it was down to somewhere between six month and a year. By the end of 2000 Chennai Telephones claims that there are no waiting times to get a phone in the estate. Quality of calls also improved as well as the satisfaction with the telephone service. However, with regard to the Internet entrepreneurs complain about the low quality of connections.

3.2. Survey design, sampling process and execution of interviews

3.2.1. Survey design

In order to explore the use of telecommunications and information technologies in Small Scale Industry enterprises in Ambattur Industrial Estate a structured questionnaire was designed. A small pilot survey in March 1999, covering 14 enterprises, revealed that the maximum time entrepreneurs are willing to spend answering questions is about one hour. Therefore, the questionnaire had to be to the point, using only closed questions, and easy to answer. The questionnaire contained three parts, starting with a couple of introductory questions about the enterprise, then asking about tele-communication and IT and ending with more in-depth general questions about the enterprise. Technologies covered by the survey were the telephone, pagers, cellular phones, computers, e-mail and the World Wide Web. For each technology users were asked about the devices they use, about usage patterns and costs as well as the perceived effects of use. Non users were asked about the reasons for not using and their plans to introduce the technology. General enterprise questions covered structural data of the enterprise (legal set-up, age etc.), characteristics of the interviewed person (entrepreneur, manager), production technologies, markets, competition, employment, wages and financial data.

3.2.2. Sampling process

The selected site for the survey was Ambattur Industrial Estate in Chennai, which has already been described in section 3.1.3. Ambattur had been chosen for two reasons. First, because of its location and composition an interesting mix of various ICT-usage levels was expected. Second, the strength of the estate's association AIEMA and its interest in the subject of the study guaranteed easy access to the enterprises in the estate.

The population, from which the survey sample was drawn, was restricted in three ways. Firstly, the survey only covered Small Scale Industry enterprises. Secondly, out of the SSI enterprises only enterprises belonging to sectors 30 to 38 of the Indian Industry standardisation were considered.[66] Thirdly, these had to be members of the Ambattur Industrial Estate Manufacturers' Association (AIEMA).

The survey was restricted to sub-sectors 30 to 38 of the Indian Industry Standardisation because of the size of SSI enterprises in other sectors. In the textile sector operations are very labour intensive. Thus, SSI enterprises in textiles, garment and leather could be very large in terms of employment reaching a size that is not considered small by any conventional definition.[67] In order to exclude these enterprises from the survey companies belonging to the sub-sectors 20 to 29 were not considered.[68]

Only AIEMA members were sampled for the survey. This was done for various reasons. Firstly, most members of AIEMA belong to the Small Scale Industry sector which has been chosen for the survey. Secondly, the association covers the large majority of Small Scale Industry Enterprises in the estate and has a good standing with its

---

[66]   The sub-sectors 30 to 38 cover: 30 Basic chemicals & chemical products (except products of petroleum and coal); 31 Rubber, plastic, petroleum and coal products; 32 Non-metallic mineral products; 33 Basic metal and alloy industries; 34 Metal products and parts (except machinery and equipment); 35 Machinery and equipment other than transport equipment; 36 Electrical machinery and apparatus; 37 Transport equipment and parts; 38 Other manufacturing industries.

[67]   During the pilot survey in March 1999 a SSI textile company was interviewed that had more than 400 employees. Its company and management structure was different from smaller companies.

[68]   The sub-sectors 20 to 29 cover: 20-21 Food products; 22 Beverages, tobacco and related products; 23 Cotton textiles; 24 Wool, silk, and man-made fibre textiles; 25 Manufacture of jute and other vegetable fibre textiles (except cotton); 26 Textile products (including wearing apparel); 27 Wood and wood products; furniture and fixtures; 28 Paper & paper products and printing, publishing & allied industries; 29 Leather and leather & fur products.

members. Thirdly, the association was used to introduce the survey and elicit support for it from the entrepreneurs.[69]

By beginning of May 1999 AIEMA had 721 members.[70] Controlling for categories (small, medium large) and sectors of the enterprises given in AIEMA publications, 80 enterprises were excluded from the list – leaving the whole population of the survey at 641. The enterprises were randomly sampled. The author and ten MBA students from Velammal College of Management and Computer Studies, located near Ambattur Industrial Estate, tried to approach 532 companies during the period from 21st May to 11th June 1999.[71] For 64 of these enterprises (twelve percent) no interview was possible because the enterprise was closed, had shifted, was locked out or the location could not be identified. 21 enterprises (four percent) had the wrong size (medium or large scale) or belonged to excluded sectors. For 62 enterprises (twelve percent) it was not possible to arrange an interview during the time of the survey. 47 enterprises (nine percent) refused to be interviewed. In the end 330 interviews were conducted successfully, i.e. 51 percent of the population were interviewed.

In the process of cleaning the data it was discovered that another 22 interviewed companies belonged to excluded sectors. These questionnaires were not included in the analysis. Another 13 questionnaires had to be excluded after cleaning because a large number of answers were obviously wrong or dubious. Consequently, 295 interviews with Small Scale Industry enterprises, belonging to Indian Industry Standardisation 30 to 38, located in Ambattur Industrial Estate constitute the sample for analysis.

3.3. General enterprise characteristics

In this section general characteristics of the interviewed enterprises are examined. In order to give a brief overview sector composition, size, age, markets and perceived problems will be displayed and a few cross-tabulations are produced.

3.3.1. Industry sectors

First the sector composition of the sample is reviewed. Ambattur Industrial Estate is a traditional engineering cluster. More than 50 percent of the enterprises in the sample process metal (see Table 3-7). Another 25 percent manufacture machinery and equipment. Other sectors, such as chemicals and rubber, are much less represented. This bias in the estate becomes clearer when the sector composition of the survey is compared to the shares of SSI enterprises in the same sectors in the whole state of Tamil Nadu. Sectors 33 to 35 only account for about 35 percent of SSI enterprises in Tamil Nadu but about 75 percent of the sample in Ambattur.[72]

---

[69] AIEMA distributed a circular prior to the survey explaining the purpose and asking for support. The interviewers, who were also carrying this letter, reported that this had made access easier.

[70] Down from 742 a year earlier. 48 exits – mainly due to closures – met 27 new members.

[71] See Annex 2 for a detailed description of the execution of interviews.

[72] Comparing data from different years is difficult because of the high entry and exit numbers in the small scale sector. However, the tendency is certainly sustained when more recent numbers for Tamil Nadu would have been available.

Table 3-7: Sectors of interviewed enterprises

Sector		Sample Ambattur 1999		Tamil Nadu 1996/97*
		Number	Percent	Percent
30	Basic chemicals and chemical products	18	6.1	8.2
31	Rubber, plastic, petroleum and coal products	19	6.4	11.9
32	Non-metallic mineral products	3	1.0	7.8
33	Basic metal and alloy industries	41	13.9	3.1
34	Metal products and parts	108	36.6	14.2
35	Machinery and equipment	73	24.7	16.6
36	Electrical machinery and apparatus	14	4.7	7.6
37	Transport equipment and parts	8	2.7	7.1
38	Other manufacturing industries	11	3.7	23.4
Total		295	100.0	100.0

* Source: Government of Tamil Nadu (1998).

3.3.2. Enterprise performance

Fluctuation in the stock of enterprises is relatively high.[73] In the year prior to the survey AIEMA lost 48 members (6.5 percent of its membership), mainly due to closures. During the survey another nine percent of the contacted enterprises were discovered to have either moved or closed. The number of enterprises in the estate, thus, seems to decrease since only seven percent of the interviewed enterprises had been less than five years in business. The average age of the interviewed enterprises is 18 years. The specific age composition is given in Figure 3-3.

The lack of new enterprises replacing closed ones – 60 percent of the enterprises operate for 15 years and more - indicates that the estate has some problems. Indeed, many entrepreneurs complain about the recession that hit Indian industry in the time after 1997. Official figures see a slowdown of growth in 1997/98 for the Small Scale Industry sector from double digit numbers to approximately eight percent in real prices only.[74] Numbers for the interviewed enterprises are worse. Combined output of the 234 enterprises that gave information on turnover (including enterprises founded later than 1996) dropped by 3.7 percent in 1997/98 but rose by 7.5 percent in 1998/99.[75]

---

[73] This is typical for developing country most small-scale enterprise sectors (Mead / Liedholm 1998).

[74] In current prices annual growth rates are 15.8% with annual inflation rate at 5.4% (1996/97), 12.7% at 4.5% (1997/98), 13.4% at 5.3% (1998/99) and 9.7 at 6.5% (1999/00) with the last one being provisional (Government of India 2001).

[75] About 25 percent of the interviewees refused to give complete information about their enterprise's financials. This number is surprisingly low. Most problematic was data on profit and past turnover.

Figure 3-3: Year enterprises were founded

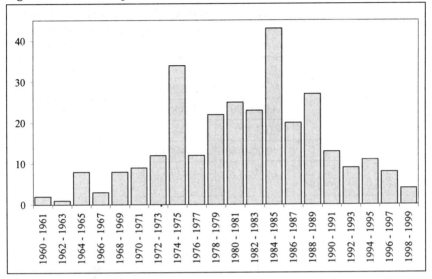

However, keeping in mind that quite a number of enterprises ceased operating in the period in question, these numbers are still too positive. For the 229 enterprises that gave this information and existed at the start of the observed period, output dropped by 3.8 percent in 1997/98 and only increased by 0.5 percent in 1998/99. On a more positive note many entrepreneurs stated that they had the feeling that the bottom had been reached and business was improving again at the time of the survey.

Looking at the size of the interviewed enterprises the following picture emerges (see Table 3-8). While generating an annual turnover in 1998/99 of about US$ 265,000 the interviewed enterprises are on average 6.6 times larger than the average Indian SSI enterprise. The average number of people working in the enterprise is five times higher than the national average, indicating that labour productivity is on average more than 30 percent higher in the interviewed enterprises than in the average Indian SSI enterprise. Annual turnover in the sample ranged from about US$ 2.500 to about US$ 5,700,000 in 1998/99, employment at the time of the survey from two to 200.

Looking at the different sectors covered by the survey there are differences in size as well as in labour productivity (see Table 3-9). In terms of turnover enterprises belonging to metal products and parts had an average turnover of just Rs. 6.4 million (about US$ 153,000) compared to an average of Rs. 18.6 million (about US$ 442,000) in the "other" category. In the latter category there are also on average, the most employees per enterprise (36.9), more than twice as many as in rubber, plastics, petroleum and coal products. The rubber et al. sector has the highest labour productivity with an average of nearly Rs. 540,000 (about US$ 12,800) per employee. Lowest labour productivity was found in metal products and parts with an average of less than Rs. 290,000 (about US$ 6,800).

Table 3-8: Size of interviewed enterprises

	Annual turnover (1998/99)		Number of people working for the enterprise at the time of the survey
	in Rs.	in US$*	
Reporting enterprises	261		290
Mean	11,158,372	265,233	27.6
Median	5,000,000	118,850	18.0
Minimum	104,379	2,481	2
Maximum	240,000,000	5,704,778	200
*Mean (for all Indian SSI enterprises in 1998/99)**	*1,690,212*	*40,176*	*5.5*

Source: Government of India (2001).
* 1 US$ = 42.07 Rs.

Table 3-9: Size and labour productivity by sector*

	Basic chemicals, chemical products	Rubber, plastic, petroleum and coal products	Basic metal and alloy industries	Metal products and parts	Machinery and equipment	Other
Annual turnover in Mio. Rs. (1998/99)						
Mean	12.099	6.737	16.196	6.428	11.058	18.609
Median	6.600	4.900	6.000	3.650	5.500	5.000
n, percentage of total	15/83.3	19/100	41/100	92/86.0	64/87.7	29/80.6
Number of people working for the enterprise at the time of the survey						
Mean	30.4	17.7	23.5	23.8	33.5	36.9
Median	22.5	13	14	15.5	20	18.5
n, percentage of total	18/100	18/94.7	41/100	108/100	70/95.9	34/94.4
Labour productivity in Rs. (1998/99)**						
Mean	474,288	537,473	406,763	287,054	339,151	481,482
n, percentage of total	15/83.3	18/94.7	38/95.0	89/83.2	62/83.8	29/82.3

* Only covering sectors that account for more than five percent of total. All others are subsumed under "other".
** Labour productivity 1998/99 is computed by dividing the turnover of 1998/99 by the average of the people working for the enterprises by the time of the survey and a year before the survey.

Table 3-10: Profit situation in the sample enterprises

Year	1996/97	1997/98	1998/99
Net profit or loss in percentage of turnover			
Mean (weighted by turnover)	8.4	6.9	8.5
Median*	8.0	7.5	7.0
Minimum	-25.0	-35.6	-166.7
Maximum	30.0	36.0	40.0
Number of enterprises reporting profit numbers (percentage of total)	_207 (71.9)_	_226 (77.9)_	_246 (83.7)_
Loss-making enterprises			
Percentage	7.6	14.2	11.6
Number of enterprises reporting profit or loss (percentage of total)	_210 (72.9)_	_233 (80.3)_	_250 (85.0)_

* including enterprises that reported a loss without specifying it (total in last row)

Table 3-11: Net profits in terms of turnover by sector*

Mean profit margin – weighted by turnover (n/percentage of total)	Basic chemical, chemical products	Rubber, plastic, petroleum and coal products	Basic metal and alloy industries	Metal products and parts	Machinery and equipment	Other
1996/97	7.8 (7/38.9)	9.8 (15/78.9)	6.7 (35/85.4)	10.5 (65/60.2)	9.7 (51/69.9)	5.7 (26/72.2)
1997/98	10.6 (9/50.0)	7.6 (15/78.9)	6.9 (35/85.4)	9.1 (75/69.4)	6.9 (57/78.1)	4.6 (27/75.0)
1998/99	10.7 (11/61.1)	10.6 (15/78.9)	10.4 (40/97.6)	9.4 (84/77.8)	7.0 (60/82.2)	6.1 (28/77.8)

* Only sectors that accounted for more than five percent of the sample are reported. All other enterprises are subsumed under "other".

Despite the difficult economic situation, the vast majority of interviewed enterprises were profitable, with 11.6 percent reporting a loss in the financial year 1998/99, down from 14.2 percent in the year before (see Table 3-10). Yet, these results are certainly positively biased since, on the one hand, loss-making enterprises that left the market in the observed period are not accounted for and, on the other hand, a higher share of loss-making enterprises is expected to be among the non-reporting enterprises. The average net profit of the enterprises that reported profit numbers was 8.5 percent of turnover in 1998/99 (up from 6.9 percent in 1997/98 and back to the level of 1996/97).

There appears to be no correlation between profit and size. Correlation coefficients for profit margin and turnover are not significant with values of -0.06 for 1996/97, -0.01 for 1997/98 and 0.05 for 1998/99. Sectorwise there are differences in profit margins (see Table 3-11). In 1998/99 in machinery and equipment as well as in the "other" category margins were well below average. In machinery and equipment margins had been going down in absolute and real terms during the reported years. A positive development for that period is observed for chemicals, as well as for basic metal and alloy industries. However, in these two industries the response rate (also reported in Table 3-11) is totally different. In the chemicals sector only about half of enterprises gave financial details which makes it questionable whether the reported margins really represent the situation in the whole sector. For basic metal and alloy industries, on the other hand, a large number of enterprises reported their figures giving a high degree of confidence in the result.

3.3.3. Exports

19 percent of the enterprises reported that they export some of their output. For five percent exports account for more than 25 percent of their total sales. Sectorwise machinery and equipment manufacturers are the most active exporters with almost one third of the enterprises reporting to export. Considering the 260 enterprises that reported turnover for 1998/99 as well as export figures, nine percent of their total turnover is sold abroad. This is almost the same rate that is reported for all Indian SSI enterprises by official sources (Government of India 2001). However, for Ambattur Industrial Estate as a whole the rate of exports will probably be higher since textile enterprises – with many producing for export only - were excluded from the survey. Exporting is related to size. Exporting enterprises had an average turnover of Rs. 23,633,581 (US$ 561,768) in 1998/99 while that of non-exporters was only 36 percent of this (Rs. 8,600,029 / US$ 204,422). The average employment in exporting enterprises is 50.8 compared with 22.9 in non-exporting ones.

3.3.4. Competition, sources of competitiveness and business problems

In an increasingly competitive business environment enterprises have to be aware of what constitutes their competitive advantage. They need to know the parameters that influence their competitive position and act in accordance to these findings.[76] In the survey the interviewed entrepreneurs were asked to rank the importance of certain criteria that determine competitiveness on a scale between 1 ("not important") to 7 ("very important"). The criteria were (a) price, (b) quality, (c) flexibility, (d) punctuality of delivery, (e) after sales services and (f) production capacity.

---

[76] Porter and Millar (1985) see the basic strategies to gain competitive advantages in either cost leadership or differentiation which can be combined with decisions on the scope of an enterprise's activities. Within this framework, Bamberger (1989) identifies categories such as costs, quality, service, image etc. as key success factors to achieve competitive advantages.

Quality, punctuality of delivery and price turned out to be the most important parameters for competition (see last row of Table 3-12). All three factors score about six and a half indicating that these factors are absolutely crucial for being competitive. With an average score of 5.6 and 5.0 flexibility and production capacity are also considered important but do not have the same weight as the other three factor. Least important are after sales services with an average score of 3.9.[77] Between the different sectors there is not much difference in the assessment of these determinants for competitiveness. Only for rubber and plastic producing enterprises the assessment of price's and quality's importance is higher than average (6.9 to 6.3). After sales services score higher by one point (4.5) for machinery and equipment manufacturers than the rest, reflecting the specific needs of the products they produce.[78]

Looking at differences between exporting and non-exporting enterprises it is interesting to note, that the price is not as important but after sales services are much more important for exporters than non-exporters (see Table 3-12). This indicates other priorities on foreign markets. Size generally does not affect the perception of the factors' importance. Only for the importance of after sales services is there a significant positive correlation with the number of people working for the enterprise.[79]

Table 3-12: Importance of various factors for competitiveness (on a scale from 1, „not important", to 7, „very important")

Export of products	Price	Quality	Flexibility	Punctuality of delivery	After sales services	Production capacity
No	6.4	6.6	5.5	6.5	3.7	5.0
Yes	5.9	6.6	5.7	6.3	4.9	5.0
Total	6.3	6.6	5.6	6.5	3.9	5.0

The entrepreneurs were also asked about their assessment of current competition in their markets. Answers were given on a scale between 1 for "no competition" to 7 for

---

[77] These results carry a lot of similarities but also some differences to the, unfortunately rather old, results from the STRATOS (Strategic Orientation of Small and Medium Enterprises) project (Bamberger 1989). STRATOS asked CEOs from more than 1000 European enterprises in clothing, food and electronics industries about the importance of 26 different factors to achieve a competitive advantage. Most important ranked "product quality" and "reliability of delivery" with values of 4.53 and 4.41 on scale from one to five. "Flexibility of the firm" comes fifth with 4.14 (preceded by "reputation of the firm" and "competence of workers (skills)". Different from the survey at Ambattur, price indicators ("low cost position" and "pricing policy") rank only in the midfield. "Service after delivery" ranks low in both surveys, being at position 22 and scoring 3.42 in the STRATOS survey.

[78] Sectorwise these results are basically in line with the results from the STRATOS survey (see previous footnote). Importance of factors is considered not much different in the three sectors clothing, food and electronics. For the service categories there are deviations. "Service after delivery" and "technical assistance before delivery" are, together with "engineering capacity", considered to a great degree more important by the electronics industry (Bamberger 1989).

[79] The correlation coefficient is 0.196 (number of observations is 279; significant at 1 percent level).

"fierce competition". On average competition was ranked at a level of 5.6 (see Table 3-13). Entrepreneurs in rubber and plastic found competition to be highest with 6.2. This coincides with their perception on the strong importance of "hard" factors such as price and quality for competitiveness. The "easiest" life report manufacturers of machinery and equipment which face competition only at a level of 5.3. There is no statistically significant difference between the perceived intensity of competition between exporters and non-exporters.

Table 3-13: Perceived intensity of competition (on a scale from 1, „no competition", to 7 „fierce competition") by sector*

	Basic chemicals, chemical products	Rubber, plastic, petroleum and coal products	Basic metal and alloy industries	Metal products and parts	Machinery and equipment	Other	Total
Perceived intensity of competition	5.7	6.2	5.5	5.6	5.3	5.8	5.6

* Only sectors that accounted for more than five percent of the sample are reported. All other enterprises are subsumed under "other".

The whole survey was basically designed to cope with the use of telecommunication and information technologies in small enterprises. However, there are a number of other areas which influence the success of a business. In the survey the entrepreneurs were asked to assess a wide range of factors that might constitute problems for their businesses.[80] The areas, that had to be rated on a scale of 1 for "no problem" to 6 for "great problem" were: (a) tax regulations, (b) electricity, (c) political situation, (d) labour standards, (e) finance, (f) telecommunication facilities, (g) special small scale regulations, (h) corruption, (i) demand, (j) infrastructure, (k) technology, and (l) foreign trade liberalisation.

The most important problem of doing business is electricity (see Table 3-14). Almost 40 percent of the interviewed entrepreneurs assign the highest rank to this area. Another 22 percent give this area a ranking of five. The second most important problem is finance with 25 percent of the entrepreneurs ranking the problem with a five or six. Least problematic are the extensive small scale industry regulation and foreign trade liberalisation. More than 60 percent of the entrepreneurs see no or only slight problems in these areas. However trade liberalisation is perceived more problematic by export-

---

[80] This question is basically borrowed from a large international private sector survey on the relation between private sector and governments, conducted in preparation of the World Development Report 1997 (World Bank 1997). Results from this specific question are presented by Brunetti et al. (1998).

ing enterprises (average score of 2.7; median of 3) than by non-exporting enterprises (average score of 1.9; median of 1).[81] Small scale industry regulations do not even hinder the larger enterprises. There is even a light but statistically not significant tendency for larger enterprises to assign less importance to this issue.

Table 3-14: Perceived problems of doing business (on a scale from 1, "no problem", to 6, "great problem")

Area	Mean	Median
Electricity	4.6	5
Finance	4.1	4
Demand	3.5	4
Tax regulation	3.4	4
Corruption	3.2	3
Labour regulations	3.1	3
Infrastructure	3.0	3
Telecommunication facilities	2.9	3
Technology	2.9	3
Political situation	2.8	2
Special Small Scale Industry regulation	2.3	2
Foreign trade liberalisation	2.2	1

3.3.5. Expectations

The entrepreneurs were asked how they expect their enterprise to change in the future. The time horizon for the expectations was given as three years. The interviewed entrepreneurs answered in various ways. After grouping the answers the following picture arose (see Table 3-15): In general, expectations concerning the future of the 271 enterprises that answered are quite positive. Only about three percent expect their situation to become worse. Although the 18 percent that do not have any idea about their future can be considered to have negative expectations as it will be extremely difficult to work successfully in an competitive environment without a vision of future business development. The metal products and parts and the rubber, plastics, petroleum and coal product sectors are gloomiest about the future, here about one third on the enterprises do not expect any positive developments. Nevertheless, about one third of the enterprises stated explicitly that they expect to grow. Surprisingly, the sector that

---

[81] Brunetti et al. (1998) unfortunately only provide answers to this question for India only aggregated together with Fiji and Malaysia. For these countries, tax regulation is most troublesome scoring more than four. This is followed by inadequate infrastructure, inflation and labour regulations. Finance is only ranked eighth, scoring about 3.5. Corruption is found in the midfield of both survey.

seems to be most gloomy also hosts the highest share of enterprises that expect to grow. In the rubber, plastics, petroleum and coal sector this was stated by almost half of the enterprises. In basic metal and alloy industries this figure was also over forty percent while the other sectors are about average. Technology is also a big issue. About 25 percent see the most important future changes in technology. Information technologies and the Internet are expected to play a leading role in this development. The leading sector here is the basic chemicals and chemical products sector. Hand in hand with the expectation to grow is the desire to conquer new markets and to produce new products. This is expected by ten percent of the interviewed entrepreneurs.

Table 3-15: Expected changes in the enterprise during the next 3 years*

	Frequency	Percent
Develop new markets	14	5.2
New products, diversification	13	4.8
Growth	73	26.9
Growth to medium scale	19	7.0
Better performance	23	8.5
Technological upgrading	40	14.8
Increase use of IT, Internet	46	17.0
Remain small	11	4.1
Reduce size	4	1.5
Close	5	1.8
No idea	49	18.1

* multiple answers were possible

The expected changes do not vary much between exporters and non-exporters. The only significant difference is that there are only five percent of exporters that quote to have no idea about the future of their enterprise whereas this figure is more than 20 percent for non-exporting enterprises.

3.3.6. Summary

The picture painted about the interviewed enterprises can be summarised as followed: The Small Scale Industry enterprises in Ambattur Industrial Estate are in general well established, most of them have been operating for more than a decade. The majority of enterprises are involved in metal processing and engineering, and in general they are larger and more productive than the Indian average. The estate was hard-hit by the industrial recession in 1997/98, which led to a decrease in turnover as well as profits and to the closure of a number of enterprises. The situation stabilised in 1998/99 and by the time of the survey the business cycle appeared to pick up again. Enterprise exports are in line with the national average. Strongest in exporting is the machinery and equipment sector. Exporting enterprises are on average much larger than non-exporting ones. The biggest problem the enterprises face is deficient electricity supply, followed by access to finance. Excessive Small Scale Industry regulations and foreign trade liberalisation are not considered very troublesome. General sentiment among the enterprises concerning the future is good. Most enterprises expect positive changes.

Sectorwise the rubber, plastics, petroleum and coal products sector is the best performer. These enterprises are on average 40 percent smaller than the overall average but report the highest labour productivity and the best profit margin. However, perceived intensity of competition is highest among the different sectors. Thus, the outlook of the enterprises is mixed. One third expect a negative development in the future while almost half expect to grow.

The backbone of the estate are the machinery and equipment manufacturers. On average they employ the most people but productivity is below average. The sector was hit hardest by the industrial recession. Profit margins went down and had not recovered by the time of the survey. Nevertheless, these enterprises are the most active exporters with one third of them claiming to sell products outside India.

Against this background the next section examines the use of telecommunications and information technology in the enterprises of the Ambattur Industrial estate.

3.4. Evidence of telecommunications and information technologies usage

The aim of this survey is to explore the use of telecommunication and information technologies in small enterprises. This chapter is supposed to provide evidence of ICT usage in Indian SSI enterprises against the background of the Indian ICT markets and the Indian small enterprise policy. The following section reviews the ICTs usage by SSI enterprise at the survey site in Ambattur Industrial Estate. First, the overall adoption rates of the different technologies are presented. Secondly, specific results for single technologies, regarding intensity of use, prices etc., are presented in more detail.

3.4.1. Overview

The enterprises were asked about telephones, fax machines, pagers, mobile phones, computers, e-mail and the World Wide Web (WWW). The number of enterprises that use these technologies are given in Table 3-16. A surprising result was the large number of enterprises using e-mail. By the time of the survey in May and June 1999 one third of the enterprises had their own access to e-mail. This was much more than expected even by entrepreneurs who were asked their opinion prior to the survey.

The diffusion of ICTs in Ambattur Industrial Estate follows normal patterns. Adding the revealed intent of introducing new technologies the following picture emerges (Figure 3-4):

The figure shows that e-mail is the fastest growing technology. The large number of entrepreneurs who stated that they are planning to install e-mail facilities in the near future is very interesting. This indicates that e-mail as a means of communication will become even more important in the future.

Table 3-16: Information and communication technologies used by the interviewed enterprises

Technology	Percentage of enterprises using the technology	Average number of devices in user enterprises
Telephone	100	2.3 (lines)
Fax	55	1.1
Pager	35	2.1
Cellular phone	37	1.4
Computer	64	2.7
E-mail	34	n.a.
WWW	19	n.a.
Web-page	4.4	n.a.

Figure 3-4: Diffusion of communication technologies over time

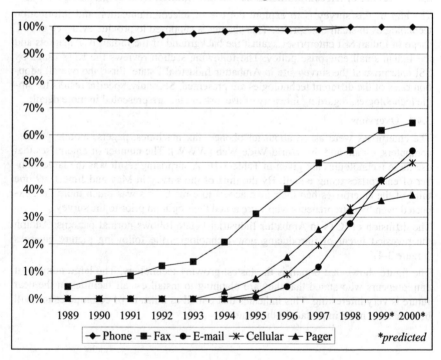

3.4.2. Telecommunication

3.4.2.1. Telephones

All of the interviewed enterprises had a basic phone connection on their premises. 60 percent had more than one line, and four percent even more than five lines. The average was 2.26 lines per enterprise. The average monthly bill per enterprise was Rs. 4,689 (about US$ 110), the average monthly bill per line was Rs. 2,082 (about US$ 50). In relative terms the enterprises spent on average (weighted by turnover) 0.59 percent of total expenditure on telephone calls (0.55 percent in terms of turnover). There is a significant positive correlation between enterprise size and absolute expenditure on telephone, but no significant correlation between enterprise size and relative expenditure.

To use telephone lines for services other than voice telephony the quality of lines an connections must be high. This has traditionally been a problem in India, but the situation seems to have been improved in the last year. Asked on the change in quality of connections during the last five years about 65 percent of those able to answer saw an improvement in local and national calls. For international calls this rate was even higher than 75 percent. Another important issue is waiting time to get a line connected. Chennai Telephones claims that there was no waiting list for Ambattur Industrial Estate by late 2000. Yet, at the time of the survey one third of the people able to answer such a question said it would take between six and twelve months. Another third stated that it would take more than twelve months. Nevertheless, situation had improved from previous years. Five years earlier these figures were 14 percent and 75 percent respectively. Thus, the perceived quality of telephone service has improved. In the 1999 more than 40 percent of the interviewed persons assigned some degree of efficiency to the service, less than 20 percent did so five years prior. Thus, despite this change for the better, there was still much scope for improvement.

3.4.2.2. Fax machines

In 55 percent of the interviewed enterprises there was a fax machine at the time of the survey. Another 19 percent used outside facilities to send and receive faxes, thus only 26 percent of enterprises did not use a fax at all. Of the non-users 18 percent stated to have plans to use a fax in the future. This result is in line with the fact that the most important reason given for not using fax was that there was no need for this. One fourth of those that use a fax outside the enterprise did this in another enterprise or at home. Three quarters used public fax offices, which were on average 1.6 kilometres (median 1 km) away from the enterprise and where they paid on average Rs. 37 (median Rs. 30) for sending and Rs. 14 (median Rs. 10) for receiving a one-page national fax.[82] Of the users of public fax offices 52 percent indicated to have plans to buy a fax machine. The most important reason for not owning a fax machine was low frequency of sending and receiving faxes. These results indicate that the demand for fax services was satisfied but there was still scope for more fax machines in the enterprises.

---

[82]   As a comparison, a one-minute national call did cost between Rs. 5 and Rs. 30, depending on distance.

The vast majority of enterprises with a fax had only one machine within the enterprise (94 percent). Data on specific fax machines in the enterprises is available for almost 90 percent of machines. On average these machines were five years old and had cost Rs. 23,142 (median Rs. 20,000). Prices dropped over the last few years, especially since 1997 when the average price fell below the Rs. 20,000 mark. In 1998 and 1999 on average about Rs. 16,000 (US$ 380) had been paid for a fax machine.

Enterprises that own a fax machine spent, on average, some 25 percent of their phone bill on fax services, i.e. on average, Rs. 2120 (about US$ 50) per month. The median enterprise that owned a fax machine sent and received five to ten faxes per week. About twenty percent of the enterprises sent and received more than 20 per week. Public fax office users utilised this service even less. The median enterprise just sent between one and five faxes per week, and half of these enterprises received less than one fax per week. Almost all faxes were sent to business partners. On average two thirds of faxes were directed to customers and one fourth to suppliers. Other destinations, e.g. public agencies, played no role. The more faxes are sent the more higher is the share of locations outside Tamil Nadu or India (see Table 3-17).

Table 3-17: Fax receivers' location in percent by frequency of fax use

Faxes sent for business purposes per week	Location of receivers			
	Chennai	Tamil Nadu	Other states	Abroad
Less than 1	59,7	22,9	12,4	5,0
1 to 5	46,5	22,4	27,2	4,0
5 to 10	43,5	22,5	31,8	2,2
10 to 20	37,9	14,1	39,6	8,4
More than 20	23,9	21,3	39,7	15,1
Total	42,1	20,8	31,0	6,2

When asked about the impact of fax on the relation between enterprises and their customers and suppliers, as well as on competitiveness and efficiency of administration a very positive picture emerges (see Table 3-18). More than 90 percent of those that use a fax within or outside their enterprises saw an improvement in customers relations, and more than three quarter an improvement in the relationship with suppliers.[83] More than three quarters of enterprises saw an improvement in their administration. Least positive was the perceived effect of fax on competitiveness which reflects the fact that fax was already widely used and therefore could not give a competitive edge. For all measures the improvement ratio is increasing with increasing frequency of fax use.[84]

---

[83]   The difference certainly reflects the higher share of faxes with customers as receivers.

[84]   For customer relations the ratio of enterprises that see an improvement through fax use increases from 50 percent for less than one per week to 100 percent for more than 20 per week. For supplier

Table 3-18: Perceived effects of fax usage (percentage of users)

	Fax has improved relationship with customers	Fax has improved relationship with suppliers	Fax makes enterprise more competitive	Fax increases efficiency of administration
Yes, significantly	58	43	24	39
Yes, slightly	34	35	28	38
No, no effect	5	16	40	18
No, even negative effect	0	0	0	1
Don't know	3	5	9	5

3.4.2.3. Pagers and cellular phones

Pagers and cellular phones, that enable mobile communication, appear to be both substitutes and complements in the interviewed enterprises. Of the about fifty percent of enterprises that used these devices forty percent used both, whereas about one third used just cellular phones and about one fourth used just pagers (see Table 3-19). The role of pagers in the enterprise might be twofold. Whereas cellular phones clearly are tools used by the enterprises' top people, pagers might be used by staff members, especially when cellular phones are used. This is indicated by three facts. First, the average number of devices in using firms was higher in the case of pagers (2.1 against 1.4, see Table 3-16) and highest in the enterprises that used both technologies (2.4 pagers

Table 3-19: The use of pagers and cellular phones in the sample enterprises

Count		Cellular phone used in the enterprise			
		yes	no, but used in the past	no	Total
Pager used in the enterprise	yes	61		42	103
	no, but in the past	4	4	5	13
	no	45	2	132	179
Total		110	6	179	295

relations this increase is from 45 to 97 percent, for competitiveness from 25 to 66 percent and for efficiency of administration from 43 to 88 percent.

on average). Second, in enterprises that used cellular phones and pagers at the same time, the most important reason to use a pager was for the entrepreneur to keep in touch with his employees when they are outside the enterprise.[85] When only pagers were used, communication with employees when they are outside, and communication with the entrepreneur when he /she is outside, scored the same value of importance. Third, enterprises that used pagers and cellular phones were on average larger than enterprises that used only one or none of these technologies (see Table 3-20).

Table 3-20: Enterprise size and use of pagers and cellular phones

Pager used	Cellular phone used	Mean	N
Yes	Yes	41.7	59
	No, but used in the past	n.a.	0
	No	30.4	42
	Total	37.0	101
No, but used in the past	Yes	26.0	4
	No, but used in the past	16.5	4
	No	20.0	4
	Total	20.8	12
No	Yes	35.1	43
	No, but used in the past	26.0	2
	No	18.7	131
	Total	22.8	176
Total	Yes	38.4	106
	No, but used in the past	19.7	6
	No	21.5	177
	Total	27.7	289

The differences in size certainly reflect the differing price of obtaining and using pagers and cellular phones. At the time of the survey pagers cost on average about Rs. 2,000 (see section 3.1.2.2 for details) and the monthly charge was Rs. 300 for alpha-numeric and Rs. 175 for numeric pagers. Costs of cellular phones were much higher. Although prices had come down the enterprises in the sample that had bought a cellular phone in 1998 or 1999 had paid, on average, more than Rs. 12,200 (US$ 290) for these phones (see Table 3-21). Besides the cost for the handset the users of cellular phones spent considerable amounts on actual use. The cellular users in the survey

---

[85]   The answer scored on average 4.5 on a scale from 1 "not importance" to 5 "great importance" for cellular phone using enterprises and just 3.4 for users of pagers only.

spent on average Rs. 2,178 per month on use per phone. 50 percent spend Rs. 1,500 and more, 25 percent Rs. 2,250 and more.[86] Compared to the costs of acquiring and using pagers these are considerable.

Table 3-21: Price of Cellular Phones (in Rs.)

Year phone was bought	Number	Mean	Minimum	Maximum
1995	8	26.375	9.000	40.000
1996	19	19.816	8.000	38.000
1997	29	16.586	7.000	30.000
1998	47	11.768	3.000	30.000
1999	13	13.769	7.500	25.000
Total	116*	15.522	3.000	40.000

* for 116 out of a total of 153 phones prices were reported

As shown in section 3.1.2.2 prospects for the paging industry in India are not very bright. This was reflected in the answers of the sample enterprises. Only a meagre eight percent of enterprises that did not use pagers were planning to get one in the future. On the other hand, six percent of non-users (12 enterprises) had had a pager but stopped using it. 50 percent had stopped using it because they no longer needed it, 33 percent had got a mobile phone and 17 percent had found the service too expensive.

By the time of the survey the situation of the mobile industry in India in general as well as in Chennai was stagnating. Only in late 1999 did growth pick up again (see Figure 3-1 and Figure 3-2 in section 3.1.2). However, even at the time of the survey the situation for cellular phones looked better than that for pagers. Of the non-using enterprises in the sample 26 percent indicated plans to get a cellular phone. Considering the exploding growth of subscribers in Chennai in the second half of 1999 and in 2000 one can expect that even more enterprises have introduced cellular phones today.[87] Of the non-users only three percent had a phone before. All of these had stopped because they considered the use to be too expensive. High cost, together with not seeing any use for a cellular phone in business, was the most important reason given for not having used a cellular phone at all.[88]

The main reason given for using a mobile phone was to keep in touch with the own enterprise when away, scoring an average of 4.3 on a scale from 1 ("no importance")

---

[86] Cellular phones can be used for personal communication. However, the cellular phones in the enterprises were largely used for business purposes. On average the interviewed persons indicated that 71 percent of calls were related to business issues.

[87] The number of cellular phone subscribers in Chennai increased from 36,218 in June 1999 to 96,224 in December 2000 (COAI 2001).

[88] Cellular phones being too expensive as a reason for not using them scored on average 3.3 on a scale from 1, "no importance", to 5, "great importance", with one third of respondents assigned the highest category. The same score was reached by "no use for business". Other possible reasons were considered less important.

to 5 ("great importance") with more than 50 percent of the interviewed person giving this argument the highest rank. Easing the contact with customers and suppliers and the expectation of customers and suppliers to be accessible scored an average of 3.9 each. These findings are also reflected by the answers about the conversation partners. The majority, with almost 50 percent, were customers, followed by the own enterprise with about 25 percent and suppliers with about 20 percent. Thus, cellular phones seem to be an important tool for the decision maker in a small company because he /she is accessible at longer periods.

Since pagers only allow for an immediate one-way communication they cannot generate comparable benefits. Consequently, the perception of effects concerning communication were much less positive for pagers than for mobile phones. While 89 percent of cellular phone users found that their relation to customers and suppliers improved through the use of the phone, only 70 percent of pager users agreed on this, but almost 80 percent of cellular as well as pager users saw an improvement in the co-ordination between employees and entrepreneurs. Relating to non-communication issues, users were more sceptical. 40 percent of cellular users and 50 percent of pager users saw no improvement in competitiveness through the use of the particular technology.

3.4.3. Information technologies

3.4.3.1. Computers

At the time of the survey 64 percent of the interviewed enterprises were using computers, and another 14 percent were planning to introduce computers in 1999 or 2000. Computer use is clearly related to enterprise size. Enterprises that use computers were more than three and a half times as large as those that did not in terms of turnover.[89] The main reason for not using a computer at that time was that there was no perceived need for it in the business.[90] For enterprises planning to use computers, the most important reason to do so was the expectation that computers would make administration easier (followed by the statement that computers have become a common tool).[91] Pressure from suppliers and customers was the least important reason given.[92] Regarding planned use 82 percent of enterprises wanted to use computers for bookkeeping and cost accounting, and 74 percent wanted to use it for salary administration. This reflects the positive expectations concerning the use of computers in administration. Using computers for design and production control was only planned by 33 percent and 44 percent of enterprises respectively.

46 percent of computerised enterprises owned only one computer; another 22 percent owned two; the remainder three or more, making up for an average of 2.7 machines per using enterprise. There was a significant correlation between the number of computers in the enterprise and enterprise size measured in turnover (correlation coeffi-

---

[89]   About Rs. 15,000,000 against about Rs. 4,000,000 turnover.

[90]   On a scale from 1, "no importance" to 5 "great importance" this statement scores on average 3.5 for the enterprises that did not plan to introduce a computer and 2.7 for enterprises that planned the use.

[91]   The former statement scored on average 4.3 on the scale from 1 to 5, the latter on average 3.9.

[92]   On average 2.5 was scored on the scale from 1 to 5.

cient of 0.403). On average the computers used were about three to four years old. However, the majority had a at least a Pentium processor, indicating that normally the latest available model is bought. This was not the case for periphery equipment. Dot-matrix printers were the most common, presumably because of their low operation costs and their low susceptibility to adverse climate conditions. Matrix printers were used in 85 percent of the using enterprises. Ink-jet printers were found in 40 percent and laser printers only in twelve percent of the enterprises. Other advanced periphery equipment, e.g. scanners, were used only in very few enterprises.

The main uses of computers were word processing, bookkeeping and cost accounting which was done by more than 85 percent of the enterprises respectively and accounted together on average for about 60 percent of time the computers were used (see Table 3-22). Design was done by 30 percent of the computer-using enterprises. These particular enterprises spent on average more than one quarter of their computer time on design.

Table 3-22: Computer applications use

	Application						
	Word processing	Bookkeeping and cost accounting	Salary calculation	Inventory control and database management	E-mail, Internet, EDI	Design	Production control
Percentage of enterprises using application	87.2	86.1	61.1	56.1	42.2	30.6	21.7
Mean of computing time (for all 180 reporting enterprises)	28.0	32.9	9.3	9.6	7.0	8.2	4.2
Mean of computing time (for application users)	32.1	38.1	15.3	17.2	16.6	26.8	19.2
Average number of computers (users)	2.59	2.58	2.86	3.21	3.63	3.76	3.31
Average number of computers (non-users)	2.26	2.40	2.07	1.41	1.77	2.02	2.35
t-test value for equality of means	0.37	0.32	1.97*	3.90*	4.99*	4.27*	2.03*

* significant at 5% level

Word-processing and bookkeeping were the basic computer applications used by almost every using enterprise. All other applications, such as design or electronic communication seem to require a more computerised enterprise. Enterprises that used these applications owned, on average, significantly more computers than enterprises that utilised computers just for basic tasks (see Table 3-22). Since the number of computers is positively correlated with enterprise size it seems that sophisticated computer use is also related size.

Even more interesting for the intensity of computer use in enterprises is the number of people who work with them. Internal penetration rates indicate the level of computerisation of an enterprise. The surveyed enterprises reported an average of 4.5 computer users per using enterprise. In 40 percent of the enterprises two people or fewer operated the computers. In 70 percent of the cases the interviewee himself was the user. In 80 percent employees had access to the machines. Thus, in the computer using enterprises about half of the people working in administration and management worked with computers some of the time. Set in relation to the whole enterprise about 16 percent of all people in using enterprises worked with computers.

The entrepreneurs considered computer knowledge of employees in administration and management very important. Almost half of the interviewed enterprises in which computers were used stated that computer skills are essential when new administrative staff is hired. In addition 60 percent of the computer using enterprises indicated a wage surcharge for computer skills for newly employed administrative staff. On average this surcharge was reported to be between ten and 25 percent.

Regarding the acquisition of computer knowledge learning by doing was by far the most important. For more than 60 percent of the interviewed entrepreneurs it was the only or the most used source of gaining experience. Other means of acquiring knowledge such as courses, mass media or advice by friends and family members were used on average only "seldom" or "sometimes". For employees that used computers, learning by doing was the most important source of acquiring computer skills. However, a great deal of emphasis was placed on the employees' own initiative. Many employers preferred to employ people with the appropriate skills rather than rely on on-the-job training. Further important source of acquiring computer skills was employees own initiative to attend courses on the matter. Sending employees to courses or hiring consultants was only done by a minority of enterprises.

This low utilisation level of outside advise and training provided by the enterprises for their employees, in addition to the low level of utilisation of external advise for the entrepreneurs, indicates a high potential for specialised training courses and facilities. In particular when more sophisticated applications are to be introduced. Relying only on on-the-job training or hiring of people with the required qualifications might, however, be short-sighted since these skills will become increasingly important and constant learning is crucial in this fast evolving area.

On the whole the interviewed persons rated the impact of computers as very positive. Almost all felt that computers increase the efficiency of administration. An effect on competitiveness was less ubiquitous with approximately one third of enterprises noting a significantly positive impact (see Table 3-23). This was probably because on the one hand computer-based applications in most companies were still very basic and therefore had not penetrated the whole processing chain. On the other hand, this result reflects in fact that computers are common only in enterprises above a certain size, and therefore were not seen as a means of increasing competitiveness.[93]

Table 3-23: Perceived effects of computer use

	Computers increase efficiency of administration	Computers make the enterprise more competitive
	%	%
Yes, significantly	72%	37%
Yes, slightly	23%	26%
No, no effect	4%	25%
No, even negative effect	0%	1%
Don´t know	1%	11%

3.4.3.2. Internet

The fastest growing technology by the time of the survey was e-mail. Approximately one third of all interviewed enterprises used this technology, a number much higher than expected, even by the people in Ambattur Industrial Estate. It is indicative of the dramatic development and growth in the use of e-mail in India at that time. In addition to the 33.9 percent who used e-mail 18.6 percent of enterprises indicated that they are planning to use e-mail either that year or in the year 2000 (11.2 percent for 1999; 7.5 percent for 2000). This results in a penetration rate of 50 percent in years after the technology became available (see Figure 3-4).

The cost-saving property of e-mails was in particular revealed by the survey.[94] Nearly one third of all e-mails sent by the interviewed enterprises were sent to locations abroad. Another half were sent to locations outside Chennai. E-mail has become, such as fax, a necessity for enterprises with international relations, just like the fax. International business partners expect their Indian counterparts to be easy and cheaply accessible. Therefore, three quarters of the interviewed enterprises that exported some part of their output had access to e-mail (compared to one quarter of non-exporting enterprises). Exporters had a very positive perception of e-mail. 60 percent of exporters that used e-mail said that it improved the relation to their customers significantly, compared to 40 percent of the non-exporting enterprises. The same holds for competitive-

---

[93] This reasoning is also used to explain the productivity paradox, i.e. the lack of evidence that spending on IT increases productivity, discussed in section 2.1.4.1. Hitt and Brynjolfsson (1996) argue that investments in IT are necessary to remain competitive but do not constitute a competitive advantage because everybody is investing.

[94] The cost aspect is often neglected in information systems literature on e-mail. Rudy (1996), for example, lists as positive features solely that discussion can occur asynchronously, that data can be shared more easily, that individuals can think before they reply and that it is unintrusive.

ness. 50 percent of the exporting enterprises felt themselves significantly more competitive through the use of e-mail. This opinion was only shared by 20 percent of the non-exporters (see Table 3-24).

Table 3-24: Perceived effects of e-mail use in relation to exporting activities

Export of products	E-mail has improved the relation to customers		E-mail increases efficiency of administration		E-mail makes enterprise more competitive	
	no	yes	no	yes	no	Yes
Yes, significantly	39%	61%	25%	55%	20%	50%
Yes, slightly	41%	29%	46%	16%	41%	18%
No, no effect	11%	8%	20%	21%	27%	21%
No, even negative effect	0%	0%	0%	0%	0%	0%
Don't know	9%	3%	9%	8%	13%	11%

In spite of the importance of e-mail described above, it should be noted that they were not used extensively at that time. The majority of users received and sent no more than ten mails per week. Less than one in ten users sent and received more than 25 mails per week. E-mails were, of course, not only sent for business purposes but private ones too. On average about two thirds of e-mails are send for business purposes. 90 percent of business related e-mails' receivers were customers and suppliers, with customers accounting for the major share. Electronic communication with private agents, e.g. chartered accountants or auditors, or with public agencies, was negligible. Developing electronic communication channels to public authorities should certainly be a large goal for the future as this has high potential for making operations more efficient and saving time and money.

An additional important internet application besides e-mail is the World Wide Web (WWW) whose use in India is still restricted by an insufficient telecommunication infrastructure. Although private internet service providers (ISPs) started operating in late 1998 the quality of connections is improving only slowly. Additionally the equipment to use the internet also hinders an effective use of the WWW in many enterprises. At the time of the survey the majority of enterprises with communication equipment used modems with a 33.6 kilobits per second transmission capacity or less. These are fine for e-mails but too slow for reasonable WWW performance. Due to these inconveniences only 45 percent of e-mail users also claimed to use the WWW. Of these users nearly two thirds spent up to 5 hours per week on the net. Business use and sending and receiving e-mails accounted for 85 percent of this time. The main uses for business purposes were to look for information on potential customers and suppliers and technical information. However, the propagated function of the WWW as being a tool to develop new business relations had not materialised on a significant scale (see Table 3-25). There were only occasional anecdotes on successes in "E-commerce".[95] Asking for the benefits of using the WWW revealed that the WWW was mainly a means by which to keep in touch with technical developments. Many entrepreneurs visited the Web-pages of leading companies in their field to get new ideas. If these ideas find their way into the development and production of own products, the Internet could become a tool in narrowing the gap to international benchmarks.

Table 3-25: Perceived benefits of using the WWW

Information found in the WWW helps ...	... being better informed about new technical developments	... finding better and cheaper supply sources	...finding new customers	... being better informed about new laws, regulations and policies
Yes, significantly	49%	25%	17%	9%
Yes, slightly	36%	36%	45%	21%
No, no effect	11%	36%	30%	53%
Don't know	4%	4%	8%	17%

The WWW can, of course, serve not only as a tool to receive, but also to disseminate, information. At the time of the survey already 13 of the 295 interviewed enterprises were present on the WWW. This presence ranged, however, from simple entries of basic enterprise information in the business section of Chennai Online (http://www.chennaionline.com) to full-fledged enterprise and product presentations under an own domain (e.g.: http://www.vanjax.com). One can be sure that the need to present enterprises on the WWW has increased since the survey. Especially enterprises that want to enter international markets or expand their international presence will find it more and more of a necessity to be present on the Internet.

3.4.4. Comparing technologies

In the previous sections characteristics of ICT use were presented technology by technology. This section aims to analyse differences between them and identify common features.

Firstly, there are only few SSI enterprises that are very fast in adopting newly available technologies. Two years after cellular phones, pagers and e-mail became available not more than 20 percent of enterprises were using them. For fax machines the 20 percent mark was only passed in 1994. However, once a certain threshold of between ten and 20 percent is reached use picks up significantly, leading to a high penetration in a couple of years. By the time of the survey all technologies were well established with penetration rates of at least one third. The reasons given by non-users for not using these technologies indicate a cost-benefit rationale behind the decision to wait with the

---

[95]   One company reported to have bought a second-hand machine from the US that it found in the Internet. Another company reported that the Internet helped to get an order from a large company. Yet, other enterprises reported that they found information on specific spare parts or on patents.

introduction. In almost all cases, lack of perceived benefits or high costs, which are of course only different sides of the same problem, were of prime importance. Mirroring this argument, most users seemed to be well-aware of the potential benefits of the technology they have chosen to adopt. A good example is the speed-enhancing and cost-reducing property of technologies, such as fax and e-mail, compared to traditional means such as telephone and letter. This is especially the case in international commu-nication. Hardly any enterprise with foreign customers did not have a fax machine, and three quarters of exporters used e-mail while only one quarter of non-exporting firms did (see Table 3-26).

Table 3-26: Relation between exports and technology use in the enterprise

		Export of products (yes/no)	
		no	yes
Fax	no	105 (46%)	4 (8%)
	yes	125 (54%)	48 (92%)
Pager	no	158 (69%)	23 (44%)
	yes	72 (31%)	29 (56%)
Cellular phone	no	155 (67%)	19 (37%)
	yes	75 (33%)	33 (63%)
Computer	no	92 (40%)	3 (6%)
	yes	138 (60%)	49 (94%)
E-mail	no	171(74%)	13 (25%)
	yes	59 (26%)	39 (75%)

In addition to cost-benefit considerations size seems to be an important determinant of ICT use. Comparing the size (in terms of turnover) of users and non-users significant differences evolve for all basic technologies (see Table 3-27).[96] Thus, either the use of ICTs involves economies of scale, or size is a proxy for other enterprise characteristics that determine ICT use. The general impression that large companies are the pioneer users of modern communication facilities, followed by SMEs, which are then followed by micro-enterprises and private users, supports the former proposition.[97] Yet, most of the technologies involved incur significant costs. The average price of a fax machine was about Rs. 16,000 (about US$ 380) in 1999. For a cellular phone one had to pay about Rs. 12,000 (about US$ 290) and a standard desk-top computer including a small monitor was between Rs. 35,000 and 50,000 (about US$ 800 to 1200) at the time of

---

[96] Only the use of the WWW revealed no significant size differences. When comparing the size of e-mail and WWW users within the group of computer users there were also no significant differ-ences in mean size.

[97] This development was outlined in section 3.1.2.3 for the Internet in India.

the survey. Nominally, these prices appear not to be very high but when compared to the average monthly wage of an employee, Rs. 2,500 (about Rs. 3,500 in administration) or the median annual turnover of Rs. 5,000,000 it becomes clear that investments in ICTs are not trivial for many enterprises. Thus, the size bias might also be a reflection of financial ability.

Table 3-27: Relation between size and technology use in the enterprise

	Average turnover 1998/99		T-value testing for equality of means
	Users	Non-users	
Fax	15,012,300	4,817,319	3.84*
Pager	18,477,621	6,964,058	4,18*
Cellular Phone	19,314,215	6,084,509	4,94*
Computer	14,378,745	3,972,692	3,77*
E-mail	16,405,449	7,857,909	3,08*
E-mail (only computer users)	16,405,449	11,853,400	1,18
WWW	15,084,341	9,850,409	1,52
WWW (only computer users)	15,084,341	14,103,390	0,22

* significant at 1% level

It is not only interesting to look at whether or not technologies are used, but also to look at the intensity of use. Use tends to become relatively intensive within SSI enterprises after adoption, hence these enterprises, although not pioneers, are quite an important user category for service providers. On average the interviewed enterprises spent nearly Rs. 4,700 (about US$ 110) per month on telephones. For fax users 25 percent of the phone bill was on average due to fax use, bringing the use up to more than Rs. 2100 (about US$ 50) on average. Cellular phone users spent on average nearly Rs. 2,200 (about US$ 52). Only utilisation of e-mail seemed to be relatively low, and is probably accounted for by the poor quality of the telecommunication infrastructure. Compared to the average wage figures given above, it becomes clear that regular spending on ICTs is a significant cost figure in SSI enterprises.

In this last section two issues are raised. The first is on differences between technology users and non-users. The second is on the intensity of use. The next chapter will explore in more detail the determinants that lead to the introduction of a technology, and the determinants of intensity of use post introduction.

4. DETERMINANTS OF ICT ADOPTION AND USE

4.1. Introduction

In the previous chapter it was shown how the use of different ICTs has developed over time in the examined enterprises. Figure 3-4 plots the diffusion curves for fax machines, mobile phones, pagers and e-mail, it shows an acceleration in the number of new users in the first years after introduction and a decrease in the additional users for older (fax) or less attractive (pager) technologies in recent years. The curves in Figure 3-4 show a pattern that is observed in most diffusion processes – the so-called S-shaped or sigmoid diffusion curve. It was also shown in the previous chapter that the users perceive the impact of ICTs on their enterprises as very positive. If this is so, the question arises, why not all enterprises have adopted these technologies and why does the speed of diffusion of the different technologies differ? This chapter will explore what factors determine enterprise behaviour with regard to ICT, i.e. the individual decision to use a new technology.

These questions are addressed by a variety of different theories and approaches on the diffusion of innovation and technological change. In section 4.2 a short overview over these different approaches is given. Several economic model families, analysing the diffusion of innovation, are examined together with a comprehensive, communication science based model, and their ability to provide answers to the questions raised above is assessed. In section 4.3 the specificity of ICT adoption is discussed in more detail and empirical evidence is reviewed. Departing from this short review a combined model of the determinants of ICT adoption and the intensity of using is developed in section 4.4. This model encloses different dimensions of adoption determinants. On the lines developed in section 4.4, and while keeping in mind the results of section 4.3, in section 4.5 the survey data is analysed. Limited dependent variable regression models are developed and tested for the impact of the determinants on the current adoption, the time of adoption and the intensity of use. The models are applied for different ICTs. So far most studies on technology adoption are focussed on one specific technology, neglecting technology specific factors. For a low-income country no multi-technology study on ICT adoption, using formal models has been undertaken.

4.2. Technology adoption: An overview over different approaches

4.2.1. Basic questions and the history of diffusion and adoption research

The examination of technology adoption in enterprises has to solve one basic question (Silverberg et al. 1988:1032): Why do not all potential users introduce new technologies at the same time? If a new technology is superior to its predecessor why is the old, inferior technology not replaced immediately? Technology diffusion and adoption research try to find answers to these questions. As a major task, all models of technology adoption have to accommodate an empirical regularity of innovation diffusion. If the ratio of individuals, firms etc. that use the innovation is plotted against time in almost all cases a S-shaped curve arises. The diffusion of an innovation starts with the use by a few innovators. It gradually increases up to a take-off point in which the speed of penetration accelerates. Later on in the diffusion process the speed by which new users join decreases until the saturation level is reached. This pattern was observed for the adoption if ICTs among the surveyed Indian Small-Scale Industry enterprises an is shown in Figure 3-4.

Research in technology adoption and diffusion can be divided into two different strands (Weiber 1992:3). First, there is adoption theory that is concerned with the individual decision to adopt or not adopt an innovation. Sustained adoption will be the final element of an innovation-decision process that comprises five stages, i.e. knowledge, persuasion, decision, implementation and confirmation (Rogers 1995:162-186). Second, there is diffusion theory, this examines the spread of an innovation in a social or economic system. It is based on the findings of adoption theory but considers aggregated adoption processes. Adoption theory, thus, is mainly concerned with decision processes within enterprises and looks towards innovation from the view of the innovator and adopter. Whereas diffusion theory focuses on the innovation itself and examines the pattern of diffusion in a specified social or economic system. Adoption theory, therefore, may be considered to cope with intra personal reasons for adoption, while diffusion theory is concerned with inter personal reasons. However, both strands of theory are closely related and only rarely is a differentiation found (Weiber 1992:3).[98]

Diffusion of technologies can be studied in two other ways. Firstly, diffusion within an organisation, i.e. the extent the innovation is used and how the use spreads. Secondly, diffusion through a set of organisations or individuals. In the latter case one is not concerned with the intensity of use but with the question whether the technology is used or not. Diffusion studies normally use this approach. This is due to the fact that intra-organisation (normally intra-firm) diffusion is hard to measure and even harder to model. As yet, not much work has been done in this field.[99]

Diffusion of innovations among organisations is a widely researched area.[100] Modern diffusion research has its starting point with a seminal study by Ryan and Gross on the use of hybrid-seed corn by farmers in Iowa published in 1943.[101] Rogers (1995:44) considers this study to be the starting point for the development of a diffusion research paradigm in the Kuhnian sense. Diffusion research reached its heights in the 1960s and 1970s. The number of new publications declined in the 1980s and 1990s. In the first

---

[98] Models of diffusion are generally concerned with the time between the first introduction of an innovation and saturation. After saturation use might drop as the innovation is succeeded by another one. This phenomenon is not accorded much prominence in this work since, the presented economic diffusion theories are not overly concerned with the substitution of technologies and the examined technologies, i.e. ICTs, are fairly new and still in the expansion phase. Only pagers are to a certain extent substitutes for mobile phones and are loosing ground with the growing popularity of mobile phones.

[99] See Stoneman and Battisti (1997) for an account of the current research and for the arising measurement problems.

[100] Rogers (1995:XV) counted a total of nearly 4,000 publications in the field by 1995. At the time of the first edition of his book "Diffusion of Innovations" in 1962 there were just 400. Currently about three quarters of the publications are of an empirical nature, and one quarter is theoretical or bibliographical (Weiber 1992:1).

[101] Ryan, Bryce / Gross, Neal C. (1943): The Diffusion of Hybrid Seed Corn in Two Iowa Communities, in: Rural Sociology, Vol. 13, pp. 273 – 285.

decades of diffusion research the work was based mainly in the United States and Europe. In the 1960s attention turned to developing countries. Based on a technology-led development strategy the diffusion of new technologies was to be explored especially in rural areas.

Rogers (1995:ch.2) identifies at least ten different major diffusion research traditions. They differ in the innovations studied, the method of data gathering and analysis as well as the unit of analysis. The most important tradition, by number of publications, is rural sociology to which the Ryan and Gross study belongs. Most interest in diffusion comes from sociology and anthropology.[102] Other important traditions are marketing and management studies as well as studies with a communication science background. Studies in economics and agricultural economics are relatively new and account for seven percent of all diffusion publications.[103]

The major traditions of diffusion research are empirical by nature. Economic approaches to technological change are, however, more theory driven. In the following section these theories are presented and conclusions about their appropriateness for the analysis of the empirical data at hand are drawn.

4.2.2. Economic approaches to the diffusion of innovations

According to Rogers' (1995) count about seven percent of total diffusion research publications belong to the economics and agricultural economics tradition. The economic approach to diffusion became prominent in the 1980s in the form of research in technology diffusion.[104] Silverberg et al. (1988) speak of three major groups of economic approaches to diffusion. These are the "epidemic approach", the "equilibrium approach" and the "evolutionary approach". Geroski (2000) adds the more empirically based "probit approach". All these approaches are presented briefly below with some simple illustrative specifications.

4.2.2.1. Epidemic models

Modern economic diffusion theory started with models resembling epidemic theories of the spread of diseases. These so-called epidemic models start on the premise that the adoption of technologies is basically determined by people's knowledge about the existence of these technologies. The simplest models assume that information on the benefits of a new technology is spread by an external information source at a constant rate α in a population of N subjects. This generates the following adoption equation:

$$y_t = N(1 - e^{-\alpha t}) \tag{4.1}$$

Equation 4.1 generates, however, not the desired s-shaped but an exponential diffusion curve. This simple epidemic model might be appropriate to model the diffusion of in-

---

[102] Rogers divides the different traditions into anthropology, early sociology, rural sociology, public health and medical sociology and general sociology.

[103] In his comprehensive account on the history of diffusion research Rogers (1995:88) devotes just three sentences to the economic approach to diffusion. This is clearly the weak point of his work.

[104] A short overview on the history of economic theories of technological diffusion is given by Karshenas and Stoneman (1995).

formation but not the adoption of technologies. This is because in order to adopt a technology, information about the existence of this specific technology is insufficient. Knowledge of how to use a technology is needed in order to use it effectively. A certain proportion of this knowledge will be tacit, i.e. it can only be transferred from person to person and not from a common information source (Geroski 2000:605). Consequently, the main information source on innovations is subjects that already use this technology. Since learning takes place through observation of the prior adopters' experience epidemic models include bounded rationality (Metcalfe 1995:481). Taking account of users as a knowledge source, a very simplistic specification of the diffusion model takes the following functional form:

$$y_t = \frac{N}{(1 + (\frac{N - y_0}{y_0})e^{\beta Nt})} \qquad (4.2)$$

where β is the probability of each existing user contacting non-users and y_0 being the number of initial users. This specification generates the observed logistic diffusion curves. Equation 4.2 was the main tool for early economic diffusion analysis examining the composition and functional form of β as the determinant of diffusion speed.[105] However, this type of model has the weakness that it cannot explain the initial diffusion of an innovation after its invention (y_0 has to be greater than 0). This problem was solved by merging the models of equations 4.1 and 4.2 to a simple mixed information source model that will generate an asymmetric S-curve (Geroski 2000:606):[106]

$$y_t = N \frac{\left[1 - e^{-(\alpha + \beta N)t}\right]}{1 + (\frac{N - y_0}{y_0})e^{-\beta(1 + \frac{\beta N}{\alpha})t}} \qquad (4.3)$$

This model can be amended by forming hypothesis about the determinants of β which can vary for different users and technologies. The assumed determinants of β, such as perceived profits, learning costs or risk, are however often difficult to measure. Nevertheless, even these sophisticated epidemic models are still too simplistic since they assume that information diffusion is the main determinant of technology diffusion. The treatment of information acquisition and provision is primitive (Karshenas / Stoneman 1995:273). Epidemic models do not take into account the fact that adoption is an autonomous choice of individuals or firms, and they ignore the dynamic character of technological progress and the business environment, assuming that these are constant and unchanged over time (Geroski 2000:607, Karshenas / Stoneman 1995:270-272,

---

[105] The most prominent example is Griliches (1957) who used a similar equation to estimate the parameters origins, slopes and ceilings of the logistic distribution curves of the diffusion of hybrid corn seeds in different states of the U.S.

[106] These kinds of models are often used in marketing studies (Geroski 2000:607).

Metcalfe 1981:349, Silverberg et al. 1988:1034-1035)[107]. The possibility of improvements of the innovations after their introduction is also not modelled (Metcalfe 1981: 351). Furthermore, it is criticised that epidemic models focus entirely on the demand for an innovation and ignore the supply side (Metcalfe 1981:350).

Using an epidemic model for the purpose of this work does not seem appropriate. Epidemic models are basically concerned with the diffusion path of an innovation. The question to be answered in this chapter, however, was on the determinants of single enterprises' adoption decisions. For epidemic models this determinant is basically knowledge, which is certainly a necessary condition for technology adoption, but does not capture cost-benefit calculations by the enterprises nor the market conditions enterprises work in. Furthermore the introduction of the majority of the examined technologies into the researched environment was too recent for a proper estimation of parameters.

4.2.2.2. Equilibrium models

Epidemic models are in essence disequilibrium models since the diffusion part is determined by an end level and end point. Being unsatisfied with this property, Karshenas and Stoneman (1995 and 1993) present a family of equilibrium diffusion models they term as rank, stock and order effect models. The central idea is that the decision of a firm to adopt a new technology depends on the benefits from adoption compared to the costs of adoption. The costs of adopting and using a new technology change over time, i.e. they fall, over time. The use of the new technology will expand over time as prices fall. However, the more enterprises already use the new technology the lower the return for the early users and the expected return for the potential users becomes. Since there is less to gain for latecomers adoption will slow down in the later stages. The rate of adoption that is observed at each point of time t, thus, reflects the profit-maximising decision of each enterprise in the population.

The three equilibrium models differ in the following ways: Rank effect models assume that the potential users of the technology differ in some dimensions so that some firms obtain a greater benefit from the new technology than others. The firms that have the highest net-benefit will adopt first. Stock effect models assume that if the number of users increases the benefits from adoption decline. The order effect models assume that the return from adopting the new technology is determined by the firm's position in the adoption order, i.e. that the firms higher in the adoption order get a higher return.

Karshenas and Stoneman (1993 and 1995) develop an empirical model that unifies the three different effects. They define a function $g_i(.)$ determining the benefits per period of use of the new technology by firm i. Arguments of $g_i(.)$ are C_i, a vector of the characteristics of the firm (representing the rank effect), K_t, the number of firms already using the new technology at time t (representing the stock effect) and S_t, the number of

---

[107] Metcalfe (1981:398-399) suggests that one cannot talk about a single diffusion curve but about "an envelope of successive diffusion curves, each appropriate to a given set of innovation and adoption environment characteristics, each with its own values of n and β."

previous adopters in the industry at time t (representing the order effect).[108] The benefits of firm i from using a new technology at time τ from adoption at time t will be:

$$g_{i\tau} = g(C_i, S_t, K_\tau) \text{ with } \tau \geq t,\ g_2 \leq 0,\ g_3 \leq 0 \tag{4.4}$$

With r as the discount rate and assuming no depreciation, the present value of the increase in gross profits arising from adoption at time t is:

$$G_{it} = \int_t^\infty g(C_i, S_t, K_\tau) e^{-r(\tau - t)} d\tau \tag{4.5}$$

The adoption will be made in the optimal time of adoption t^* if the acquisition is profitable in t (profitability condition) and if it is not more profitable to wait beyond t^* (arbitrage condition). Defining Γ_{it} as the net present value of acquisition in time t and P_t is the cost of acquiring the technology in t then these two conditions can be formulated as follows:

$$\Gamma_{it} = -P_t + G_{it} \geq 0 \tag{4.6}$$

and

$$y_{it} = \frac{d(\Gamma_{it} e^{-rt})}{dt} \leq 0 \tag{4.7}$$

If profit maximising behaviour of the enterprises is assumed then the profitability condition determines the set of potential adopters. The arbitrage condition defines the individual adoption time. Assuming that in t^* $y_{it^*} = 0$, then: [109]

$$y_{it} = rP_t - p_t - g(C_i, S_t, K_t) + \int_t^\infty g_2(C_i, S_t, K_\tau) s_t\, e^{-r(\tau - 1)} d\tau \tag{4.8}$$

Equation 4.8 generates the following results: (a) Expected reductions in the cost of acquisition of a technology delay its adoption ($-p_t$); (b) Increases in the price of a new technology will also delay its adoption (rP_t); (c) Faster expected increases in the number of adopters would lead to an earlier adoption (integral term); (d) The more adopters there are in t the fewer new adopters will join in t ($-g(C_i, S_t, K_t)$); (e) The profile of the diffusion process generated by this model will furthermore depend upon the distribution of the characteristics C across the firms. If these are not specified the sign is not determined.

The model shows as well that the diffusion depends on demand-side and supply-side factors. The cost function of the technology suppliers has importance for the diffusion process as well the changing of cost over time or the market structure because the technology supplier's pricing and service decision influence the relative advantage of the technology. The supplier can influence the diffusion process by providing informa-

---

[108] S_t equals K_t.

[109] Lower case letters represent derivatives with respect to time. s_t and p_t represent expected changes in the number of users and the price of technology.

tion on the technology (Geroski 2000:612). The model can be extended in various ways, e.g. by including the improvement of technologies over time, product differentiation or standardisation. On the user side adaptation costs can be included, i.e. the adaptation costs of the technologies itself, as well as training and organisational costs (Karshenas / Stoneman 1995:278-279).

Karshenas and Stoneman (1993) applied this model to data on the diffusion of CNC machines in Great Britain. Estimating a number of model specifications they conclude that rank effects and endogenous learning effects (as described by epidemic models) seem to play an important role on in the diffusion process, while the existence of stock and order effects was not supported. From their point of view this gives greater empirical importance to probit-type and epidemic-type models of diffusion than to game-theoretic models of diffusion.[110]

The equilibrium model presented provides comprehensive explanations for the speed of technology diffusion, accounting both for supply and demand factors. However, empirical verification poses comprehensive requirements on the data which cannot be met by the current survey on Indian Small Scale Industry enterprises, which is cross-sectional in nature. The empirical results by Karshenas and Stoneman (1993) also indicate that the most decisive category of influencing factors is in the dimension of enterprise characteristics, i.e. rank effects. Yet simpler tools, as shown in the next sections, can also assess the impact of enterprise characteristics.

4.2.2.3. Evolutional economics approach to diffusion

Evolutionary economics approaches to innovation and technology diffusion consider themselves as alternatives to neo-classical equilibrium models, such as the one presented above. With reference to Schumpeter's notion of creative destruction they try to develop models of continuous economic change rather than the adjustment to equilibrium stages. Metcalfe (1995:448) points out that "evolution is not to be interpreted as change in response to exogenous variations in data, but rather change which occurs endogenously without reference to adjustment to some equilibrium state." Thus, evolutionary economics comprises a behavioural approach, i.e. "a firm at any time operates largely according to a set of decision rules that link a domain of environmental stimuli to a range of responses on the part of firms' (Nelson / Winter 1974:891). This means firms are governed by routines (operating characteristics, investment rules, search rules etc.) that do not change in response to small changes in the environment, i.e. evolutionary economics sees inertia in the behaviour of enterprises. Routines only change in the course of cumulative learning processes. The examination of processes is a way through which entrepreneurial behaviour becomes intelligible. The equilibrium approach cannot accommodate entrepreneurial rewards that go beyond profit maximising. Evolutionary economics focuses on the strategic, cognitive and organisational aspects of the firm to explain the different behaviour of different enterprises.

---

[110] Karshenas and Stoneman (1993:523) also found in their comprehensive data set support for the importance of expectations in the diffusion process. Static or myopic specifications, that only consider single-period profitability, performed worse than dynamic counterparts, i.e. expectations of adopters play a significant role in adoption.

The evolution of industrial dynamics is explained by evolutionary economists in the following way: In the short-run the mentioned routines and decision rules are stable. Only in the long run will they change. Processes of rule changes may involve "goal-oriented 'search' and 'problem-solving' activity" that lead to innovation (Nelson / Winter 1974:892). The question is about the selection mechanisms of new rules, which lead to the expansion of firms using favourable rules and the contraction of firms using unfavourable rules. The selection mechanism works in the way that current decision rules determine the firm's decision on supplies and production and, hence, market prices. Realised prices determine profitability and therefore (together with investment and capital market rules) expansion or contraction of the firm. If the size is altered firms decision rules generate different decisions concerning supplies and sales and, hence, different price and profitability signals. In this way dynamic change is achieved (Nelson / Winter 1974:893). Innovation is, however, happening in the presence of counteracting risks. On the one hand, innovation carries some risk because it changes processes and routines in the enterprise, which can threaten the enterprise's perform-ance. On the other the lack of innovation carries the risk of declining performance within a changing environment (Meeus / Oerlemans 2000:41-42). In the described dy-namic environment phenomena such as the coexistence of different technologies, the existence of multiple equilibria and the change of relative advantage within the diffu-sion process are explained. The dynamics of enterprise performance are, thus, the out-come of innovative learning, diffusion of innovative knowledge and selection of inno-vations by enterprises (Dosi 1988:1159).

Considering this evolutionary understanding of innovation processes it becomes clear that these are difficult to measure. Evolutionary economics is very much concerned with entrepreneurial behaviour, which, cannot be traced by standard economic frame-works and, is difficult to model quantitatively. Another particular feature of evolution-ary innovation theory is the assumption of technological trajectories, i.e. innovation and the subsequent use of technologies is path dependent. For these reasons it is nearly impossible to incorporate evolutional thinking into quantitative, cross-sectional ex-aminations of technology use and innovation. What can be done in this work is the attempt to include entrepreneurial characteristics and entrepreneurial assessments of technological developments into the analysis of technology adoption decisions.

4.2.2.4. Probit models

Another economic approach to analyse adoption decisions is to apply a probit model. The name is derived from the use of Probit and Logit regression models.[111] The basic assumption of this type of model is that individuals or organisations differ in certain characteristics. These characteristics affect the probability of adopting new technolo-gies because of their influence on perceived benefits and costs of a technological inno-vation (Geroski 2000:610). With this assumption the probit models stress that adoption is an individual choice. Technically, adoption takes place if the value of a characteris-

---

[111] Dependent variable is a latent variable that cannot be observed. For adoption modelling this will be the propensity to adopt a certain technology. What is observed is whether the technology is adopted of not. If the estimated propensity reaches a defined threshold (normally 0.5) the predic-tion changes from non-adoption to adoption (see section 4.5.2.1 and Annex 6 for details).

tic exceeds a certain threshold. The threshold is assumed to move over time leading to a rise in the number of adopting units. The increase of use, i.e. the adoption pattern, is determined by the movement of the threshold and the distribution of the characteristics' values over the population. To generate a S-shaped diffusion curve there are two options. First, if there is a uniform distribution of the characteristic the speed of the threshold's movement is initially slow, then accelerates and later slows again. Second, if the distribution follows the normal or a comparable distribution the movement of the threshold may also be at a constant rate (Geroski 2000: 610-611).[112] Probit type models are well suited for empirical analysis since the influence of different characteristics can be studied easily. The drawback of the model is the neglect of interaction between the potential adopters. This aspect is better addressed by epidemic models. However, adoption analysis using the probit model has been done by a number of different studies. Geroski (2000:612) cites typical characteristics whose influence on adoption decisions is often studied: enterprise size, suppliers, technological expectations, learning and search costs, switching costs and opportunity costs.

Probit models are well suited to analyse the influence of the same determinants on the adoption of different innovations. This approach, which emphasises the importance of the innovations' properties on the adoption decision, was pioneered by Dewees and Hawkes (1988) who examined the adoption of innovations by coast trawl fishermen at the U.S. Pacific coast. Dewees and Hawkes consider three groups of variables important in predicting the adoption or rejection of innovations. These are firstly personal characteristics and the personal situation of the fisher, secondly attitudinal variables and thirdly perceived attributes of innovations. For these three groups altogether 21 variables are defined.[113] These variables are tested with a Logit regression model for adoption or non-adoption of six different innovations in the fishing industry. Only size turns out to be a significant factor for all but one innovation. In general the profile of significant factors is very different for each innovation. Dewees and Hawkes argue that this coincides with findings by Downs and Mohr (1976) who argue that the effect of different variables on the adoption of innovation will differ with different attributes of the innovation.

For the problem to be analysed in this work a probit type model seems appropriate. It will be possible to identify single determinants of the adoption of different ICTs. However, this approach concentrates on the adopter alone. It should also be considered, especially when more than one innovation is examined, to identify differences in the character of innovations that influence their adoption.

---

[112] An asymmetric diffusion curve may best be modelled by an asymmetric distribution of the characteristic.

[113] For personal characteristics and situation variables: age, education, firm size, kinship ties, access to information, cosmopoliteness, percentage of income from fishing and years of experience. Attitudinal variables are the current economic fishing conditions, the anticipated economic fishing conditions, risk aversion, loan difficulties and financial commitment to fishing. Perceived innovation attributes are economic advantage, simplicity, prestige, perceived risk, compatibility, trialability, plasticity and other advantages. (Dewees and Hawkes 1988:225-226)

4.2.3. Diffusion framework by Rogers

Besides economic models of diffusion, the communication related approach by Rogers is relevant to any discussion on diffusion. Rogers (1995) gives the most comprehensive account of the diffusion of innovations in his eponymous book. Although the economic models presented in the previous section are largely neglected, Rogers gives a complete overview of fifty years of innovation research and offers his own account of the innovation process. Elements of the diffusion process, as he understands it, are the innovation itself, the relevant communication channels, time and the social system.[114] Rogers greatly stresses the importance of subjective elements in the diffusion process. Perceptions and behaviour of individuals are factors that determine adoption. Thus, the innovation itself and its characteristics are important determinants for the speed of diffusion. This is progress from the economic models presented above, which focus on individual characteristics, enterprise characteristics and market conditions as determining factors.

In more detail, the picture Rogers draws is as follows: Starting point is the innovation that is considered "an idea, practice, or object that is perceived as new by an individual or other unit of adoption" (Rogers 1995:11). Important is the notion of the perceived newness not the real newness. The innovative technology itself might be very old.

Rogers identifies five characteristics of innovations that help to explain the speed of adoption (Rogers 1995:15-16): (a) *relative advantage* ("the degree to which an innovation is perceived better than the idea it supersedes"), (b) *compatibility* ("the degree to which an innovation is perceived as being consistent with existing values, past experiences, and needs of potential users"), (c) *complexity* ("the degree to which an innovation is perceived as difficult to understand and to use"), (d) *trialability* ("the degree to which an innovation may be experimented with on a limited basis"), and (e) *observability* ("the degree to which the results of an innovation are visible to others").

Knowledge of innovations is distributed through communication channels, which are "the means by which messages get from one individual to another" (Rogers 1995:18). Important channels for the diffusion of innovations are mass-media channels and interpersonal channels. The former are more important in early stages of diffusion, the latter become more important during later stages. Important for communication is that individuals who communicate with each other are similar in certain attributes, such as social status, education etc. (Rogers 1995:19).

Another important and interesting aspect of diffusion is the time that is involved in the process as such. Time plays a role in the innovation-decision process, the innovativeness of an individual and the rate of adoption in a system (Rogers 1995:20-23). The innovation-decision process takes time because the adopting individual has to pass through different phases, i.e. knowledge, persuasion, decision, implementation and, finally, confirmation of the decision. Individuals can also be divided into groups depending on the time of adoption. The common groups are: innovators, early adopters, early majority, late majority and laggards. Finally, different innovations have different

---

[114] "Diffusion is the process by which an innovation is communicated through certain channels over time among the members of a social system." (Rogers 1995:5)

rates of adoption, i.e. "the speed by which an innovation is adopted by members of a social system" (Rogers 1995:23). Plotting the number of individuals that have innovated against time, the usual S-shaped diffusion curve arises. However, the slope of this curve is different for each innovation.

Important for the diffusion of an innovation is the structure of the social system in which the innovation is diffusing. How are communication flows organized in the system? What is the position of opinion leaders towards an innovation? Are the change agents homophilous, e.g. are they similar to the individuals in the system? What is the nature of the innovation decision? Is it optional, collective or authoritarian? Considering all these aspects, i.e. innovation, communication channels, time and social system, diffusion processes in its totality can be analysed.

This framework developed by Rogers, a communication scientist, is very much biased to social anthropology, i.e. basically qualitative. Applying quantitative tools to the factors addressed by this theory is rather difficult as the importance and the structure of the social system and the structure of communication channels are difficult to capture. As described above, economic approaches to diffusion are more concerned with individual decisions on the basis of cost-benefit-analysis. The social anthropology approach, which focused mainly on characteristics of the individual, is also challenged by a number of empirical studies. These studies stress that it is not the characteristics and attitude of the potential adopter alone that determines the diffusion process, but the different characteristics of innovations, which lead to differing diffusion patterns (Batz et al. 1999; Deewes / Hawkes 1988; Thong 1999). Therefore, the impact of the technological dimension on the adoption of the technologies is a factor that has to be examined closely in the following analysis. For this purpose of this study, i.e. exploring the determinants for the use of different technologies, and because it is applied by a number of studies on the adoption of innovations in small-scale enterprises, Rogers' framework appears to be a good reference model.[115]

4.3. Evidence of ICT adoption in small-scale enterprises

Before a specific model will be developed empirical evidence is reviewed. In the following section first the specific features of innovation adoption in small-scale enterprises are discussed. Then empirical evidence of ICT adoption and use by small-scale enterprises from industrialised countries is reviewed, followed by a review of ICT adoption and use in developing countries.

4.3.1. Adoption of innovations in small-scale enterprises

In the discussion about innovation size of the potential innovator plays an important role. Whether large or small enterprises are more innovative, and how size affects the speed of adopting new technologies are important research issues. The latter issue is

---

[115] Rogers' framework is referred to partially or in total for example in Harrison et al. (1997), Iacouvou et al. (1995), Nooteboom (1994), Thong (1999), Thong and Yap (1995).

the one we are concerned within this piece of work.[116] Size is suspected to be a determining factor because small-scale enterprises are assigned specific characteristics, for instance relative resource poverty or higher flexibility, that have been discussed in section 2.2.2.

Empirical evidence indicates that small enterprise lag behind in the adoption of innovations (Nooteboom 1994:342). A classical study, which supports the argument of a higher speed of technology adoption in larger enterprises, is conducted by Mansfield (1963). Mansfield gives three reasons for this phenomenon. First, larger firms face relatively smaller costs and risks involved with innovation. Second, larger firms have a wider range of "operating conditions", therefore the likelihood that conditions favourable for the particular innovation are among these is greater. Third, large firms have more units of a particular type of equipment, which increases the chance of an early replacement.[117]

In the area of new ICTs it is also well established that small-scale enterprises lag behind large firms in adoption (Julien 1995:460-466; la Rovere 1998). This may be because these technologies are not appropriate, i.e. their profitability is too low for a small-scale enterprise, or because of a lack of resources to screen viable technological options. For many small enterprises scanning for information is only of an informal nature in which the entrepreneur plays a pivotal role (see section 2.2.2.3 for a detailed discussion).[118] The argument that the lack of resources constraints technological adoption is not shared by all authors. Meeus and Oerlemans (2000) explore empirically the validity of the evolutionary adaptiationist perspective[119] on innovation and the epi-

---

[116] The discussion whether small firms are more innovative than large ones goes back to Schumpeter who, however, produces contradicting evidence which was not solved by later work (Acs / Audretsch 1991; Brouwer 1998 and 2000; Nooteboom 1994).

Acs and Audretsch (1991:739-740) attribute this to different measures used to quantify technological change, notably input measures, e.g. R&D spending, and output measures, e.g. patents, and to the truncated distribution of firm sizes in most empirical work. Brouwer (1998:391) points out that the R&D input indicator might be wrong in assigning innovativeness. She is proposing to look at output measures, i.e. direct innovation counts, which will change the picture in favour of small enterprises because these need less R&D per innovation. This reasoning is in line with the results of an empirical test on U.S. enterprise data by Acs and Audretsch (1991), which tests whether specific variables influence the differences in innovation activities between large and small companies (see van Dijk et al. (1997) for a summary). Nooteboom (1994:338) argues that the variation of results is a result of mixing between the questions of participation in R&D, of expense and of effectiveness. He sees evidence that there is "a lesser participation in R&D of small enterprises but a greater intensity and a greater productivity when they participate" (p.338).

[117] Testing for fourteen innovations in four industries Mansfield finds that size is the most important determinant for the speed of adoption, followed by the profitability of investment. Other factors, that were expected to have a positive effect on adoption speed, such as firm profitability, growth rate, liquidity, the age of the enterprise and its profit trend, emerged as not significant (Mansfield 1963: 309-310).

[118] Other factors influencing technological scanning are the firm's characteristics, the information networks, such as associations, and environmental uncertainty (Julien et al. 1999:285).

[119] The adaptation perspective stresses the importance of flexibility, i.e. the propensity to adjust behaviour to environmental changes, for enterprise success (Meeus /Oerlemans 2000:43).

demical selection perspective.[120] Analysing data from the Dutch manufacturing sector they claim that adaptation is of importance, i.e. even with a limited resource base small enterprises can find appropriate technological solutions when they efficiently exploit their potential flexibility. Whether this is possible is, however, questionable. The fewer resources of small enterprises lead to weaknesses in finance, training, planning, organisation as well as to a more informal structure which leads to an intuitive and reactive decision making process (Blili / Raymond 1993:443). Thus, small-scale enterprises will only innovate if clear business opportunities are realised or if strong outside pressure – from customers or suppliers – forces them to do so (Gagnon / Toulouse 1996; la Rovere 1998:197). In these cases environmental uncertainty is reduced.

Another very important factor for technology adoption in small-scale enterprises is the personality and the behaviour of the entrepreneur, which is at the centre of a study by Gagnon and Toulouse (1996). They model the decision-making process during technology adoption in smaller enterprises in the following way. Five dimensions of entrepreneurial behaviour are identified (see Table 4-1):

Table 4-1: Model of entrepreneurial behaviour in technology adoption

Dimension	Behaviour
Strategic orientation	Driven by perception of opportunity
Commitment to size opportunities	Revolutionary, with short duration
Commitment of resources	Multi-staged with minimal exposure at each stage
Control of resources	Episodic use or rent of required resources
Management structure	Flat, with multiple informal networks

Source: Gagnon / Toulouse (1996:61).

The strategic orientation of the entrepreneur is driven by the perception of opportunity. However, the commitment to size opportunities is only of short duration. Resources are committed not only at one, but at various stages of the process, whereby only a minimal exposure of resources in that stages is aimed at. As a consequence, resources are, ideally, rented during the adoption process. Consequently, control of the resources is not total. Finally, entrepreneurial decision-making behaviour will depend on a flat management structure in which informal networks are heavily used. This model indicates that the adoption of technologies, requiring many resources over a long period of time, will change the enterprise significantly. Therefore, there will be barriers to successful adoption.[121] The importance of the entrepreneur or the enterprise's CEO for technology adoption in small-scale enterprises' decisions is stressed by other studies as well (e.g. Fink 1998; Thong 1999). This is especially the case if an innovation can be assigned strategic importance (Blili / Raymond 1993).

---

[120] The selection perspective stresses resource constraints, i.e. there are cognitive limits on choices which increase the risks associated with changes. Thus, the larger the constraints the more appropriate is inert, i.e. routine, behaviour (Meeus / Oerlemans 2000:43).

[121] Gagnon and Toulouse (1996) corroborate these presumptions with a case study on the adoption of new technologies in eleven small and medium-sized Canadian enterprises.

4.3.2. Specific characteristics of ICT innovations

It is not only the size of the innovation adopting enterprise which calls for a consideration of different determinants for technology adoption and use, but also the character
of the innovation itself. An innovation might be characterised along four lines (Thong
1999:190-191). First, it might be a process or a product innovation, i.e. it improves the
production process or it is involved in the development and production of new products and services. Second, an innovation can be radical or incremental, where the latter
represent only minor changes in products or processes and the former represent fun-
damental changes. Third, the incentive to innovate can be from the supply side (tech-
nology-push) or from the demand side (market-pull). Fourth, an innovation might be
planned or incidental, i.e. it might be carried out due to strategical deliberations for
market control or as a reaction to new demand.

Thong (1999) claims that the computer-based information system he examines are a
process innovation and that they are radical because to use them is nontrivial.[122] For
the remaining two categories both forms are possible. Regarding ICTs, as defined in
this work, it seems questionable – at least for relatively unsophisticated communication tools such as fax machines, cellular phones and pagers - whether their adoption
constitutes a radical innovation.[123] For the last two dimensions the ambiguity certainly
also exists for ICTs. As it has been stated before, due to the lack of resources and lack
of formalised information scanning, it can be expected that in general innovations are
demand driven and not of strategic purpose in small-scale enterprises (Blili / Raymond
1993; Julien et al. 1999).

4.3.3. Selected empirical evidence of ICT adoption in industrialised country SMEs

In general the literature on ICT adoption and use in SMEs is diverse and not integrated
into specific aspects and schools, often neglecting formal modelling (Harrison et al.
1997:173; Thong 1999:191). Diversity also stems from the diversity of technologies
subsumed under IT and ICT, which leads to different study objectives in almost all
surveys. This section will review empirical evidence collected on ICT adoption and
use in industrialised countries' SMEs. The subsequent section will review similar studies undertaken in developing countries. In industrialised countries, recent literature
about ICT adoption and use is especially concerned with advanced technologies, such
as the Internet, and connected topics, e.g. e-commerce. Most of these studies are conducted by consultancies and contain no analytical or sophisticated empirical analysis.
As examples the results of two recent surveys on Internet use of German SMEs, and a
study on e-mail adoption by British small-scale enterprises, are briefly reviewed.

Beck and Köppen (1999) interviewed 311 enterprises from the German small business
and skilled crafts (Handwerk) sector on Internet use. Their results are, however, not
representative since 56 percent of the enterprises took part by Internet, consequently

---

[122] Blili and Raymond (1993:442), for example, state, that computerisation affects the cost of co-
ordination rather than production.

[123] However, literature on productivity effects of IT claims that positive effects will only be realised if
enterprise organisation and processes are adapted (see section 2.1.4.1).

leading to biased results.[124] At the beginning of 1998 75 percent of the enterprises had access to the Internet (43 percent of the off-line responses); 41 percent even had their own Internet presence (with another 26 percent planning the introduction) where the majority displayed information about the enterprise and its services. The growth rate for this service was very high since three-quarters started just in the year before the survey. The relation between costs and benefits was ranked on average at 38 on a scale between 0 and 100 but was expected to improve to an average of 54 during the next twelve months. The most important motive to build up an Internet presentation was to reach customers. This was expected by more than 60 percent of users, but materialised for only about a third of these. The authors conclude that the enterprises have in general a positive perception of the Internet. The biggest fear is whether potential customers, which are normally found on the local level, are reached by this tool. For non-users the authors identify first and foremost a lack of information as a constraint.

Covering more than 1500 German SMEs with between 10 and 500 employees from industry, trade and service sectors TechConsult (2000) provide wider evidence on SMEs' use of the Internet. About 62 percent of the enterprises interviewed in January 2000 had their own web-page. Only six percent of enterprises were offline (14 percent of the enterprises below 50 employees but only four percent of the ones above 100 employees). In the on-line enterprises on average 36 percent of all employees had access to the Internet, with a tendency of a higher share in small enterprises. Of the whole sample about 16 percent did on-line sales, conducted any B2B integration or defined business processes on the Internet. This was regardless of size, but industry sectors do play a role with trade being more advanced (21 percent) than industry (10 percent). Assessing the problems of e-business use, small enterprises complained more about higher costs and about a lack of compatibility of enterprise and products with the Internet. The decision in favour of e-business was mainly triggered by the expected positive impact on competitiveness. Advanced users also understood global competition as a chance rather than a threat. For active e-business users better communication with customers and suppliers was expected. In general the largest potential was seen in marketing and in contacting new customers.

Sillince et al. (1998) claim to have conducted the first survey on adoption, diffusion, use and impact of e-mail, most previous research being more of a theoretical nature.[125] In 1996 360 British small-scale enterprises were interviewed, of which only 24 percent had adopted e-mail. The diffusion took off in 1995. In 1994 only three percent had adopted the technology. Looking at their descriptive results on an _ad-hoc_ basis, Sillince et al. suggest that the diffusion depends on characteristics of the company (i.e. size as well as promotion and encouragement inside the company), on the trading partners (i.e. the existence of a critical mass) and on the technology (i.e. the improvement of e-mail products). External factors seemed to be most important since the majority of the non-users menioned the fact that their customers, suppliers or other organisations

---

[124] The survey was not guided by any formal considerations and the results displayed are descriptive without any cross-tabulation.

[125] See Rudy (1996) for a review of this literature.

do not use the technology as a reason not to adopt e-mail. On the user side, external factors proved to be important too, together with the technology's properties of "speed" and "ease of communication". However, the use of e-mail itself was not really sophisticated in the majority of companies, being mainly used to speed up existing communication channels. Negotiations, e-business or participation played only a minor role. Sillince et al. (1998:242) talk about a second learning stage that has yet to be reached.

Business surveys, such as those by Beck and Köppen (1999) or TechConsult (2000), give an overview about ICT use but do not provide a deeper analysis of the determinants of technology adoption and usage. However, even surveys with a scientific background often do not provide more formalised evidence (e.g. Sillince et al.). Harrison et al. (1997:173-174) review half a dozen different empirical surveys, which did not apply any existing model or framework. Findings of these studies comprise the importance of IT knowledge by entrepreneurs and CEOs as well as the importance of external agencies.

In their own work Harrison et al. use a framework based on the "Theory of Planned Behaviour" to explore small-scale enterprises' executives decisions on the adoption of IT.[126] They assume that the main reason to adopt IT is the expectation of executives to improve competitiveness of the business. 166 small businesses with 25 to 200 employees were examined in a multi-phased survey. From the results they conclude that IT adoption is a function of attitude, subjective norms about adoption and perceived control over adoption.[127]

A wider approach is taken by Fink (1998). He identifies the unique characteristics of SMEs with respect to ICTs in the fields of environment, organisation, decision-making and psychology. He tested ten factors comprising four different variables, each of which were supposed to increase or decrease ICT adoption on 87 Australian SMEs (10 to 500 employees). Using cluster analysis he produced three major groupings. The most significant group comprised "IT benefits", "organisational culture", "IT availability" and "inhouse IT expertise". The second group, which had a smaller positive influence, comprised "internal resources", "IT selection" and "IT implementation". A third group comprised "external environment", "outside support"

---

[126] The Theory of Planned Behaviour is constructed as follows: A "person's behaviour [...], such as an executive adopting an IT to gain a competitive advantage, is a positive function of the intention [...] to perform it – as long as the behaviour is under a person's volitional control [...]. Intention is defined as the strength of conscious plans to perform the target behaviour" (Harrison et al. 1997:176). Intention is a function of three variables: (1) attitude towards performing the behaviour, (2) subjective norm regarding the behaviour and (3) the perceived availability of abilities and resources to perform the behaviour, i.e. perceived control over the behaviour.

[127] "Attitudes are a function of the positive and negative consequences executives see. Subjective norms flow from stakeholder positions inside and outside the firm regarding the IT adoption decision. Perceived control reflects anticipated resources and barriers to adopting the new IT, as well as executives' beliefs about overcoming them. These are empirically and conceptually distinct factors. They make independent and important contributions to the decision process." (Harrison at al. 1997:189)

and "external resources". Size only played a role in "IT availability". Fink concludes that internal factors are more important for technology adoption than external factors. Earlier studies (e.g. Yap et al. 1992; Iacovou et al. 1995) had placed more emphasis on external factors, including consultant support or external pressure.

Iacovou ct al. (1995) examined the adoption and impact of Electronic Data Interchange (EDI) in seven Canadian enterprises from different sectors, ranging in size from four to 175 employees. EDI adoption and integration were assumed to be influenced by the perceived benefits, organisational readiness and external pressure. The cases revealed that the main factor for adoption was external pressure by trading partners. The successful integration which will lead to significant benefits require organisational readiness and awareness of the potential benefits, which induces the willingness to spend sufficient resources for adoption and integration. Especially in small enterprises the last factors are often lacking.

4.3.4. Empirical evidence of ICT adoption in developing country small-scale enterprises

This section reviews results of studies undertaken on the adoption of ICTs by enterprises in developing countries. These enterprises face different economic framework conditions to similar enterprises in industrialised countries (see section 2.2.3) and should therefore show different innovation performance. However, the frameworks used for analysing determinants of ICT adoption are often the same and also generate similar results (Dasgupta et al. 1999). Different is the penetration of ICTs among and within developing countries' small-scale enterprises. The focus of most studies is, therefore, not on e-business but on the use and adoption of basic ICT technologies.[128] This is especially the case for studies on low-income countries.

There are only a limited number of studies on the adoption of ICTs in small industry and service enterprises in developing countries. Out of these studies only a small number employ quantitative techniques to analyse the adoption process (e.g. Lal 1999, Lal 1999a, Seyal et al. 2000, Thong 1999, Thong / Yap 1995).[129] Other empirical works conduct case studies (e.g. Khan 1998, Lal 1998) or simply use descriptive analysis (e.g. Duncombe 1999, Duncombe / Heeks 1999, la Rovere 1998). Descriptive studies mainly explore the extent to which ICTs are used, surveys that employ more formal methods try to analyse the determinants of the reported use. Again, individual results vary from study to study. This may be due to different objectives, different environments and different survey set-ups.

Although providing some conceptualisation of developing country small-scale enterprises' information needs Duncombe reports only basic descriptive results from a survey undertaken on Botswanian small-scale enterprises (Duncombe 1999; Duncombe /

---

[128] Studies on the basic uses of ICT were undertaken in industrialised countries in the 1980s and before. At this time new communication technologies, e. g. fax and first data exchange applications (e.g. BTX), as well as microcomputers and PCs came into wide use in small enterprises (see for example Wittstock (1990) for a survey on German small businesses in the mid 1980s).

[129] Thong (1999), whose work is reviewed later in this section, claims that he was the first to apply a quantitative model to analyse IT adoption and intensity of adoption in small enterprises.

Heeks 1999 and 2001). 61 formal enterprises from manufacturing and service responded to a mailed survey, hardly making it representative.[130] However, it turned out that ICTs were more widely used in the service sector, especially in tourism, technical services and IT. Duncombe (1999:73) divides the enterprises into five groups: non-ICT users (no immediate access to ICTs), non-IT users (access to telephone, fax within the enterprise but no computer use), non-networked IT users (computers but no network connection), networked IT users (external data connection) and intensive IT users (external and internal network connection). The survey shows that the intensity of IT use (i.e. belonging to a group with more advanced ICT and IT use) is positively related to size, affiliation to the service sector, being an exporting manufacturer and being owned by a foreigner.

La Rovere (1998) concentrates on the barriers to use ICTs in developing countries. She cites a study on the ICT use of Brazilian SMEs in 1997 by a Brazilian SME promotion organisation, which reported a usage level relatively similar to the survey presented in this work.[131] The main reason for not using computers was found in factors inherent to the enterprises, i.e. a lack of resources and a lack of systematic information gathering and processing in the enterprises. To apply computers efficiently Brazilian SMEs face additional difficulties in that few adequate software exists for SMEs in Portuguese. Moreover, SMEs have difficulties in choosing and evaluating adequate technological solutions.

A more specific account is given by Khan (1998) who conducted a detailed case study on eight innovating SMEs in Pakistan. His investigation is based on a qualitative framework of technological innovation in SMEs which contains, on the one hand, environmental factors (i.e. various variables belonging to the general business framework conditions, "enabling and disabling environment", and specific market conditions), and on the other, driving factors for innovation (i.e. various variables characterising the entrepreneur, motivation, opportunity recognition and evaluation and technology assessment). Implementation of the innovation is influenced by finance, technical expertise, time, networks and problems. Interviewing eight SMEs that recently introduced an innovation and had some innovation record Khan concluded that environmental factors, especially on the policy side, are rather disabling. The entrepreneurs need "a high degree of determination and commitment to operate within a weak supporting infrastructure of technological innovation, and to tolerate a high degree of ambiguity and uncertainty in the hope of achieving a challenge of making profits." (Khan 1998:308) In such an environment innovators act demand-led, satisfying a clearly identified product need and aiming at reachable customers. At all stages of the innovation process the enterprises' own informal networks were used to help. However, innovative success was often constrained, besides the already mentioned adverse general environment, by the general technological lag in a developing country and by a lack of managerial skills. With these results Khan stresses the importance of the entrepreneurs

---

[130]   About 50 percent of the enterprises were e-mail users, 60 percent were using a mobile phone. This clearly indicates a pro-technology bias within the sample.

[131]   57 percent of Brazilian SMEs owned computer equipment in 1997, 22 percent used the Internet (la Rovere 1998:201-202).

perception of opportunities for technological innovation especially in an innovation unfriendly environment.

A more formal approach is applied by Seyal et al. (2000). Investigating the degree of IT usage in 54 SMEs from different sectors in Brunei they concentrate on internal determinants of technology adoption, i.e. CEO and organisational characteristics. Seyal et al. examine the influence of four CEO parameters (ownership of a PC at home, educational level, computer literacy and computer experience) and organisational parameters (size of organisation, type of business and sales of business) on IT usage. After controlling for the non-existence of multicollinearity Seyal et al. regress the variables on IT usage which was measured on a five point scale from "not at all" to "all of the time". Only the influence of businesses' sales, the type of business and the occurrence of in-house training are significant. Size of business, ownership of a PC, outside training, self-taught training, CEO's educational level and CEO's total experience do not turn out to be significant.

A similar study was undertaken by Lal (1999 and 2000) for the adoption of IT in 59 Indian electronic goods manufacturers. Since all enterprises are located in the same industrial area he only pays attention to factors within the companies, i.e. entrepreneurial characteristics, international orientation, workforce and size of the enterprise. Lal divides the enterprises into four categories: non-IT firms (no use of IT-tools); low level IT firms (use of management information systems - MIS); moderate level IT users (use of CAD/CAM in addition to MIS) and high level IT firms (use of flexible manufacturing systems in addition to CAD/CAM and MIS). Using descriptive and univariate techniques Lal denies any influence of export activity and the importance given to product quality on ICT adoption. The perception of R&D spending importance, the importance given to market share as well as the entrepreneurs' education, size and skill intensity of the enterprise are tested in a variety of ordered probit models, in which only skill intensity do not prove to be significant. Thus, Lal concludes, that the entrepreneur and his / her perception are most important for technology adoption.

Lal (1999a and 2000) also conducted a survey on Indian garment manufacturers with a slightly different focus. The question was whether IT use influences export performance, i.e. ICT adoption is not the dependent variable in this study. 74 enterprises in a Delhi industrial estate, which is one of India's garment centres, were interviewed. IT adoption is again categorised into non-IT firms, firms that use IT in office automation and firms that use IT in manufacturing activities (mainly integrated CAD applications). As there were almost no non-IT using enterprises, the degree of IT-adoption is reformulated as a dummy variable, which indicates whether IT was used in manufacturing. Using a Tobit regression model on the intensity of exports, the IT-dummy turns out to be a significantly positive determinant.[132] Lal concludes that the advanced use of IT tools is crucial for garment companies to remain internationally competitive.

The most structured and comprehensive model of IT adoption and intensity of use in small enterprises is probably that developed by Thong (1999). A predecessor of this

---

[132] Other significant variables are the quality of raw material used, the perceived importance of flexibility in design and the wage rate.

work, with the same data set of 166 Singaporean small businesses is Thong and Yap (1995), which concentrates on CEO and organisational characteristics as determinants of IT adoption. Thong and Yap focus especially on the characteristics of the CEO, which is usually the owner of a small business, because he plays the major role in these businesses. Characteristics of the CEO and the organisation are represented by a number of variables. Thong and Yap assume that adoption of IT in a small business depends on the CEO's innovativeness, the CEO's attitude towards adoption of IT, the CEO's IT knowledge, business size, competitiveness of the environment and information intensity of the business. Data is used from interviews of small companies (below 100 employees and less than S$15 million sales) from manufacturing, trade and service sectors. The independent variable is a dichotomous variable, indicating whether the enterprise is computerised (defined by specific software applications). Bivariate testing and discriminant analysis for the multivariate analysis show a significant positive effect of the three CEO characteristics and business size of IT adoption.

Thong (1999) develops this model further, including environmental characteristics as well as technological characteristics, and extends the model to cater for the intensity of IT use.[133] Thong identifies different parameters for the four influencing dimensions. In this study, CEO characteristics comprise indices of the CEO's innovativeness and the CEO's IT knowledge. Organisational characteristics are business size, the information intensity of the business, and in this case, indices for the employees' IT knowledge. The IT characteristics are indices of the relative advantage of the particular IT, its compatibility and complexity.[134] These factors are directly borrowed from Rogers (1995). Environmental characteristics are reduced to an index of competition intensity. Since the last factor was counted as an organisational characteristics in Thong and Yap (1995) the innovation of this model lies in the inclusion of technological influences.

The models are tested with the same data set as in Thong and Yap (1995). The results of a discriminant analysis show that the likelihood of IT adoption is significantly influenced by CEO's innovativeness and IT knowledge, by relative advantage / compatibility and complexity, as well as by business size and employees' knowledge. Information intensity and environmental characteristics, i.e. competition intensity turns out not to be significant. These results are similar to Thong and Yap (1995) but add for technology characteristics. For the extent of IT adoption only organisational characteristics (business size, employees' IT knowledge and information intensity) show a significant influence. CEO and technological characteristics show no effect.

Thong concludes firstly that the study highlights the importance of having "innovative and IS-knowledgeable CEOs" (Thong 1999:208) for IT adoption. Secondly, he concludes that IT are only adopted when they offer a better alternative to existing business practices. Thirdly, the presence of sufficient financial resources and IS-knowledgeable

---

[133] The likelihood of IT adoption is again a dichotomous variable, whether the enterprise is computerised or not. An enterprise is considered computerised if it has a computer and uses it beyond word processing. The extent of IT adoption is operationalised by the number of computers.

[134] A principal component analysis of the survey data groups the variables representing relative advantage and compatibility together. Both characteristics are therefore analysed together (Thong 1999:200-201).

employees is crucial for successful IT adoption (i.e. understanding size as a proxy of financial power). Finally, the information needs of a business will be the main trigger for the extent of IT adoption. He admits, however, that more research on the specific determining factors is needed to understand the adoption of IT and especially the extent to which they are used.

Reviewing the results presented one can conclude that there are no specific results of what determines the use of ICTs in small enterprises. Only size is with certainty a decisive determinant. Almost all studies could establish the influence on size.[135] For all other variable groups records are mixed.

Differences might be due to different methods of designing dependent factors and variables. In most cases a number of dimensions is identified in which determinants can be found. These dimensions are, however, not used as variates in the analysis. They only structure the adoption decision. Normally a number of variates is subsumed under the dimensions. Either this is done for clarification purposes and each single variable is tested individually (e.g. Fink 1998, Lal 1999 and Lal 1999a) or variables are combined to a reduced number of factors (e.g. Harrison et al. 1997 and Thong 1999).

The explained variables also differ. In most cases the use or non-use of a technology at a specified point in time is examined. Only a few authors try to explain the intensity of adoption either in categories of use (Lal 1999) or in continuous forms (Thong 1999). To identify the driving factors behind information technology adoption and to test the hypothesis single equation limited dependent regression models are normally used (Lal 1999, Lal 1999a, Seyal et al. 2000, Deewes / Hawkes 1988). An alternative is the use of discriminant analysis to identify differences between the users and non-users of the technology in question (Thong 1999, Thong / Yap 1995).

Most importantly, the objects of research differ from study to study. In the previous section's survey of the adoption of ICT a wide range of technologies was presented. These variations in observed technologies should also lead to difference in the identified determining adoption factors. This result is in line with Deewes and Hawks (1988) who showed that the adoption of different technologies is due to different determinants even in the same population. Nevertheless, departing from the evidence presented in the last two sections, a general model of ICT adoption in developing country small-scale enterprises is developed in the next section.

4.4. Towards a model of ICT adoption in developing country small-scale enterprises

4.4.1. General remarks

Most of the formal studies presented above structure the determinants of an adoption decision into different dimension. Within these dimensions different factors or vari-

---

[135] Where this is not the case fallacies in the analysis can be assumed. Seyal et al. (2000), for example, should have controlled for the sector when examining IT usage because different sectors need different degrees of IT.

ables are identified and tested for their influence on ICT adoption. An extensive list of possible factors and variables is provided by Lefebvre and Lefebvre (1996), which they partially derive from a review of IT adoption literature from the 1980s and early 90s. The two long lists the authors provide for "factors affecting adoption" and "measures for the characteristics of the decision-making process with respect to IT adoption" are, however, not operational in detail but can provide a first starting point for the model to develop. Lefebvre and Lefebvre (1996:42-43) divide the factors potentially influencing the adoption of IT applications into two main fields: factors external to the firm and factors internal to the firm.[136] Additionally they give high importance to influences on the decision making process, which they consider as a separate prime adoption factor.[137] The list contains personal characteristics of the involved persons, the actual external impulse to adopt, the availability of information and characteristics of the technology (Lefebvre and Lefebvre 1996:54-56).[138]

Most empirical studies examine only internal determinants (e.g. Lal 1999, Lal 1999a, Seyal et al. 2000, Thong / Yap 1995). This can be assigned to the fact that only enterprises that work in the same political and macroeconomic environment are examined and that only one technology is considered. In these cases CEO characteristics and specific organisational characteristics are examined. However, as Rogers (1995), and Deewes and Hawks (1988) propose, the importance and significance of different potential determinants differs with the technology in question. Most studies that account for technology characteristics apply Rogers (1995) categorisation (relative advantage, compatibility, complexity, trialability and observability), either in total or as a selection, as technological parameters (e.g. Iacovou et al. 1995, Lefebvre / Lefebvre 1996, Thong 1999). However, an assessment of the technological determinants, especially

---

[136]   Factors external to the firm are:
- industry characteristics (overall competition, characteristics of demand, degree of diffusion of technologies in the industry, availability of external know-how),
- macroeconomic environment (availability of capital and human resources, quality of industrial relations, inflation, business cycle),
- national policies (especially trade policies, industry regulation and taxation).
Internal factors are:
- firm's past experience (e.g. internal diffusion of technologies, number of technologies adopted),
- firm's characteristics (e.g. size, financial resources, organisation),
- firm's pursued strategy (e.g. strategic orientation, technological awareness).

[137]   This distinction is rather strange because the mentioned external and internal factors also have an influence on the decision and do to some extent overlap with these factors. The rationale behind this distinction is also not clarified by the authors.

[138]   In detail the reported factors are:
- influences of internal proponents, i.e. CEO's and employees' characteristics (e.g. age, education, experience),
- influences of external proponents (e.g. influence by customers, competitors, associations, consultants, governments),
- availability of internal and external technical information sources (e.g. groups within the enterprise, trade fairs, journals, consultants),
- characteristics of IT applications (perceived characteristics as proposed by Rogers (1995) and relative cost),
- characteristics of the justification process (e.g. organisational and technological feasibility).

the technology's relative advantage is not possible without knowing about the external environment of an enterprise. These environmental determinants can be of general nature, as proposed by Lefebvre and Lefebvre (1996), or more enterprise specific, i.e. they relate to the market environment.

These deliberations suggest to structure a model of technology adoption determinants into four dimensions: individual characteristics of the decision maker (entrepreneur, CEO, lead manager), organisational characteristics, environmental characteristics and technology characteristics. This general model structure was successfully applied by Thong (1999). His model will be the basis for a general model of technology adoption determinants' dimensions and sub-dimensions.

4.4.2. Personal dimension

As it was stressed in the discussion on technology adoption these processes are driven by the subjective perception of the people involved. The personality of the decision maker is therefore of prime importance in determining the extent and timing of technology adoption. Small enterprises are characterised by the fact that many decisions are made by the CEO alone, who will be the owner-entrepreneur in most cases. There is normally no elaborate managerial hierarchy. Even when enterprises become larger and administrative functions are divided, the majority of decisions is still taken by the CEO. Delegation of tasks is often not a strength of entrepreneurs who enlarged their enterprise from a very small scale. The introduction of new technologies as a strategic decision will therefore depend to a large extent on the personality of the CEO.

From the surveys reviewed above some CEO characteristics that influence technology adoption can be derived. These are foremost attitude and motivation (e.g. Harrison et al. 1997, Khan 1998, Thong / Yap 1995) as well as the ability to conduct the adoption process (e.g. La Rovere 1998, Khan 1998, Thong / Yap 1995, Thong 1999), i.e. on the one hand characteristics of the CEOs personality and on the other hand characteristics of his acquired knowledge. Thong's (1999) division into "CEO's innovativeness", i.e. the degree to which an CEO is likely to adopt an innovation earlier than others, and "CEO's IS knowledge" captures this distinction best and will be used to represent the personal dimension of the adoption decision. The question will be how to define these characteristics since they are not directly observable. In the survey used by Thong (1999) and Thong and Yap (1995) the CEO's had to state the extent to which they agree with given statements. The scaled answers were combined and indicators that were supposed to represent the dimension in question were formed. However, this is a relatively soft method, requiring specific, not undisputed methods of grouping and clustering. Baumol (1995:22) stresses that looking at attributes of the individual who is taking the decision is the only possible way to capture innovative performance. Identifying easily observable attributes such as age, education, IT experience etc, as proxies, to represent the desired dimension is therefore used by a variety of surveys (e.g. Lal 1999, Seyal et al. 2000).[139]

---

[139] Using proxies for entrepreneurial ability is common for small enterprise studies in general. Goedhuys and Sleuwaegen (2000), for example, find in a survey on small enterprises in Côte d'Ivoire,

4.4.3. Organisational dimension

In previous sections is has been elaborated that small enterprise behave differently to large ones. Thus, size is often tested for in adoption studies (e.g. Sillince et al. 1998, Duncombe 1999, Sayal et al. 2000, Thong 1999). Size is considered an indicator of resources available to the enterprise. Resources are not only quantitative but also qualitative, e.g. enterprise culture (e.g. Fink 1998). The knowledge of enterprise staff will thus be of importance too (e.g. Sillince et al. 1998, Thong 1999). Some of these aspects are, however, given by a structure of the enterprise, which is determined by its area of business, i.e. the sector it belongs to (Pavitt 1984). Enterprises of different size and lines of business will have differing technology requirements (Barten / Bear 1999:8-9). The adoption of ICTs will also depend on technological penetration in other sections of the enterprise, i.e. the use technology intensive production technologies will influence the adoption of office automation tools (Lefebvre et al. 1995).

In order to keep the model fairly general, the organisational dimension should be represented by "enterprise structure" and "enterprise performance". Enterprise structure refers to aspects related to the type of business, i.e. the sector, IT requirements. Enterprise performance refers to all aspects that are actively achieved by the enterprise, i.e. size, enterprise culture, and employees' knowledge. It is not easy to assign all possible variables completely to one of the sub-dimensions, but in order to distinguish between required and achieved organisational characteristics this distinction seems reasonable.

4.4.4. Environmental dimension

The two former dimensions cover determinants internal to the enterprise. In addition, factors external to the enterprise will determine whether a technology is adopted. These include the general conditions in which the business is operating, e.g. the infrastructure, general and specific policies, available support institutions. The importance of these factors for ICT adoption is stressed, for example, by Khan (1998), Fink (1998) and Lefebvre and Lefebvre (1996). This aspect will be extremely important for studies in developing countries because the business environment is often adverse (see the description given by Khan (1998)) and may vary significantly between, but also within, countries, as shown by a World Bank study on the relation of governments and business (Brunetti, et al. 1998).

Other external determinants belong to the specific market environment of the adopter. Thong (1999) refers to competition intensity, Duncombe (1999) to the markets served. Lal (1999) clearly shows how intense ICT adoption is related to export performance. In another study Nassimbeni (2001) elaborates that the propensity of a small business to export is linked to its ability to innovate and to its technological profile.[140] However, the market environment does not cover only markets served in general, but also direct links with divers business partners, which may influence or pressure the adoption of new technologies (e.g. Iacovou et al. 1995, Lefebvre / Lefebvre 1996).

---

that success of these enterprises depends on entrepreneurial capabilities. They measure these through age, education , experience etc.

[140] The study is based on a survey of small Italian manufacturing companies from the furniture, mechanics and electronics sectors.

The sources of competitiveness in specific markets might also affect technology use. Lal (1996) shows in a survey on Indian electrical and electronic goods manufacturers that an increased perception of the importance of quality of products and after sales services are positively related to IT use.[141]

4.4.5. Technological dimension

The importance of an innovation's characteristics in the decision to adopt it is especially stressed by Rogers (1995). He characterises innovations by their relative advantage, compatibility, complexity, trialability and observability, while stressing that these characteristics are not considered objectively, but perceived by the decision maker. Innovations' perceived characteristics become an important issue for research when the diffusion of different technologies is compared, e.g. in Deewes and Hawkes (1988) study on variety of innovation in fishery. Most studies on diffusion of single innovation do not attach much importance to the influence of the technologies properties.

However, technology characteristics, as mentioned before, are not only static but might change over time. This holds true especially for ICTs in two ways. First, most ICTs are prone to network externalities, i.e. with each additional user the utility of the already existing applications increases. With increasing user base the relative advantage of specific ICTs will change. Second, ICTs themselves are not static but change over time. For most ICTs prices of acquiring and using them fall continuously.[142] Many ICTs are subject to constant modifications, adding new properties or simply power.[143] Thus with reduced price a technology's relative advantage will increase and it might become more trialable. Modifications of technologies can make them more compatible for their using environments and less complex, e.g. moving to an intuitive graphic machine-user interface. Taking this into account a number of single-technology studies accounted for the perception of ICT's relative advantages (e.g. Sillince et al. 1998, Fink 1998, Thong 1999) or the adequacy (compatibility) of ICTs (e.g. La Rovere 1998, Thong 1999).

For developing countries an additional technological characteristic becomes important: availability. Network and technology development is in many cases retarded. Large parts of countries are not served by any IT infrastructure.[144]

4.4.6. The general model

For a general model of technology adoption four dimensions of technology adoption decision's determinants have been identified:

1. Personal dimension (with CEO's innovativeness and technology knowledge).

2. Organisational dimension (with enterprise performance and enterprise structure).

---

[141] Flexibility in design, delivery schedule and low overhead costs proved not significant (Lal 1996).

[142] See World Bank (1998:3) for a graphical account of the falling cost of sending information.

[143] For example Moore's law, named after the co-founder of Intel, states that the power of microchips doubles every 18 to 24 months.

[144] The importance of availability was described in the case of the Indian mobile phones and paging services. Owing to the problems in issuing mobile phone licences, paging services started earlier than cellular services in the Indian cities, leading to a strong initial growth for pagers.

3. Environmental dimension (with specific market environment and general business environment).

4. Technological dimension (with availability, relative advantage, compatibility, complexity, trialability and observability).

The impact of the first three dimensions on the adoption decision will, however, depend very much on the properties of the technological dimension. Changes in the technological dimension, may they result from the outcome of adoption or non-adoption or external development, will alter the influence of the other dimensions leading to reconsideration of the previously taken decision not to adopt. This reasoning is graphically displayed in Figure 4-1. In the next section analysis on the data on the ICT use of Small Scale Industry enterprises in Ambattur Industrial Estate is undertaken along these lines.

4.5. Analysis of technology adoption and intensity of use from survey data

4.5.1. Identifying adoption determinants

4.5.1.1. General problems

In the former section a general model of ICT adoption has been developed in which four main dimensions of determining factors were identified. For each of these main dimensions there are various sub-dimensions and influencing variables. As shown above all of these are valid, depending on the research question and the empirical setting. However, empirical research has to concentrate on specific aspects because the data required to cover all aspects would be too extensive, and the willingness of entrepreneurs to answer surveys is limited.[145]

It is not easy to identify the appropriate variables representing the determining factors. Firstly, it is often not possible to observe the influence of a dimension directly, which then constitutes the need to identify indirect proxy variables. Secondly, in many cases, different dimensions and sub-dimensions cannot be considered to be one-dimensional, i.e. a number of different variables constitute one dimension or sub-dimension.[146] Different variables that fit into one dimension are often highly correlated which violates the assumptions for multivariate regression models and inhibits a proper interpretation

---

[145] Lefebvre and Lefebvre (1996), for example, do not dare to test the long list of determining variables they have compiled. The survey used in this work had to be restricted to a questionnaire that took not longer than 45 minutes to complete. Spending more than one hour on answering questions on their enterprise seemed to be too long for the entrepreneurs. The willingness to answer dropped considerably when interviews went on for a long time. Therefore, the number of questions concerning each technology as well as questions on attitudes and financial data was restricted.

[146] See for example the lists provided by Lefebvre and Lefebvre (1996) or by Thong (1999).

Figure 4-1: Determinants of individual technology adoption decisions

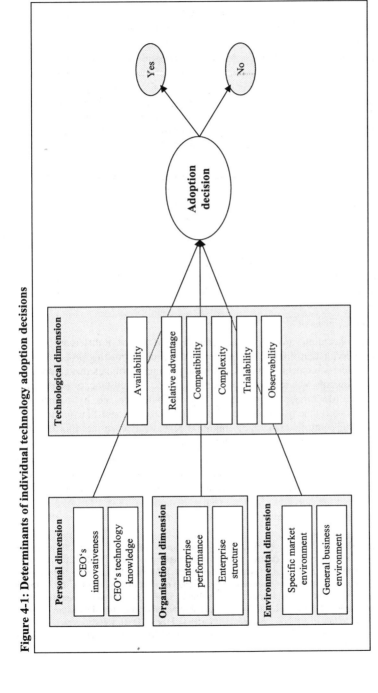

of regression results. To mitigate this problem factor analysis techniques can be used to identify representative variables that feed into regression analysis.

The adoption model specified in this section will explicitly exclude the technological dimension, i.e. explaining variables for technology adoption cover only the personal, the organisational and the environmental dimensions of the adoption decision. As it has been developed in the previous section, properties of the technology will mediate the influence of the other factors. The method of this work is to apply the same model with the same explanatory variables to different technologies. Differences in the impact of the explanatory variables on the adoption of different technologies can then be accounted for by the characteristics of technologies and will be discussed with the regression results.

The sample of this survey has been described in Section 3.2. However, the analysis in this section is restricted to enterprises in which the entrepreneur or a leading executive participated in the survey. As mentioned previously, in small enterprises the CEO, who will normally be the owner-manager, takes all relevant decisions. Strategic decisions, such as the introduction of new technologies, are not taken by subordinate personnel, and are influenced by the personal attributes and perceptions of the decision maker. Therefore, only those cases where the interviewee claimed to be proprietor, partner, director, general manager or chief executive officer are considered in the analysis of diffusion decisions. This reduces the analysed sample size from the 295 considered in Chapter 3 to 266.[147]

4.5.1.2. Personal dimension

Since this work concentrates mainly on the comparison of the use of different ICTs the exploration of individual attributes' importance to the decision-making process had to be neglected to a certain extent. Nevertheless main personal attributes that could indicate the attitude towards new technologies were acquired. This attitude, or innovativeness, will then influence adoption decisions. The attributes are age, experience and education. Additionally, the use of advanced production technologies, i.e. numerically and microprocessor controlled machines, might be considered as an indicator of innovativeness as well as an indicator for knowledge about advanced technologies.

Experience can be measured by the number of years the entrepreneur has spent with the current enterprise. This is, however, an incomplete measure since the working experience before joining or founding the current enterprise is not accounted for. Therefore age is used as a measure of experience (variable name: **AGE_CEO**). Age and the number of years spent in the current enterprise are significantly correlated with a cor-

---

[147] The excluded enterprises are not significantly different from the rest which makes this operation feasible. Comparing the means of the two groups for basic enterprise characteristics (size, exports, imports, technology use) and ICT use reveals no significant differences for all variables except the natural logarithm of the number of employees. The average number of employees in the excluded companies is 35.5 against 26.8 in the included. This finding is not surprising since enterprises with more persons employed are expected to have a more formalised organisational structure, i.e. it is more likely only to talk to a subordinate manager instead of the CEO. However, average turnover is only marginally different (12.1 against 10.7 million Rupees) letting the size bias not appear too severe. For details see Annex 3.

relation coefficient of 0.451. Principal component analysis of the personal attributes groups these variables together too. Aside being a proxy for experience, age is, however, an influencing factor in itself. Younger entrepreneurs, who gained experience with ICTs at college for example, will be more geared to modern technologies and ideas than older entrepreneurs, who have been in business for a long time and work with established routines. This suggests a negative correlation between age and ICT adoption. The age of the interviewee in the survey, however, might be misleading for this deliberation. In many enterprises two generations run the business. Thus, it might be that the senior entrepreneur was interviewed but his son or daughter had introduced modern technologies. Taking all these issues about age and experience into consideration it can be assumed that both young and old interviewees use modern technologies in their businesses. In order take this assumption into account the squared age is also added into the model.

Education is represented by the years of formal education derived from the degrees held by the interviewed entrepreneurs (variable name: **EDU_YEAR**).[148] Education is assumed to have a positive influence on forming a positive attitude towards new technologies and innovation.[149]

The willingness to introduce new ICTs is assumed to correlated greatly to willingness to introduce other modern technologies. Using advanced production technologies will lower the threshold to introduce modern technologies in office automation (Lefebvre et al 1995). However, production technology is also dependent on the business of the enterprise, and will therefore be discussed in detail in the next section.

Altogether, these variables are arguments representing the personal propensity to innovate and indicate the CEO's technological knowledge. They form the personal dimension's elements for the diffusion model at hand.

4.5.1.3. Organisational dimension

The second dimension that influences adoption decisions consists of genuine enterprise characteristics. These characteristics can be divided into structural characteristics, related to the business of the enterprise, and to performance related characteristics, depending on the success of enterprise operations. These two categories are, not unequivocal, but they can serve as a guide to structure the organisational attributes of the diffusion decision. Structure related factors are the sector the enterprise works in, the production technologies it uses, its employment and its cost structure. It is clear that technologies and the cost structure are dependent on enterprise performance too, but in general they should be more dependent on the business of the enterprise.[150] Per-

---

[148] "Matriculation" = 10 years; "12th Standard" and "vocational training" = 12 years; diploma = 13 years (10 years schooling + 3 for diploma); graduates in science, arts, commerce = 15 years (12+3); graduates engineering = 16 years (12+4); postgraduates management = additional 2 years; postgraduates engineering = additional 1.5 years.

[149] Education is a standard variable in many technology adoption studies being a proxy for technological knowledge as well as open-mindedness (see for example Seyal et al. 2000 or Lal 1999).

[150] The importance of the business sector for technology adoption and innovation behaviour is showed conceptionally by Pavitt (1984) and empirically in multi-sector surveys, for example Duncombe (1999) or Seyal et al. (2000).

formance related factors are the size of the enterprise, the age of the enterprise and its profitability. Again, these attributes depend on the overall enterprise structure and the sector, but it can be assumed that much of the variance is derived from differing operations. Nevertheless, one should be cautious using performance related variables in the analysis of determining factors of technology adoption. The use of technologies is supposed to change the performance of enterprises. Therefore, one can expect a correlation between performance and technology adoption but causality might be in the opposite way, as suggested by the adoption model.

The variables, representing structure related factors for the adoption analysis, are defined as follows: The enterprises have been asked about the production technologies they use. 20 percent of the enterprises claim to use advanced technologies, i.e. numerically controlled and microprocessor controlled machinery. The use of advanced production technologies is represented by a dummy variable indicating the use of numerically controlled and microprocessor controlled machinery in production (variable name: **ADV_TECH**).

Cost structure could be represented by raw material costs expressed in terms of turnover, which was asked in the survey. However, as only two thirds of the enterprises responded to this question it is excluded from the model in order to keep the number of cases that are part of the analysis high. Different cost structures, in general, are taken care of by including sector dummies into the regression equation. The sectors are defined according to the two-digit Indian Industry Standardisation. For the regression only sectors with a significant share in the sample are considered. Two similar sectors with a smaller share are joined for analysis. The following four sector dummies are then added to the regression model:

- Sectors 30 and 31: basic chemicals, chemical products, rubber, plastic, petroleum and coal products (11.7 percent of the sample, variable name: **SEC_3031**);
- Sector 33: basic metal and alloy industries (13.5 percent of the sample, variable name: **SEC_33**);
- Sector 34: metal products and parts (37.2 percent of the sample, variable name: **SEC_34**) and
- Sector 35: machinery and equipment (24.1 percent of the sample, variable name: **SEC_35**).

Variables used for the performance related factors are age and size of the enterprise. Profitability could have been used but, as in the cost structure case, these financial figures were not answered by a number of enterprises. In order to keep the number of enterprises analysed high and to avoid problems with causality mentioned above, it is omitted. Age indicates sustained success of the operations. This is an achievement in the environment of relatively high entry and exit numbers and it indicates the ability to adapt to changing business environments (variable name: **AGE_ENT**).

Size is an indicator for enterprise performance as it indicates past growth.[151] Size is represented in this analysis by the number of employees, i.e. by the internationally most commonly used identification criteria for enterprise size. The distribution of employment figures is highly skewed to the right. In order to reduce the leverage of the few firms at the upper end, the number of employees is transformed by taking the natural logarithm (variable name: **LN_SIZE**).[152]

4.5.1.4. Environmental dimension

The adoption decision is influenced by the enterprise's environment. It cannot be assumed that small enterprises have the chance to influence their environment significantly. Therefore, in the context of this work, the environmental dimension comprises variables that cannot be influenced by the enterprise. Since the enterprises covered by the survey are located in the same area and belong to similar sectors of the economy one can expect a number of environmental dimensions to be fairly equal for all enterprises. All enterprises will basically have the same potential access to physical infrastructure, e.g. electricity, transport, telecommunication etc., they work under the same policy regime and deal with the same institutions and organisations. If enterprises of different locations had been interviewed, differences in infrastructure endowments, policies and institutions would have been a major explanatory factor for the use of technologies.

Besides differences in the general business environment, differences in the market environment are assumed to have a major impact on technology adoption differences. Enterprises, even when they are at the same location, face differences in their product and factor markets due to the different products and services they produce and to differing business strategies. The operation of enterprises will also depend on the perception of the market environment by the decision maker (Thong 1999).

In the survey several questions on market conditions were asked. Information was requested on the number of customers and suppliers, the share of the three largest customers / suppliers and the destination of sales as well as the origin of supplies ("local", "national", "international"). On competition the location of main competitors was acquired ("Chennai", "India", "abroad"). The interviewees also had to assess the general level of competition on a seven-point scale (from 1, "no competition" to 7, "fierce competition") and the importance of certain attributes for competitiveness (from 1,"not important", to 7, "very important"). These attributes were "price", "quality", "flexibility / responsiveness", "punctuality of delivery", "after sales services" and "production capacity".[153]

---

[151] The importance of size for technology adoption has been elaborated in section 4.3.1. Most studies, even when concentrating on small enterprises only, include size as a determining variable (e.g. Duncombe 1999, Lal 1999, Sillince et al. 1998, Thong 1999)

[152] After transformation the distribution is close to the normal distribution. Working with log-transformations for size is common in many enterprise studies (e.g. Harrison et al. 1997).

[153] The categories are borrowed partially from Lal (1996) who examines sources of competitiveness in 59 Indian electrical and electronic goods companies. He proposes quality of products, flexibility in design, after sales services, delivery schedule and low overhead costs as possible sources. Quality and after sales services proved to be significantly more important for IT using enterprises.

To reduce and structure this information for further analysis factor analysis techniques, i.e. Principal Component Analysis (PCA), are applied to these market environment variables. As a result six factors are identified (see Annex 4 for details). From each factor one variable is selected to represent it in the regression equation:[154]

Factor 1 (*"Quantity of business contacts"*): A combination of two variables is chosen to be the representative variable of this factor. Adding up the number of customers and the number of suppliers gives the total number of business contacts of the enterprise (variable name: **CONTACT**).[155] Since ICTs help to communicate and to manage business relations it can be assumed that benefits from using them are different for differing numbers of business partners.

Factor 2 (*"National market focus"*): To build a representative variable, again, supplies and sales are aggregated by adding up the percentages of supplies bought nationally and the percentage of national sales which gives (divided by two) the share of business at the national level (variable name: **NAT_BUSI**). ICTs enable long-distance communication. Therefore, it can be assumed that their use is influenced by the amount of business that requires long-distance communication.

Factor 3 (*"International focus"*): For international business the same arguments apply as for national business. ICTs are even more advantageous for international business contacts as their use can save even more time and costs. The representative variable is built in the same way as above, adding up the percentages of supplies sourced from abroad and the international sales (variable name: **INT_BUSI**).

From each of the last three factors one representative variable should be chosen. As a starting point the ones with the highest factor loadings are advisable, but the assumed relation to ICT usage should also be taken into account. This leads to the choice of flexibility as the representative variable for factor 4 (*"Customer orientation"*), because ICTs are said to influence flexibility (variable name: **IM_FLEX**).[156]

For factor 5 (*"Quality competition"*) importance of quality is chosen as a representative variable (variable name: **IM_QUAL**).[157] The perception of quality as a major determinant of competitiveness can be assumed to reflect a more advanced way of doing business, indicating greater space for the application of ICTs.

"Importance of price" is chosen as a representative variable for factor 6 (*"Price competition"*). The perception of strong competition, mainly felt through price pressure, can be assumed to indicate a negative perception of opportunities and therefore a lack of openness towards new technologies (variable name: **IM_PRIC**).[158]

---

[154] In some cases two variables are combined in order to save as much information as possible.

[155] The ranges given for these variables had been transferred for the PCA. The new values are 2.5 for "less than 5", 7.5 for "5-10", 15.5 for "11-20",35.5 for "21-50" and 75 for "more than 50".

[156] IM_FLEX is a dummy variable, which assumes the value one if "flexibility" is given the top rank among the six categories assessed for their importance in competitiveness.

[157] IM_QUAL is a dummy variable, which assumes the value one if "quality" is given the top rank among the six categories assessed for their importance in competitiveness.

[158] IM_PRIC is a dummy variable, which assumes the value one if "price" is given the top rank among the six categories assessed for their importance in competitiveness.

It turns out that the correlation between the last three variables is low with correlation coefficients not exceeding 0.07. Therefore, they are well suited for a regression equation. In total, all six environmental variables reflect different aspects of the enterprises' perceived market environment and should, therefore, differently affect technology adoption.

4.5.1.5. Summary

The basic descriptive statistics of the explanatory variables described in the previous section are displayed in Table 4-2 for the continuous variables, and in Table 4-3 for the

Table 4-2: Selected descriptive statistics for continuous explanatory variables

Variable	Mean	Std.Dev.	Median	Minimum	Maximum	NumCases
AGE_CEO	45,97	10,49	48,00	22	72	265
EDU_YEAR	15,24	1,42	16,00	10	18	263
AGE_ENT	17,63	8,01	17,00	0	39	265
LN_SIZE	2,88	0,88	2,83	0,69	5,30	260
CONTACT	40,66	39,77	23,00	5	150	259
NAT_BUSI	25,66	25,93	20,00	0	100	252
INT_BUSI	3,46	9,26	0,00	0	50	252

Table 4-3: Selected descriptive statistics for dummy explanatory variables

Variable	Percentage (x=1)	NumCases
ADV_TECH	19,9	266
SEC_3031	11,7	266
SEC_33	13,5	266
SEC_34	37,2	266
SEC_35	24,1	266
IM_FLEX	33,3	249
IM_PRIC	65,3	262
IM_QUAL	79,8	262

dummy variables. None of the relevant bivariate correlation coefficients exceeds 0.4 indicating that there is no serious multicollinearity problem left in the selected data.[159]

The overall structure of the model is displayed in Figure 4-2. This model will be specified and tested for different questions in the following sections. First, a logistic regression model explores the determinants of current use or non-use (Section 0). Second, the determinants for the year of adoption are analysed by a Tobit regression model (Section 4.5.3). Third, with a slightly different model set-up, the determinants of the intensity of use are explored by ordinary least squares (OLS) regression model, by Tobit regression model and by Heckman's sample selection model (Section 4.5.4).

4.5.2. Determinants of ICT adoption at the time of the survey

4.5.2.1. Problem setting and selection of models

In this section the determinants for the adoption or non-adoption of a specific ICT at the time of the survey are explored. The determinants belong to the personal, the enterprise, and the environmental dimension, as developed in the previous section. Differences on the technology side will be reflected in different results from the analysis. The dependent variable is dichotomous. It can take the value "yes", for adoption of the technology in question, and "no" for not using it at the time of the survey. An appropriate technique to estimate models that regress on a dichotomous dependent variable is the Probit regression.[160]

The binomial Probit regression model is

$$y_i^* = \beta_0 + \sum_{j=1}^{k} \beta_j x_{ij} + u_i \tag{4.9}$$

with y_i^* being a not observable, so-called "latent" variable, which in this case represents the propensity to adopt the examined technology.[161] Observed is a dummy variable y_i defined as:

$$y_i = \begin{cases} 1 & if \ y^* > 0 \\ 0 & otherwise \end{cases} \tag{4.10}$$

Since the estimated coefficients of the Probit regression are difficult to interpret marginal effects are calculated and reported. Probit coefficients are reported in the Annex.

Ordered response models are used in order to analyse problems in which more than two discrete outcomes are observed. These discrete outcomes are not scaleable but

---

[159] The correlation matrix for these variables is displayed in Table A-5-1 in Annex 5.

[160] As an alternative to the binomial Probit regression the binomial Logit model could have been chosen. The Probit model is preferred as its results can also be used for analysis in later sections. Logit and Probit models only differ in their underlying distributions, which is the logistic distribution for the Logit model and the standard normal for the Probit model. Besides some differences in the size of the tails both distributions are fairly equal. Therefore, results from both models, are nearly identical in the following regressions (Maddala 1983:23).

[161] See Annex 6.1 for a detailed derivation of the binomial Probit regression model.

Figure 4-2: Model of ICT adoption and usage decisions

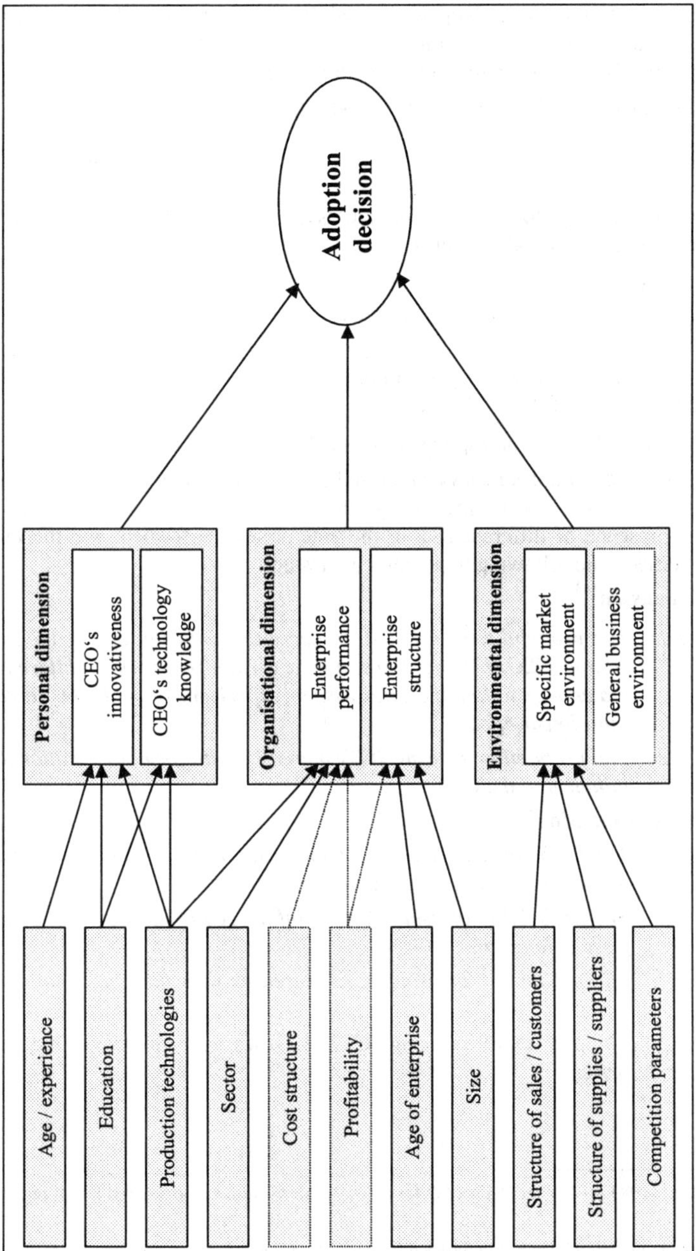

have a defined order, e.g. a) no computer is used, b) computer is used but no e-mail, c) computer is used for e-mail too. Again, both Probit and Logit models can be used for analysis. Ordered Probit and Logit models are defined in the following way:[162]

The regression model for the ordered model is given by:

$$y_{ij}^* = \beta_0 + \sum_{k=1}^{l} \beta_k x_{ik} + u_i \, , \tag{4.11}$$

The variable y_{ij}^* belongs to the jth of m categories if $\alpha_{j-1} < y^* < \alpha_j$ ($j = 1,2,...,m$). Hence, there is a set of ordinal variables:

$$y_{ij} = \begin{cases} 1 & if \, y_{ij}^* \in j \\ 0 & otherwise \end{cases} \text{(with } i=1,2,...,n, \, j=1,2,...,m) \tag{4.12}$$

Estimation of parameters is done by maximum likelihood estimation. Marginal effects will be displayed for the category borders.

4.5.2.2. Hypotheses building and specification of the regression model

The dimensions and variables that are supposed to influence the adoption of ICT were presented in section 4.5.1. Now, specific hypothesis about the influence of these variables on the presence of different ICT in the enterprises are formed, and the Probit model is specified. The following hypothesis are tested:

Personal dimension[163]

Hypothesis 1.1:   *The probability of using ICTs decreases with the age of the interviewed CEO, but increases after a certain point when children are old enough to join the enterprise or experience of the CEO increases (non-linear effect).*

Hypothesis 1.2:   *The probability of using ICTs increases with formal educational attainment of the CEO.*

Organisational dimension[164]

Hypothesis 1.3:   *The probability of using ICTs increases when advanced production technologies are used in the enterprise.*

Hypothesis 1.4:   *The probability of using ICTs is influenced by the sector the enterprise belongs to.*

Hypothesis 1.5:   *The probability of using ICTs increases with the age of the enterprise.*

Hypothesis 1.6:   *The probability of using ICTs increases with the size of the enterprise.*

---

[162] See Maddala (1983:46-49) and Annex 6.2 for a detailed derivation of the ordered Probit regression model.

[163] For the reasoning behind these hypotheses refer back to section 4.5.1.2.

[164] For the reasoning behind these hypotheses refer back to section 4.5.1.3.

Environmental dimension[165]

Hypothesis 1.7: *The probability of using ICTs increases with the number of business contacts.*

Hypothesis 1.8: *The probability of using ICTs increases with the share of national business relations, i.e. relations outside the local area.*

Hypothesis 1.9: *The probability of using ICTs increases with the share of international business relations.*

Hypothesis 1.10: *The probability of using ICTs increases when flexibility is perceived as the most important determinant of being competitive.*

Hypothesis 1.11: *The probability of using ICTs increases when quality is perceived as the most important determinant of being competitive.*

Hypothesis 1.12: *The probability of using ICTs decreases when price is perceived as the most important determinant of being competitive.*

Fitting the hypothesis into (4.9) leads to the following regression model, which will be tested on its predictive value for the adoption of different technologies.

$$y_i^* = \beta_0 + \beta_1 * AGE\_CEO_i{}^2 + \beta_2 * AGE\_CEO_i + \beta_3 * EDU\_YEAR_i + \quad (4.13)$$
$$+ \beta_4 * ADV\_TECH_i + \beta_5 * SEC\_3031_i + \beta_6 * SEC\_33_i +$$
$$+ \beta_7 * SEC\_34_i + \beta_8 * SEC\_35_i + \beta_9 * AGE\_ENT_i + \beta_{10} * LN\_SIZE_i +$$
$$+ \beta_{11} * CONTACT_i + \beta_{12} * NAT\_BUSI_i + \beta_{13} * INT\_BUSI_i +$$
$$+ \beta_{14} * IM\_FLEX_i + \beta_{15} * IM\_PRIC_i + \beta_{16} * IM\_QUAL_i + u_i$$

With these specifications of the independent variables 225 of the 266 enterprises are considered for analysis. Binominal Probit regressions are run on fax, pagers, cellular phones, computers and e-mail. For fax machines the first dependent variable y_i is **FAX_OWN**. FAX_OWN is a dummy variable that takes the value one if there is a fax either in the interviewed enterprise or in another enterprise owned by the interviewed CEO or at the CEO's home. Otherwise FAX_OWN assumes zero. A second regression for fax is done on the use of fax, including the use outside the enterprise, e.g. at public fax facilities. The dummy dependent variable is **FAX_USE**. For pagers the variable is **PAG_NOW** and for cellular phone the variable is **CEL_NOW**. They assume the value one if a pager or a mobile phone is currently used in the enterprise or by the interviewed CEO. Enterprises or CEOs that introduced the technology but discontinued its use were excluded from the analysis because the reasons for quitting the use were diverse. Nine enterprises stopped using pagers and five enterprises stopped using cellular phones. The variable for computer usage is **COMP_OWN** and indicates whether computers are used in the enterprise or at the CEO's home. The variable for e-mail usage in the enterprise, **E_MAIL**, assumes the value one if the computers are used for e-mail (see Table 4-4 for details of these variables).

Following the binomial Probit regression two ordered Probit regressions of the following form are conducted:

---

[165] For the reasoning behind these hypotheses refer back to section 4.5.1.4.

$$y_{ij}^* = \beta_0 + \beta_1 * AGE\_CEO_i{}^2 + \beta_2 * AGE\_CEO_i + \beta_3 * EDU\_YEAR_i + \qquad (4.14)$$
$$+ \beta_4 * ADV\_TECH_i + \beta_5 * SEC\_3031_i + \beta_6 * SEC\_33_i +$$
$$+ \beta_7 * SEC\_34_i + \beta_8 * SEC\_35_i + \beta_9 * AGE\_ENT_i + \beta_{10} * LN\_SIZE_i +$$
$$+ \beta_{11} * CONTACT_i + \beta_{12} * NAT\_BUSI_i + \beta_{13} * INT\_BUSI_i +$$
$$+ \beta_{14} * IM\_FLEX_i + \beta_{15} * IM\_PRIC_i + \beta_{16} * IM\_QUAL_i + u_i$$

The first observed variable y_{ij} that should be predicted with the latent variable y_{ij}^* is the ordinal variable **FAX_CAT**, which assumes the values zero for no use of fax, one for the use of outside fax facilities and two for the ownership of a fax machine. The second observed variable is **COMP_CAT**, which assumes the value zero for no computer use, one for computer use without using e-mail and two for using the computer as a communication tool, i.e. using e-mail (see Table 4-4 for details of these variables).

Table 4-4: Values assumed by dependent variables

	N	0	1	2
FAX_OWN	225	87 (39%)	138 (61%)	-
FAX_USE	225	51 (23%)	174 (77%)	-
PAG_NOW	216	137 (63%)	79 (37%)	-
CEL_NOW	220	140 (64%)	80 (36%)	-
COMP_OWN	225	75 (33%)	150 (67%)	-
E_MAIL	223	149 (67%)	74 (33%)	-
FAX_CAT	225	51 (23%)	36 (16%)	138 (61%)
COMP_CAT	223	73 (33%)	76 (34%)	74 (33%)

4.5.2.3. Results

Goodness of fit

The results of the binomial Probit regressions are shown in Table 4-5.[166] Before looking at the marginal effects goodness of fit of the models is examined.

The Chi-Squared statistic test tests for the validity of the model.[167] The Chi-Squared test values for the six binomial models range from 34.71 to 95.14, which indicates at 16 degrees of freedom a high significance level of at least 0.005 for all technologies.

To measure the goodness of fit, calculation of R^2 measures should be done. However, due to the non-linear nature of the Probit regression it is not possible to derive appropriate results by using the Ordinary Least Squares (OLS) R^2. Thus, two Pseudo-R^2 measures are displayed.[168] McFadden-Pseudo-R^2 values for the estimated models

---

[166] Estimated Probit coefficients are displayed in Annex 8. Regressions are run by the econometrics package LIMDEP 7.0.

[167] See Annex 7.1.1 for details how to derive these measures.

[168] See Annex 7.1.2 for details how to derive these measures.

range between 0.122 for pagers and 0.395 for fax usage. Values of the Cragg and Uhler-Pseudo-R^2 are between 0.203 for pagers and 0.525 for fax usage, i.e. they are higher than the McFadden values. The order, however, remains the same.

The most important goodness of fit measure is the prediction accuracy of the estimated Probit models.[169] Overall prediction accuracy ranges from 70.8 percent for pagers to 87.6 percent for fax users, i.e. it is reasonably high.

Comparing the goodness of fit measures for all six regressions it turns out that the order is basically similar for all techniques.[170] The derived model fits best for the usage of fax and worst for the usage of pagers. The goodness of fit for the usage of cellular phones also lags behind other model specifications. Therefore, results for the latter two technologies should be interpreted more cautiously because there seem to be more omitted arguments.

The same goodness of fit measures that are used for the binomial Probit can also be used for the ordered Probit regression models (see Table 4-6 for results). However, their values should not be compared directly with the values calculated for the former models. For the categorised fax and computer adoption the Chi-Squared test indicates a high significance level for the models. The McFadden-Pseudo-R^2 values are at 0.247 for fax and 0.207 for computers respectively. The Cragg and Uhler-Pseudo-R^2 values are at 0.437 and 0.410. From these indicators both models perform fairly equal. However, if the prediction accuracy is considered two features emerge. First, it seems that for the adoption of fax the distribution of the probabilities is such that the middle category is neglected, i.e. the probabilities group at the top and at the lower end. Second, the overall prediction accuracy is better for fax usage than for computer usage but it is more unevenly distributed over the categories, which again raises doubt over the distribution of the probability of using fax.

Discussion of parameters

For the **age of the CEO**, it was assumed that the probability to adopt ICTs first decreases with the age and starts to increase again later, when for example children join in the enterprise. This hypothesis is supported for the ownership of fax, the usage of fax and the adoption of computers. However, the significance level for ownership of fax and computer are, below the normally accepted threshold, between the ten and twenty percent level. For the usage of fax age is significant at the five percent level. In the ordered Probit model for fax usage age is significant just above the ten percent level. Interesting are the values of the vertex, i.e. the age above which the probability of having adopted the technology rises. The local minima for the ownership of fax are 48.3 years, for the usage of fax 47.1 years and for the adoption of computers 43.2 years. Demographically these values make sense. For the adoption of pagers and e-mail there is no significant influence of age. For cellular phones the influence is significant but opposite to that expected. The probability to adopt a cellular phone rises until the age of 39.0 and then declines again.

---

[169] See Annex 7.1.3 for details how to derive these measures.
[170] See Annex 7.1.4 for details.

Table 4-5: Results of (binominal) Probit regression on adoption of ICTs

Dependent variables:	FAX_OWN		FAX_USE		PAG_NOW		CEL_NOW		COMP_OWN		E_MAIL	
N	225		225		216		220		225		223	
Validity of model:												
Log likelihood function	-107,81		-72,85		-124,48		-116,43		-107,45		-100,53	
Restricted log likelihood	-150,13		-120,42		-141,84		-144,21		-143,22		-141,71	
Chi^2 - test value	84,63		95,14		34,71		55,54		71,52		82,37	
Degrees of freedom	16		16		16		16		16		16	
Significance level	0,0000		0,0000		0,0043		0,0000		0,0000		0,0000	
McFadden Pseudo-R^2	0,282		0,395		0,122		0,193		0,248		0,290	
Cragg/Uhler Pseudo-R^2	0,423		0,525		0,203		0,378		0,532		0,429	
Prediction accuracy (%):												
no use	65,5		62,7		86,1		87,1		58,7		94,0	
use	79,0		94,8		43,0		52,5		86,7		58,1	
overall	73,8		87,6		70,8		74,5		77,3		82,1	
Independent variables:	Mar.eff.	t-ratio	Mar.eff.	t-ratio	Mar.eff.	t-ratio	Mar.eff.	t-ratio	Mar.eff.	t-ratio	Mar.eff.	t-ratio
Constant	0,2047	0,222	0,6199	1,317	-0,9490	-1,168	-1,3930	-1,692 *	0,1608	0,202	-1,6992	-2,058 **
AGE_CEO	-0,0535	-1,551	-0,0375	-2,065 **	-0,0022	-0,079	0,0427	1,472	-0,0381	-1,298	-0,0077	-0,270
AGE_CEO^2	0,0006	1,459	0,0004	2,011 **	-0,0001	-0,158	-0,0005	-1,668 *	0,0004	1,358	0,0001	0,347
EDU_YEAR	0,0117	0,425	-0,0119	-0,881	0,0357	1,306	-0,0007	-0,026	-0,0050	-0,207	0,0496	1,833 *
ADV_TECH	0,1675	1,647 *	0,1414	2,228 **	-0,0028	-0,032	0,0469	0,510	0,2086	2,144 **	0,0219	0,234
SEC_3031	-0,0447	-0,305	0,0913	1,194	0,1148	0,829	-0,1117	-0,796	0,0639	0,480	0,0148	0,095
SEC_33	0,1778	1,232	0,1768	2,363 **	0,2730	2,014 **	0,1836	1,358	0,3679	2,798 ***	0,1635	1,042
SEC_34	-0,0520	-0,421	0,0940	1,586	0,0404	0,355	-0,0478	-0,419	0,1780	1,593	0,2015	1,542
SEC_35	0,0167	0,126	0,0921	1,367	-0,0288	-0,238	0,0259	0,217	0,0475	0,407	0,0702	0,533
AGE_ENT	-0,0002	-0,034	-0,0020	-0,759	-0,0004	-0,084	-0,0082	-1,685 *	0,0023	0,484	0,0058	1,182
LN_SIZE	0,2690	5,119 ***	0,1226	3,729 ***	0,1552	3,289 ***	0,1756	3,651 ***	0,1786	3,857 ***	0,1350	2,812 ***
CONTACT	0,0000	0,008	0,0016	2,136 **	0,0027	2,569 **	0,0012	1,101	0,0001	0,045	0,0027	2,551 **
NAT_BUSI	0,0059	3,381 ***	0,0025	2,494 **	-0,0008	-0,493	0,0015	0,934	0,0048	3,097 ***	0,0044	2,837 ***
INT_BUSI	0,0066	1,138	0,0062	1,604	-0,0092	-1,748 *	0,0126	2,297 **	0,0177	2,014 **	0,0160	2,577 ***
IM_FLEX	0,0509	0,619	0,1161	2,615 ***	0,0569	0,738	-0,1299	-1,944 *	0,0004	0,006	0,0275	0,336
IM_PRIC	0,1066	1,300	0,1198	2,657 ***	-0,0765	-0,986	0,1163	1,391	0,0040	0,054	0,0044	0,054
IM_QUAL	-0,0678	-0,746	-0,1189	-2,279 **	-0,0738	-0,850	-0,0251	-0,277	-0,0242	-0,305	0,0484	-0,526

* significant at 10% level; ** significant at 5% level; *** significant at 1% level; coefficients are reported in Table A-8-1 in Annex 8.

Table 4-6: Results of ordered Probit regression on adoption of ICTs

Dependent variables:	FAX_CAT					COM_CAT				
N	225					223				
Validity of model:										
Log likelihood function	-157,38					-194,35				
Restricted log likelihood	-209,13					-244,96				
Chi² - test value	103,50					101,21				
Degrees of freedom	16					16				
Significance level	0,0000					0,0000				
Mc Fadden Pseudo R²	0,247					0,207				
Cragg/Uhler- Pseudo-R²	0,437					0,410				
Prediction accuracy (%):										
0: no fax use / no computer	74,5					60,3				
1: outside use / computer only	0,0					44,7				
2: fax owned / computer & e-mail	89,1					62,2				
overall	70,2					55,6				
			Marginal effects					Marginal effects		
Independent variables:	Coeff.	t-ratio	0	1	2	Coeff.	t-ratio	0	1	2
Constant	2,2695	0,786	-0,4688	-0,3401	0,8089	-1,6972	-0,851	0,5444	0,0442	-0,5886
AGE_CEO	-0,1815	-1,596	0,0375	0,0272	-0,0647	-0,0556	-0,777	0,0178	0,0014	-0,0193
AGE_CEO²	0,0019	1,539	-0,0004	-0,0003	0,0007	0,0007	0,852	-0,0002	0,0000	0,0002
EDU_YEAR	-0,0134	-0,157	0,0028	0,0020	-0,0048	0,0624	0,998	-0,0200	-0,0016	0,0216
ADV_TECH	0,6493	2,354 **	-0,1341	-0,0973	0,2314	0,3485	1,334	-0,1118	-0,0091	0,1209
SEC_3031	0,0122	0,033	-0,0025	-0,0018	0,0043	0,0756	0,212	-0,0242	-0,0020	0,0262
SEC_33	0,6804	1,798 *	-0,1405	-0,1020	0,2425	0,7570	2,093 **	-0,2428	-0,0197	0,2626
SEC_34	0,0705	0,218	-0,0146	-0,0106	0,0251	0,4570	1,466	-0,1466	-0,0119	0,1585
SEC_35	0,2765	0,757	-0,0571	-0,0414	0,0986	0,0897	0,287	-0,0288	-0,0023	0,0311
AGE_ENT	-0,0064	-0,448	0,0013	0,0010	-0,0023	0,0113	0,889	-0,0036	-0,0003	0,0039
LN_SIZE	0,7898	5,398 ***	-0,1632	-0,1184	0,2815	0,4691	3,871 ***	-0,1505	-0,0122	0,1627
CONTACT	0,0017	0,620	-0,0004	-0,0003	0,0006	0,0045	1,724 *	-0,0014	-0,0001	0,0016
NAT_BUSI	0,0170	3,419 ***	-0,0035	-0,0025	0,0061	0,0127	3,384 ***	-0,0041	-0,0003	0,0044
INT_BUSI	0,0218	1,492	-0,0045	-0,0033	0,0078	0,0489	2,680 ***	-0,0157	-0,0013	0,0170
IM_FLEX	0,2912	1,230	-0,0602	-0,0436	0,1038	0,0576	0,291	-0,0185	-0,0015	0,0200
IM_PRIC	0,4754	1,956 **	-0,0982	-0,0713	0,1695	-0,0098	-0,050	0,0032	0,0003	-0,0034
IM_QUAL	-0,4031	-1,431	0,0833	0,0604	-0,1437	-0,1645	-0,792	0,0528	0,0043	-0,0570

* significant at 10% level; ** significant at 5% level; *** significant at 1% level

For the same reasons that were given for the age / experience of the CEO the effect of the **CEO's educational attainment** on ICT use is difficult to observe. The hypothesis assumes a positive relation between these measures. The only positive relation with an acceptable significance level is given for the use of e-mail, which is, of course the most recent and complex technology. Increasing the time of education by one year above the mean of 15.2 years increases the probability of using e-mail by almost five percentage points.

The coefficients for the **use of advanced technologies** carry the expected signs for all ICTs except for the pager, which is, however, not significantly different from zero. A positive correlation at an acceptable level is only visible for the ownership of a fax machine, use of fax and ownership of a computer. The use of mobile ICTs, i.e. pagers and mobile phones, does not have any relation to the use of numerically and micro-processor controlled production tools. The marginal effects in the regressions on fax use and ownership, as well as on computer ownership are relatively high. Using advanced production technologies raises the probability of owning a computer by almost 21 percentage points, using a fax by nearly 17 percentage points and owning a fax by more than 14 percentage points.

In the ordered regression the use of advanced production technologies significantly influence the way fax is used but not the way computers are used. Using advanced technologies makes it more than 13 percentage points less likely to use fax at all, makes it about ten percentage points less likely to use outside facilities and increased the probability to own a fax machine by more than 23 percentage points.

Belonging to a particular **sector** of industry does not appear to have a great effect. Signs differ from technology to technology for most of the sectors. One sector that stands out is basic metal and alloy industries (sector 33). It is positively related to the adoption of all technologies. For the usage of fax, the adoption of pagers and the own-ership of computers the positive sign is significant.[171] In the ordered variant both re-gressions are significant for metal and alloy industry.[172] The reason for these results might be, in the case of fax and pagers, the service character of many of this sectors enterprises' operations. Another reason for the above average use in this sector might also be the large average size of the enterprises (see section 3.3.1). Surprisingly, enter-prises of sector 35 (machinery and equipment) are less prone to use ICTs. One could have expected an influence on this sector in particular because many of its enterprises produce relatively sophisticated products. Thus, besides this tendency for the enter-prises of the basic metal and alloy industry to be more prone to use ICTs, affiliation to a certain sector does not seem to have a major influence on ICT adoption. However,

---

[171] Marginal effects are high. Belonging to sector 33 raises the probability of using a fax by 17.7 per-centage points, a pager by 27.3 percentage points and a computer by 36.8 percentage points.

[172] In these regressions belonging to metal and alloy industry raises the probability of owning a fax by more than 24 percentage points while lowering the probability of using outside facilities by ten percentage points and using no fax at all be 14 percentage points. For IT use, belonging to that sec-tor raises the probability to use a computer and e-mail by 26 percentage points, lowers the prob-ability of owning a computer without using it for e-mail by two percentage points and lowers the probability of not using a computer at all by 24 percentage points.

this is not too surprising if one keeps in mind that all enterprises belong to the manufacturing sector and are not as different as, for example, enterprises from manufacturing and service sector.

The **age of the enterprise** was expected to be positively correlated with the use of ICTs. This hypothesis is not confirmed for any of the technologies examined. The only significant relation, for cellular phones, is even negative, but with a very small marginal effect. The probability of using a cellular phone drops by 0.9 percentage points when the age of the enterprise is increased by one year from the mean of 17.9. The direction of relation coincides with the negative relation between age of the CEO and cellular phone use. This can be interpreted in the way that cellular phones are a technology that appeals rather to the "young" than to the "old".

The most significant and important determinant of ICT use is the **size of the enterprise**. For all technologies the logarithm of the number of employees is significant at the one percent level. Marginal effects are considerable for some of the technologies. Increasing the number of employees by one unit from the mean (i.e. from about 18 to 49 employees) increases the probability of owning a fax by about 27 percentage points, of using a fax by 12 percentage points, of owning a computer by about 18 percentage points, of using e-mail by 13.5 percentage points, of using a pager by 15.5 percentage points and of using a cellular phone by 17.5 percentage points (see Figure 4-3).

Figure 4-3: Influence of size on technology adoption

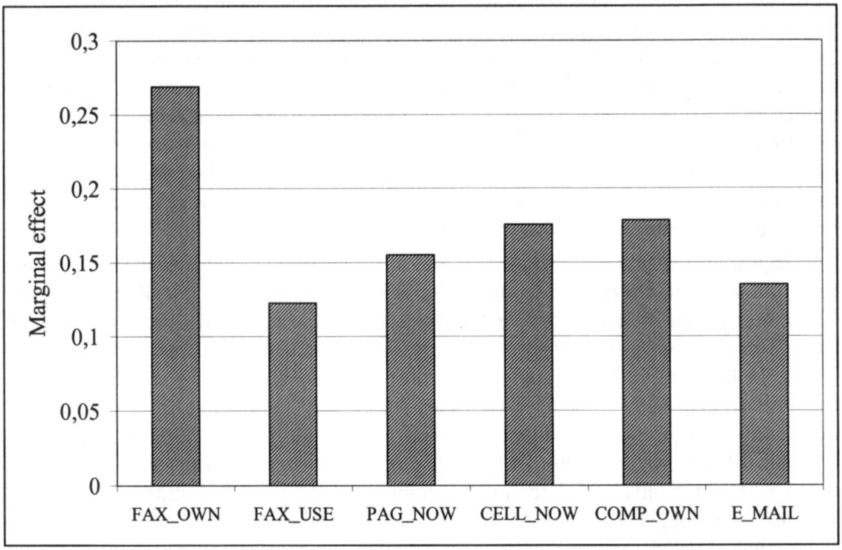

For the ordered regressions size is also highly significant. Raising size by one unit above the average will lower the probability of using no fax by 16 percentage points, of using outside facilities by almost twelve percentage points but increases the probability of owning a fax machine by 28 percentage points. Raising the size by one unit will lower the probability of not using a computer by 15 percentage points and will increase the probability of using e-mail by 16 percentage points. The probability of using a computer without connecting it to the Internet is hardly affected by size.

The **number of business contacts** is significantly positively related to the use of fax, the use of pagers and of e-mail at the five percent level. There is no relation for the ownership of a fax machine or computers. This result is surprising for the ownership of fax machines, as these were assumed to improve the management of sales and orders, but not so much for computers, as these are not only communication tools. It seems that it is sufficient to simply have access to a fax. For cellular phones the coefficient is positive but not significant. Marginal effects for both pagers and e-mail are relatively equal. Raising the number of business partners by one unit above the mean of 41 raises the probability of using these technologies by about 0.27 percentage points. The increase in the probability of using fax is 0.16 percentage points. The ordered regression for computers and e-mail is significant at the 10 percent level. It corroborates the results for these technologies. Increasing the number of business contacts by one increases the probability of using e-mail by 0.16 and lowers the probability of not using a computer at all by 0.14 percentage points. The use of computers only is not affected.

The **proportion of business at the national level** is a significant determinant, for the ownership and use of fax, computers and e-mail. All signs are positive except for pagers, but this is not significant. The marginal effects for fax, ownership of computer, and e-mail are considerable. Increasing the proportion of national business by one percentage point over the mean of 26 percent increases the probability of using the technology by nearly 0.6 percentage points for the ownership of fax machines, nearly 0.5 percentage points for computers and more than 0.4 percentage points for e-mail. In the ordered regressions, the marginal effect for fax ownership is 0.6 percentage points, too. For the use of computers and e-mail it is 0.4 percentage point. The probability of not using a computer at all is lowered at about the same rate.

Less significant than national business, but still with highly significant effects is the **proportion of international business**. The sign is positive for almost all technologies. The effect is significantly positive for the use of cellular phones, computers and e-mail. The ownership and usage of fax is positive but below acceptable significance levels. In the ordered Probit analysis the proportion of international business is, like the proportion of national business, a highly significant determinant for the intensity of computer adoption. For the adoption of fax it is not significant (slightly below the acceptable 10 percent threshold). Only the use of pagers carries a negative sign, indicating that it is basically a tool for local communication used by enterprises with local business. Looking at the marginal effects reveals that these are higher for an increase in international than in national business. Increasing the proportion of international business contacts by one percentage point above the mean of three percent increases the probability of using the technology by nearly 1.8 percentage points for computers and by 1.6 percentage points for e-mail. The probability of using a cellular phone increases by more than 1.2 percentage points. In the ordered regression results for computer use are highly significant. Raising the export ratio by one percent of turnover will increase the probability of using e-mail by 1.7 percentage points. These results indicate the increase in relative savings of communication costs by using technologies such as e-mail with increasing distance and the crossing of borders.

The results for the **perceived importance of certain parameters for competitiveness** are weak and ambiguous for most technologies. Only in the case of fax usage do all three variables show a significant relation. Seeing flexibility or price as the most important determinants for competitiveness will have a positive influence of the use of fax. Quality, as the most important determinant, will have a negative influence, i.e. for price and quality the signs are different than expected.[173] These results might be an indicator of a fax being a tool for price negotiations. The positive effect of prices' importance is also significant determining the level of fax usage in the ordered Probit model.[174] The only other coefficient significant at an acceptable level is flexibility for cellular phones. Contrary to expectations it is negative, indicating that the probability of using a cellular phone increases if flexibility is not of prime importance for competitiveness. This is counterintuitive since cellular phones are assumed to increase flexibility in the sense that the owner can be reached and consulted immediately. In general, one can conclude from the results that the perception of the competitive environment's determinants has no visible and conclusive effect on the use of advanced ICTs, such as cellular phones, computers and e-mail.

4.5.2.4. Conclusion

The regression results show different determinants for the adoption of different ICTs. However, there are some similarities between the different technologies. The probability of using ICTs is strongly influenced by the size of the enterprises as well as the proportion of business relations outside the local area. These results reflect on the one hand certain economies of scale using ICTs and, on the other, their cost and time saving potential, i.e. a relative advantage in long distance communication. The latter aspect is also reflected in higher marginal effects on the probability of adopting ICTs for international business relations compared to national business relations. The observation about the reach of business holds for each technology except pagers, that can be considered tools for local communication used by enterprises with local business.

The ownership of fax and computers show relatively similar patterns of adoption determinants. For both technologies age of the enterprise as well as the number of business contacts and education of the CEO do not have any influence. Both technologies have, meanwhile, become a common tool for the kind of enterprises interviewed. This is reflected in the high penetration rates for both technologies (about two thirds each).

Although being similar technologies that are used for similar purposes (being accessible outside the enterprise) pagers and mobile phones have a different structure of determinants. This indicates that these two technologies are not that similar. Cellular

---

[173] For Importance of flexibility the marginal effect is 0.116, for importance of price it is 0.120 and for importance of quality it is –0.119.

[174] The probability of fax ownership is raised by 17 percent if price is considered most important.

phones can be a substitute as well as a complement to the use of pagers. Moreover, cellular phones are almost solely used by the CEOs themselves whereas pagers are, especially in larger enterprises, a tool used by subordinate managers, too.[175] Furthermore, it became clear from the diffusion pattern that pagers will not become a widely used technology. For cellular phones and e-mail a pervasive use can be expected. This might also explain the relatively bad model fit for pager usage.

Looking at the different dimensions that determine technology adoption, it emerges that market environment as well as enterprise performance are the strongest factors. The markets an enterprise serves determine the relative advantage of using a specific ICT compared to other less sophisticated or more costly communication techniques. Although the utilisation of specific markets will be very much determined by the products and services an enterprise produces, the sector as such is not a strong determining factor. This leaves scope for entrepreneurial influence. However, the entrepreneurial proxies used in this work seem insufficient to capture this influence fully. Regarding the technological as such it becomes clear that relative advantage – may it be in terms of cost or flexibility – is the main trigger to adopt a specific technology.

4.5.3. Determinants of the timing of ICT adoption

4.5.3.1. Problem setting and Tobit regression model

The analysis conducted in the previous section presented just a snapshot of ICT adoption within the Ambattur Small Scale enterprises. It only looked at the determinants of using ICTs exactly at the time of the survey. However, different technologies are around for a different number of years and have different diffusion speeds, i.e. we are dealing with a dynamic process. In order to capture some of these dynamics one should look at the time a technology is adopted by a specific enterprise.

We assume that the time of adoption is basically determined by the same factors, which have been already presented, i.e. the same independent variables are fit into the model. What is different from the previous section is the dependent variable, which in this case is the time a technology had been used at the time of the survey. The dependent variable becomes a numerical variable that assumes a positive value for all users and zero for non-users. Using OLS-regression to estimate the determinants' effects will not lead to efficient and consistent estimators because this method ignores the fact that non-users will adopt the technology at different points of time in the future (Dhrymes 1986:1586-1588). The visible distribution of adoption among enterprises is censored at the time of the survey. To take this into account, a censored regression model, the Tobit model, named after Nobel laureate James Tobin who introduced this method in 1958, is used for analysis.

The standard Tobit model is defined in the following way:[176]

---

[175] This was already assumed from the descriptive date presented in Section 3.4.2.3 and in Table 3-19 in the same section.

[176] See Maddala (1983:151-156).

$$y_i = \beta_0 + \sum_{j=1}^{k} \beta_j x_{ij} + u_i \quad \text{if RHS} > 0$$
$$y_i = 0 \qquad \qquad \text{otherwise} \qquad \qquad (4.15)$$

The u_i are assumed to be normally distributed with mean zero and common variance σ^2. The parameters β_0 and β_j are estimated by maximum likelihood estimation in an iterative process. Extensions of the model allow for different lower limits and the introduction of upper limits to the value of y_i.

4.5.3.2. Hypotheses and specification of the Tobit model

For the analysis of the time of ICT adoption the same dimensions and independent variables are considered as in the previous section. This is not without problems because these variables refer to characteristics of the entrepreneurs, the enterprises and the enterprises' environment as they were at the time of the survey. The decision to adopt was taken at an earlier point in time, when these characteristics might have been different. For some variables there might even be the possibility that they were themselves influenced by the adoption of the examined ICTs. Exogenous and endogenous changes in the (presumably) independent variables therefore occurred in the time between adoption and the survey. In most cases, however, this time has not been very long. These changes might not be that large. Furthermore, changes in the variables are path dependent, i.e. they depend on previous values. Considering these points it seems acceptable to consider the current values of the independent variables as good proxies for their values at the time of adoption. Thus, hypotheses and the overall model tested are similar to the model presented in the previous section.

Personal dimension

Hypothesis 2.1:   *The time of ICT adoption is later the higher the age of the interviewed CEO is, but becomes earlier after a certain point, when children are old enough to join the enterprise or experience of the CEO increases.*

Hypothesis 2.2:   *The time of ICT adoption is earlier the higher the formal educational attainment of the CEO is.*

Organisational dimension

Hypothesis 2.3:   *The time of ICT adoption is earlier when advanced production technologies are used in the enterprise.*

Hypothesis 2.4:   *The time of ICT adoption is influenced by the sector the enterprise belongs to.*

Hypothesis 2.5:   *The time of ICT adoption is earlier the older the enterprise is.*

Hypothesis 2.6:   *The time of ICT adoption is earlier the larger the enterprise is.*

Environmental dimension

Hypothesis 2.7:   *The time of ICT adoption is earlier the higher the number of business contacts is.*

Hypothesis 2.8:   *The time of ICT adoption is earlier the higher the share of national business relations is, i.e. relations outside the local area.*

Hypothesis 2.9:   The time of ICT adoption is earlier the higher the share of international business relations is.

Hypothesis 2.10: The time of ICT adoption is earlier if flexibility is perceived as the most important determinant of being competitive.

Hypothesis 2.11: The time of ICT adoption is earlier if quality is perceived as the most important determinant of being competitive.

Hypothesis 2.12: The time of ICT adoption is later if price is perceived as the most important determinant of being competitive.

Fitting the hypothesis into (4.15) leads to the following regression model that will be tested on its prediction value for the time since adoption of the different ICTs.

$$y_i = \beta_0 + \beta_1 * AGE\_CEO_i{}^2 + \beta_2 * AGE\_CEO_i + \beta_3 * EDU\_YEAR_i + \quad (4.16)$$
$$+ \beta_4 * ADV\_TECH_i + \beta_5 * SEC\_3031_i + \beta_6 * SEC\_33_i +$$
$$+ \beta_7 * SEC\_34_i + \beta_8 * SEC\_35_i + \beta_9 * AGE\_ENT_i + \beta_{10} * LN\_SIZE_i +$$
$$+ \beta_{11} * CONTACT_i + \beta_{12} * NAT\_BUSI_i + \beta_{13} * INT\_BUSI_i +$$
$$+ \beta_{14} * IM\_FLEX_i + \beta_{15} * IM\_PRIC_i + \beta_{16} * IM\_QUAL_i + u_i$$

Tobit regressions are run in two ways. First a regression is run on the time of buying a fax machine, using a pager, cellular phone and e-mail.[177] In the second round of regressions future use is included.[178] Accounting for the planned time of introduction, the lower censoring point becomes -2.[179]

Again, 225 out of 266 cases could be considered for analysis due to missing values in the independent variables. The dependent variables are: **YE_FAX** for the time of owning a fax machine (**YEF_FAX** with future plans included). Three cases are excluded by the founding restriction (see footnote 177). Furthermore three outliers that stated to have used a fax for more than twelve years are excluded.[180] This leaves 219 cases for analysis. The time a pager is used is denoted by **YE_PAG** (**YEF_PAG** with future

---

[177] In the survey enterprises were asked about the year of introduction. This value is adjusted for analysis purpose by assuming the adoption to have taken place in the middle of the period and calculating the duration of use from the time of the survey. Since the survey took place in mid 1999 this leads to the following values: 1999 becomes 0.25 years, 1998 becomes 1 year, 1997 becomes 2 years etc.

Excluded from the analysis are cases in which the examined technology was introduced directly from the start of the enterprises operation, i.e. in the same year as the founding year. This will avoid disturbances that would occur from a late adoption that is simply due to a late founding date.

[178] For all technologies non-users were asked about their plans of introducing the technologies in the future. One has to be aware, that the answers given might be biased in two – however opposite – ways. First, in order to appear more modern, an intention was shown that does not really exist. Second, non-users might not really know yet about the properties of the examined ICTs and could decide for a faster adoption or to adoption at all if they get to know more about the technology.

[179] The answers given are converted in the following way (according to the schedule given above): "Soon" and "This year" becomes -0.25 years; "Next year" becomes -1 year. The category "Later", which was, however, given be only a few entrepreneurs, is ignored. The values for the non-users with no intention to use are adjusted accordingly to the censoring point to -2.

[180] Fax services only became available in India after 1985 (Singh 1999:134).

plans included). Seven cases are excluded because of the founding restriction. Since we are interested in the adoption date enterprises that introduced pagers and later discontinued their use are – contrary to the simple adoption analysis – not excluded. 218 cases are analysed. **YE_CELL** is the dependent variable for the time cellular phones are used (**YEF_CELL** with future plans included). Former users that discontinued the use are included, but two cases had to be excluded because of the founding restriction, leaving 223 cases for analysis. For the time of using e-mail **YE_MAIL** is the dependent variable (**YEF_MAIL** with future plans included). Four cases are excluded because of the founding restriction leaving 221 cases for analysis. Descriptive details of the variables are displayed in Table 4-7.

Table 4-7: Details of dependent variables

	Number of observations	Number of non-limit observations (Percentage)	Mean of non-limit observations
YE_FAX	219	123 (56%)	4.1
YE_PAG	218	85 (39%)	2.3
YE_CELL	223	84 (38%)	1.7
YE_MAIL	221	76 (34%)	1.3
YEF_FAX	219	141 (64%)	3.5
YEF_PAG	218	97 (44%)	1.9
YEF_CELL	223	115 (52%)	1.1
YEF_MAIL	219	117 (53%)	0.6

4.5.3.3. Results

The results of the Tobit regressions are shown in Table 4-8. Before looking at the estimated coefficients and marginal effects, goodness of fit measures for the models are examined. As for the Probit regression model in the previous section, goodness of fit can be tested. Chi-squared test values for the applied Tobit models range from 40.83 to 92.51, i.e. at 16 degrees of freedom they are all highly significant at the one per mill level and above.

Pseudo-R^2 measures for the Tobit models show the following values:[181] The Weighted Aldrich and Nelson-R^2 are between 0.240 for YEF_PAG and 0.457 for YEF_MAIL. The values for the model including future plans are higher for fax and e-mail. They are lower for pagers and about the same for cellular phones. The order within the two groups (with and without future plans) is the same for both goodness of fit measures. Thus, the Tobit fits best for e-mail and fax and worst for pagers.

---

[181] For the derivation of these measures see Annex 7.2.

Table 4-8: Results of Tobit regression on time of adoption

Dependent variables:	YE_CELL		YEF_CELL		YE_MAIL		YEF_MAIL	
N	223		223		221		221	
Validity of model:								
Log likelihood function	-239,62		-347,96		-191,22		-309,72	
Chi² - test value	55,53		56,45		81,67		92,51	
Degrees of freedom	17		17		17		17	
Significance level	0,0000		0,0000		0,0000		0,0000	
Weighted Aldrich/Nelson Pseudo-R²	0,322		0,320		0,424		0,457	
Independent variables:	Mar.eff.	t-ratio	Mar.eff.	t-ratio	Mar.eff.	t-ratio	Mar.eff.	t-ratio
Constant	-1,0335	-0,762	-1,8767	-0,688	-2,3324	-2,495 **	-6,2163	-2,780 ***
AGE_CEO	0,0411	0,853	0,0663	0,693	0,0074	0,238	-0,0121	-0,157
AGE_CEO²	-0,0006	-1,078	-0,0010	-0,912	-0,0001	-0,143	0,0002	0,239
EDU_YEAR	-0,0569	-1,391	-0,1078	-1,283	0,0686	2,283 **	0,2086	2,888 ***
ADV_TECH	0,0725	0,489	0,1989	0,668	-0,0381	-0,386	0,0507	0,212
SEC_3031	-0,0004	-0,002	-0,1229	-0,268	0,1168	0,781	0,0498	0,137
SEC_33	0,3284	1,426	0,5201	1,112	0,1038	0,626	0,2987	0,789
SEC_34	0,0443	0,236	0,1402	0,371	0,1471	1,130	0,4338	1,416
SEC_35	0,0598	0,309	-0,0329	-0,083	0,0920	0,703	0,1836	0,572
AGE_ENT	-0,0126	-1,552	-0,0317	-1,914 *	0,0058	1,105	-0,0003	-0,025
LN_SIZE	0,3074	3,933 ***	0,6173	3,932 ***	0,1535	3,002 ***	0,3943	3,177 ***
CONTACT	0,0016	0,920	0,0043	1,239	0,0019	1,756 *	0,0066	2,453 **
NAT_BUSI	0,0031	1,232	0,0061	1,178	0,0041	1,178	0,0139	3,480 ***
INT_BUSI	0,0179	2,577 ***	0,0351	2,412 **	0,0163	3,472 ***	0,0394	3,185 ***
IM_FLEX	-0,1212	-0,921	-0,3499	-1,340	0,0033	0,038	-0,0674	-0,324
IM_PRIC	0,2137	1,613	0,2040	0,780	-0,0042	-0,049	0,2094	0,995
IM_QUAL	0,0264	0,181	-0,0721	-0,250	-0,0223	-0,237	0,0095	0,041

* significant at 10% level; ** significant at 5% level; *** significant at 1% level; Tobit coefficients are reported in Table A-8-2 in Annex 8.

Table 4-8 continued

Dependent variables:	YE_CELL		YEF_CELL		YE_MAIL		YEF_MAIL	
N	223		223		221		221	
Validity of model:								
Log likelihood function	-239,62		-347,96		-191,22		-309,72	
Chi² - test value	55,53		56,45		81,67		92,51	
Degrees of freedom	17		17		17		17	
Significance level	0,0000		0,0000		0,0000		0,0000	
Weighted Aldrich/Nelson Pseudo-R^2	0,322		0,320		0,424		0,457	
Independent variables:	*Mar.eff.*	*t-ratio*	*Mar.eff.*	*t-ratio*	*Mar.eff.*	*t-ratio*	*Mar.eff.*	*t-ratio*
Constant	-1,0335	-0,762	-1,8767	-0,688	-2,3324	-2,495 **	-6,2163	-2,780 ***
AGE_CEO	0,0411	0,853	0,0663	0,693	0,0074	0,238	-0,0121	-0,157
AGE_CEO²	-0,0006	-1,078	-0,0010	-0,912	-0,0001	-0,143	0,0002	0,239
EDU_YEAR	-0,0569	-1,391	-0,1078	-1,283	0,0686	2,283 **	0,2086	2,888 ***
ADV_TECH	0,0725	0,489	0,1989	0,668	-0,0381	-0,386	0,0507	0,212
SEC_3031	-0,0004	-0,002	-0,1229	-0,268	0,1168	0,781	0,0498	0,137
SEC_33	0,3284	1,426	0,5201	1,112	0,1038	0,626	0,2987	0,789
SEC_34	0,0443	0,236	0,1402	0,371	0,1471	1,130	0,4338	1,416
SEC_35	0,0598	0,309	-0,0329	-0,083	0,0920	0,703	0,1836	0,572
AGE_ENT	-0,0126	-1,552	-0,0317	-1,914 *	0,0058	1,105	-0,0003	-0,025
LN_SIZE	0,3074	3,933 ***	0,6173	3,932 ***	0,1535	3,002 ***	0,3943	3,177 ***
CONTACT	0,0016	0,920	0,0043	1,239	0,0019	1,756 *	0,0066	2,453 **
NAT_BUSI	0,0031	1,232	0,0061	1,178	0,0041	2,522 **	0,0139	3,480 ***
INT_BUSI	0,0179	2,577 ***	0,0351	2,412 **	0,0163	3,472 ***	0,0394	3,185 ***
IM_FLEX	-0,1212	-0,921	-0,3499	-1,340	0,0033	0,038	-0,0674	-0,324
IM_PRIC	0,2137	1,613	0,2040	0,780	-0,0042	-0,049	0,2094	0,995
IM_QUAL	0,0264	0,181	-0,0721	-0,250	-0,0223	-0,237	0,0095	0,041

* significant at 10% level; ** significant at 5% level; *** significant at 1% level; Tobit coefficients are reported in Table A-8-2 in Annex 8.

Looking at the single variables the following picture emerges:

The **age of the CEO** does not have any significant influence on the time of adoption.

Education only has a significant positive influence on the time of adopting e-mail. For all other technologies there is no significant influence. Marginal effects for both regressions on e-mail adoption time are different. For the current users extending education by one year above the mean of 15.2 years will make adoption occur about 0.07 years earlier. Including the planned users this become 0.21 years. It seems that higher education raises, at least, the awareness of e-mail.

The **use of advanced production technologies** has no significant relation to the time of ICT adoption.

The **sector** enterprises belong to seems to have no impact in general on the time of adoption. Only for pagers does belonging to a sector, the basic metal and alloy industries, lead to an earlier adoption of pagers by one year for current users and by 1.5 years if planned future use is included in the analysis. For all other technologies and sectors there is no significance influence at an acceptable level.

Age of the enterprise is only significant for the time cellular phones are introduced and the introduction is planned. However, the sign is negative, i.e. the younger the enterprise the earlier it has adopted or plans to adopt the technology.

Size is again the most obvious determining factor for the adoption of ICTs. The log of enterprises' employees is positively significant at the one percent level for all models. Marginal effects are different. Raising the number of employees from about 18 to 48 only speeds up the introduction of e-mail by about 0.15 years for current users and 0.40 years if planned use is included. For cellular phones it is 0.31 (0.62), for pagers 0.35 (0.60) and for fax machines 1.09 (1.57) (see Figure 4-4).

The **number of business contacts** is highly significant for the time of introducing pagers and e-mail. Marginal effects are, however, quite low. Raising contacts by one unit above the mean of about 42 leads to an earlier adoption of pager by the current users of 0.008 years and including planned users by 0.014 years. For e-mail these effects are 0.002 years for current and 0.007 years including planned users.

Again the amount of non-local, i.e. **national and international business** is very important. Only for pagers is there no significant influence for both the amount of national business and international business. This indicates the local character of pagers. For the use of mobile phones the amount of international business influences the time of adoption significantly. This might be explained by the fact that use of cellular phones of foreign partners was observed at an early stage. Raising the amount of international business by one percentage point above the mean of 3.1 percent would influence the introduction time by 0.018 year for current users and 0.035 years including planned users. For fax machines the trigger seems to be advantages in national long-distance communication, which significantly influences the adoption time (international business carries a positive sign but is not significant). Raising national business by one percentage point above the mean of 26.3 percent of total business will change adoption time by 0.019 years for current owners and 0.027 years for future users. For

Figure 4-4: Influence of size on time of technology adoption

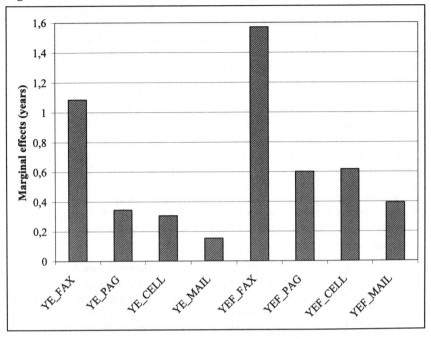

the use of e-mail the amount of national and international business are positively re-lated and highly significant, reflecting the cost advantage of e-mail for long-distance communication above other technologies. Marginal effects are 0.004 (0.014) years for a one percentage point increase of national business by current (including future) users and 0.016 (0.039) for an one percentage point increase of international business.

Competition parameters do not have an pervasive influence on adoption time. For the adoption time of e-mail the perception of the importance of flexibility, price and quality does not seem to matter at all. Just as the adoption rate at the time of the sur-vey, the importance of flexibility seems, to be negatively correlated with adoption time of cellular phones. This is opposite to what was expected. For the adoption time of pagers the perceived importance of quality has a negative influence, indicating again the simple character of pagers. For fax machines there is a similar picture to the Probit model. Signs for price and flexibility have positive signs, quality a negative sign. However, only the effects of quality and flexibility on the ownership of fax machines, including the planning users, are significant.

4.5.3.4. Conclusion

Market environment and enterprise performance parameters are the most important determinants just as they were in the analysis of adoption at the time of the survey. Personal characteristics are even less important, as are structural parameters of the enterprise. Adoption time's most important determinant is size for all examined ICTs. This might indicate positive economies of scale associate with the use of ICTs on the one hand and on the other induced growth from ICT use. The latter proposition, however, is not really corroborated since the inclusion of planned use does not weaken the results.[182] Size is followed by the share of national business for fax and e-mail and the share of international business for e-mail. This result reflects the relative cost advantage of these ICTs for long-distance and international communication. Competition parameters do not play an important role. Only for fax machines does the perception of flexibility as the most important determinant of competitiveness seem to have an influence on adoption time. The larger effect when future users are included indicates that flexibility is a perceived characteristic of that technology.

Comparing the results of the regression on time of adoption with the regression on adoption as such, it appears that the results are similar. In particular for fax ownership and e-mail usage the same variables have a significant influence. For pagers and cellular phones there are slight differences. What stands out is that age of the CEO loses its influence when time of adoption is examined. Variations in all other variables do not follow specific patterns or are not strong enough to assign meaning to.

4.5.4. Determinants of the intensity of ICT use

4.5.4.1. Identifying intensity parameters and appropriate regression models

After discussing the determinants of technology adoption and the time of adoption we now turn to the determinants of the usage intensity after adoption has taken place. The dimensions are assumed to be the same, i.e. entrepreneurial characteristics, structure and performance of the enterprise, market and general environment, and characteristics of the adopted ICT itself. This allows to test for the influence of the same variables as in the previous analysis. However, impact of these variables on use is expected to be different from the adoption decision. Adoption was described as a discrete, dichotomous process in which adoption takes place when an unobserved variable, probability to adopt, crosses a certain threshold. After adoption has taken place the intensity of use is a continuous variable (Thong 1999).

Intensity of ICT use can be measured quantitatively in two ways, either in time the technology is used, or how much money is spent on use. Qualitative measures would consider the kind of information processed and transmitted. For the purpose of this work only quantitative measures are taken into account. For fax and e-mail the number of faxes and mails sent and received are used as indicators of the intensity of use. Weekly numbers of faxes and e-mails - sent as well as received - are added up in order to account for total use.[183] For cellular phones we referred to the average monthly phone bill, which proved to be easy to recall for the interviewees.

---

[182] Marginal effects are even larger for all ICTs when planned use is included. This might be due to technical reasons of calculating the marginal effects. If it is not it would indicate that size is the cause for ICT adoption and not the reverse.

[183] The interviewees were asked to indicate the usage in ranges. In order to create scalars these ranges are transformed in the following way: 0.5 for "less than 1", 3 for "1 to 5", 7.5 for "5 to 10", 15.5 for "10 to 20" and 35.5 for "more than 20".

In the case of cellular phones and e-mail one should be aware, that substantial private use could occur. Since this work is interested in business, private use, as indicated by the users, is deducted from the total cellular phone bill and from the number of e-mails sent and received.[184] Thus, in the following analysis the total number of faxes sent and received (variable name: **FR_FAX**)[185], the monthly expenditure for business use of cellular phones (**EX_CEL_B**) and the number of business related e-mails sent and received (**FR_EMA_B**) will be used as dependent variables (see Table 4-9 for details).

Table 4-9: Descriptive statistics of intensity variables*

	Number of observations	Number of non-limit observations (Percentage)	Mean of non-limit observations
FR_FAX**	225	174 (77%)	20.0
FR_FAX***	225	138 (61%)	23.4
EX_CEL_B	217	77 (35%)	1958
FR_EMA_B	217	66 (30%)	12.6

*   Only cases that are used for Tobit regression are included. For other models less cases are in-cluded in analysis. Values will change accordingly.
**   Analysis done for fax users (including use outside the enterprise)
*** Analysis done for fax owners only.

To analyse the described problem Tobit regression models, as presented in the previous section, seem to be the best method since they include information on users and non-users and produce well-behaved estimates. However, the Tobit regression is restricted to independent variables that are available for all cases. To examine the current intensity of use it might be interesting to include variables specific to the users, e.g. the experience with the technology or perception of the technology.[186] Including such variables could give more importance to variates belonging to the technological dimension. The easiest option to achieve this goal is to use OLS regression for the subsample that uses the examined technology y:

$$y_i = \beta_0 + \sum_{j=1}^{k} \beta_j x_{ij} + u_i \text{ for all } y_i > 0. \tag{4.17}$$

---

[184] The following analysis was also done on total use, i.e. including private use. Results are fairly similar. Interesting deviations will nevertheless be reported.

[185] The frequency of fax use will be tested for two model specifications. The first considers the frequency of use by all users, i.e. users which own a fax and those that do not. The second only counts uses by fax owners.

[186] Perception of technology use could have been considered as a determinant of the time of adoption, analysed in the previous section. It was excluded because current perceptions and opinions would have been used to analyse a decision taken in the past. In this section it is assumed that current perception is a determinant of current intensity of use.

However, the estimates of coefficients β are biased because the sample that is used is not representative for the whole population, i.e. we face a sample selection bias. To provide a remedy to this problem Heckman (1976) proposed a correction method based on the following model (see Nawata (1994) and Puhani (2000)):

$$y_{1i} = \beta_0 + \sum_{j=1}^{k} \beta_j x_{ij} + u_i$$

$$y_{2i} = \alpha_0 + \sum_{j=1}^{l} \alpha_j x_{ij} + v_i$$

$$d_i = 1(y_{2i} > 0), \, i = 1,2,...,N. \tag{4.18}$$

d_i assumes one if the argument in the parenthesis is true otherwise $d_i = 0$. d_i indicates the sign of y_{2i} that is not observed itself. u_i and v_i are assumed to be binary normal distributed:

$$\begin{bmatrix} u_i \\ v_i \end{bmatrix} \sim BN \left[\begin{bmatrix} 0 \\ 0 \end{bmatrix}, \begin{bmatrix} \sigma_1^2 & \sigma_{12} \\ \sigma_{12} & 1 \end{bmatrix} \right] \, [187] \tag{4.19}$$

The conditional expectation of y_{1i} given $d_i > 0$ is:

$$E(y_{1i} \mid d_i = 1) = \beta_0 + \sum_{j=1}^{k} \beta_j x_{ij} + E(u_i \mid v_i > -(\alpha_0 + \sum_{j=1}^{l} \alpha_j x_{ij})) \quad \text{with} \tag{4.20}$$

$$E(u_i \mid v_i > -(\alpha_0 + \sum_{j=1}^{l} \alpha_j x_{ij})) = \sigma_{12} \lambda (\alpha_0 + \sum_{j=1}^{l} \alpha_j x_{ij}). \tag{4.21}$$

with σ_{12} is the covariance of u_i and v_i and λ is the so-called inverse Mills ratio

$$\lambda(z) = \frac{\phi(z)}{\Phi(z)}, \tag{4.22}$$

with $\phi(.)$ denoting the density and $\Phi(.)$ the cumulative density function of standard normal. Heckman proposes to first estimate $\lambda(\alpha_0 + \sum_{j=1}^{l} \alpha_j x_{ij})$ by way of a Probit model and then estimate in the second step

$$y_{1i} = \beta_0 + \sum_{j=1}^{k} \beta_j x_{ij} + \rho \sigma_1 \lambda (\alpha_0 + \sum_{j=1}^{l} \alpha_j x_{ij}) + \varepsilon_i \tag{4.23}$$

---

[187] The variance of v_i is set to be 1 because it cannot be observed due to the nature of the model (Greene 1998:712 and Davidson / MacKinnon 1993:542).

by way of OLS.[188] The Heckman estimator is consistent as long as v_i has a normal distribution and ε_i is independent of λ. It is not efficient if ε_i is heteroscedastic (Puhani 2000:55). Davidson and MacKinnon (1993:544) suggest to use the coefficient $\rho\sigma_l$ on the selectivity regressor λ as a test for the presence of a selectivity bias. Since $\sigma_1 \neq 0$ the hypothesis that $\rho = 0$ can be tested by looking at the t-statistic for the coefficient. If the coefficient is not significantly different from zero selectivity is not a problem and sub-sample OLS regression is expected to yield consistent estimates.

The Heckman model offers the possibility to divide the argument in the tested model into two parts. The first part, i.e. the Probit estimation, identifies determinants of the cases' affiliation to the examined sub-sample. The second part, i.e. the OLS regression, examines characteristics of the sub-sample. In the present case, the Probit regression identifies variables that determine the decision to adopt the technology. The OLS regression identifies determinants of the intensity of using the examined technology.

However, Heckman's limited information model (in contrast to the full information model of the Tobit type) is not without problems. The main problem is unrobust results due to multicollinearity in the arguments of equation y_{1i} (Puhani 2000:57, Nawata 1994:40). Consequently the Heckman model works best when variables that are good predictors of y_2 do not appear in x. This condition is difficult to achieve because it can be contrary to the economic reasoning behind the two equations. In the current case we can think of variables that are considered to influence the decision to adopt as well as the usage intensity after adoption has taken place, e.g. the size of the enterprise or the share of international business contacts. Thus, a trade-off between economic meaningfulness and econometric appropriateness can be suspected when applying the Heckman method. A remedy would be to use maximum likelihood estimators (MLE) for equation 4.23 instead of OLS. MLE perform better, i.e. they are more efficient, in the presence of multicollinearity but they are difficult to compute.[189] In order to make sure that the right determinants are identified, i.e. to account for unrobustness, different models and model specifications will be presented in the following analysis.

4.5.4.2. Hypotheses and specification of models

In addition to the independent variables presented in section 4.5.1 and the ones used in the previous analyses, a few more variables, that are only acquired from the users, will be presented. First, experience with a technology can be considered to influence the intensity of its use. Experience will be represented by the length of time the technology has already been used. These were dependent variables in section 4.5.3, i.e. YE_FAX, YE_CELL and YE_MAIL (see for Table 4-7 details).[190]

---

[188] σ_{12} is substituted by the correlation coefficient between u_t and v_t, ρ, and the standard deviation of u_t, σ_l due to $\sigma_{12} = \dfrac{\rho}{\sqrt{\sigma_1^2}\sqrt{\sigma_2^2}}$.

[189] See Nawata (1994) for a detailed discussion on the comparison of Heckman's estimator and MLE. For the present analysis MLE estimates for 4.22 are not applied because of computing difficulties. For most model specifications LIMDEP was not able to generate appropriate results.

[190] YE_FAX is the time a fax machine is owned. Thus, the variable is not applicable when considering the use of fax, which includes enterprises that use outside facilities only.

The other set of variables comprises questions about the importance assigned to different reasons of using a technology. Enterprises could mark the answers to the options given on a five point Likert scale ranking from 1, "no importance", to 5, "great importance". This information was requested for fax and cellular phones but not for e-mail. The options are presented in Table 4-10 and Table 4-11.

Table 4-10: Reasons of using and owning fax

Variable name	Variable description	Number of observations	Mean
IM_F_SPE	Fax is more reliable and faster than postal service	166 (128)	4.46 (4.42)
IM_F_BIN	Fax is more binding than a phone call	166 (128)	4.37 (4.38)
IM_F_EAS	Fax makes communication with customers / suppliers easier	166 (128)	4.30 (4.36)
IM_F_COS	Fax is a cheap way to send documents	166 (128)	3.01 (2.95)
IM_F_COM	Fax is commonly used	166 (128)	3.03 (3.08)
IM_F_EXP	Being accessible by fax is expected by customers / suppliers	166 (128)	3.27 (3.40)

* Numbers in parenthesis are for fax owners only.

Table 4-11: Reasons of using cellular phones

Variable name	Variable description	Number of observations	Mean
IM_C_EMP	Cellular phone is used to stay in touch with employees when outside the enterprise	66	4.33
IM_C_EAS	Cellular phone makes communication with customers / suppliers easier	66	3.91
IM_C_STA	Cellular phone is a status symbol	66	2.03
IM_C_COM	Cellular phone is commonly used	66	2.39
IM_C_EXP	Use of a cellular phone is expected by customers / suppliers	66	3.86

Most of this reasoning refers to specific advantages gained when using the technology (IM_F_SPE, IM_F_BIN, IM_F_EAS, IM_F_COS, IM_C_EAS, IM_C_EMP). Others indicate direct or indirect outside pressure (IM_F_EXP, IM_F_COM, IM_C_EXP, IM_C_COM, IM_C_STA). Since the variables are fairly similar one might expect some correlation. Testing for bivariate correlation between the variables for each specific technology reveals, however, no major correlation problem. The highest observed correlation coefficients are about 0.3 for the variables concerning cellular phones and 0.4 for the variables concerning the use of fax machines.[191] It is therefore possible to include all variables into the regressions.

In addition perceived effects of using ICTs influence the intensity of their use. Causality can, of course, also be assumed to be the other way, but for the analysis in this section it is argued that a positive perception of the technologies' possibilities will spur its use. Since ICTs, as understood in this work, are management tools their impact should be on administration not on production. Enterprises were asked whether they perceive ICTs to improve efficiency of administration specifically and the competitiveness of the enterprise in general.[192] Answer options were "yes, significantly", "yes, slightly", "no, no effect", "no, even negative effect", "don't know" (see section 3.4 for detailed results). Since negative effects were hardly reported and "don't know" can be assumed to indicate only negligible impacts three major categories of perceived effects can be identified, i.e. significantly positive, slightly positive, non-positive. These are transferred to dummy variables. The variables are presented in Table 4-12 to Table 4-14.

Table 4-12: Perceived effects of fax use*

Variable name	Variable description	Observations	% of non-zero observations
EF_F_SIG	Fax has a significant positive effect on the efficiency of administration	166 (128)	38.6 (42.2)
EF_F_SLI	Fax has a slight positive effect on the efficiency of administration	166 (128)	38.0 (36.7)
CO_F_SIG	Fax has a significant positive effect on the competitiveness of the enterprise	166 (128)	25.3 (24.2)
CO_F_SLI	Fax has a slight positive effect on the competitiveness of the enterprise	166 (128)	26.5 (27.3)

* Numbers in parenthesis are for fax owners only.

Table 4-13: Perceived effects of cellular phone use

Variable name	Variable description	Observations	% of non-zero observations
CO_C_SIG	Cellular phone has a significant positive effect on competitiveness of the enterprise	66	24.2
CO_C_SLI	Cellular phone has a slight positive effect on competitiveness of the enterprise	66	31.8

---

[191] See Table A-5-2 and Table A-5-3 in Annex 5.

[192] The former question was not asked in connection with mobile phones.

Table 4-14: Perceived effects of e-mail use

Variable name	Variable description	Obser-vations	% of non-zero observations
EF_M_SIG	E-mail has a significant positive effect on the efficiency of administration	63	38.1
EF_M_SLI	E-mail has a slight positive effect on the efficiency of administration	63	31.7
CO_M_SIG	E-mail has a significant positive effect on competitiveness of the enterprise	63	34.9
CO_M_SLI	E-mail has a slight positive effect on com-petitiveness of the enterprise	63	31.7

Adding these variables to the established ones the following hypotheses to be emerge:

Personal dimension

Hypothesis 3.1:   *ICT use is less intense the higher the age of the interviewed CEO is, but becomes more intense after a certain point, when children are old enough to join the enterprise or experience of the CEO increases.*

Hypothesis 3.2:   *ICT use is more intense the higher the formal educational attainment of the CEO is.*

Organisational dimension

Hypothesis 3.3:   *ICT use is more intense when advanced production technologies are used in the enterprise.*

Hypothesis 3.4:   *The intensity of ICT use is influenced by the sector the enterprise belongs to.*

Hypothesis 3.5:   *ICT use is more intense the older the enterprise is.*

Hypothesis 3.6:   *ICT use is more intense the larger the enterprise is.*

Environmental dimension

Hypothesis 3.7:   *ICT use is more intense the higher the number of business contacts is.*

Hypothesis 3.8:   *ICT use is more intense the higher the share of national business relations is, i.e. relations outside the local area.*

Hypothesis 3.9:   *ICT use is more intense the higher the share of international business relations is.*

Hypothesis 3.10: *ICT use is more intense if flexibility is perceived as the most important determinant of being competitive.*

Hypothesis 3.11: *ICT use is more intense if quality is perceived as the most important determinant of being competitive.*

Hypothesis 3.12: ICT use is less intense if price is perceived as the most important determinant of being competitive.

Technological dimension

Hypothesis 3.13: ICT use is more intense the longer it is already used in the enterprise.[193]

Hypothesis 3.14: ICT use is more intense the more important technology specific advantages are perceived to be.[194]

Hypothesis 3.15: ICT use is less intense the more important outside pressure of using this particular ICT is perceived to be.[195]

Hypothesis 3.16: ICT use is more intense if the particular ICT is perceived to positively influence efficiency of administration.[196]

Hypothesis 3.17: ICT use is more if the particular ICT is perceived to positively influence competitiveness of the enterprise.

As mentioned above, it is not clear which specific model and model specification is best to analyse the problem at hand. Therefore, a number of different models (i.e. OLS, Tobit, Heckman) and different model specifications (i.e. different samples of independent variables) will be presented:

1. The basic equation for the sub-sample OLS will be based on equation 4.16 from section 4.5.3.2 to which the previously presented variables will be added. In order to compare it to the following Tobit regression, which can only account for variables surveyed for users and non-users, OLS regressions for the basic variables only are reported as well.

2. The equations of the Tobit models will be based on equation 4.16 from section 4.5.3.2 covering only the basic variables.

3. The Probit equation for the Heckman model will be equation 4.14 from section 4.5.2.2 leading to the same results as in that section. For the following OLS regression an equation similar to equation 4.19 is used. As for the sub-sample OLS regression results are reported for the basic variables only as well as for the basic variables plus the newly identified ones. In a second variation, groups of variables that appear in the selection equation are not considered in the intensity equation. These are personal characteristics and the enterprises' structural characteristics which can be considered to be determinants of the decision to adopt a technology but are assumed not to be important when the actual intensity of use is determined. For the same reason the perceptions of the importance of specific determinants of competitiveness are also not considered. The remaining variables to determine the intensity of use are indicators of enterprise performance and specific market environment.

---

[193] Not tested for the usage of fax including the use of outside facilities.

[194] Not tested for e-mail users.

[195] Not tested for e-mail users.

[196] Not tested for users of cellular phones.

4.5.4.3. Results

To determine which are the appropriate results to refer to for proper interpretation we first look at the basic model results. After identifying one or several best model specifications the results of these are discussed in more detail.

For the **intensity of fax use (including fax office users)** all models tested appear to be valid since they show good goodness of fit measures (see Table 4-15). Adding additional variables to the basic variables from the adoption analysis appears to improve the goodness of fit, therefore it seems advisable to include them in the analysis. Results from the Heckman regression indicate that sample selection bias seems to be no problem in the current sample. The correlation ρ of the error terms of selection and intensity equation are very small, rendering the inverse mills ratio λ to be insignificant. Thus, one may refer to the OLS regressions for detailed results.[197] Indeed, results from both the sub sample and the Heckman OLS appear to be fairly similar.

A good fit for all models is also observed for the **intensity of fax usage in the enterprises** (see Table 4-16). Adding additional variables increases the goodness of fit and should therefore be considered. The coefficient of λ in the Heckman regression is not significantly different from zero, indicating that we cannot observe any severe sample selection bias. Therefore, it seems, again, advisable to refer to the sub-sample OLS. Comparing of sub-sample OLS and Heckman OLS reveals differences in the coefficients of variables that are highly significant in the selection equation, i.e. we can conclude that λ exerts an influence on the Heckman OLS results even if it is considered insignificant. In the presence of multicollinearity problems Puhani (2000) suggests to refer to sub-sample OLS because it generates more robust results.

The results of sub-sample OLS regressions for the intensity of fax use show the following pattern: The main determinants are enterprises' performance and their market environment variables. Fax machines owned by the enterprises are more intensively used with decreasing enterprise age. Size has again a positive influence for all specifications with marginal effects between seven and eight. The number of business contacts and the number of faxes are sent and received are positively correlated. For all three variables, effects are larger for the regression of fax machine use in the enterprise. The share of national business is also significantly positively correlated to fax use. The marginal effect in this case is larger when fax office users are included (0.14 and 0.12 against 0.17 and 0.18). Perceiving price as the most important component for competitiveness increases the intensity of fax usage (only significant in the extended model specification). Personal characteristics of the CEO have no influence on the intensity of fax use as well as structure parameters.

Looking at perceived characteristics of fax machines, only ease of using a fax machine and the binding character of faxes, compared to telephone calls, carry negative signs, all other characteristics carry positive signs. However, only the importance of the bind-

---

[197] Puhani (2000) prefers OLS over Heckman regression because it leads to more robust results in the face of even mild multicollinearity in the data of the Heckman OLS equation. Applying the test on multicollinearity suggested by Puhani shows a degree of multicollinearity that makes the application of OLS preferable.

ing characteristic of fax is significant at an acceptable level, indicating that CEOs that assign a special status to faxes will use them less frequently. Cost deliberations, network effects and pressure from business partners seem to play no role. Although there seems to be no clear opinion about single characteristics of fax machines, overall perception is positive. Intensity of use rises with a positive perception of fax machines' effects on efficiency of administration (significant for all users) and with the perception of significantly positive effects of fax on the competitiveness of the enterprise (significant for in-house users).

For **intensity of cellular phone use** for business purposes the model fit is not as good as for fax (see Table 4-17). However, all estimated models still pass F-tests and likelihood ratio tests at the five percent level. The coefficients of λ in the Heckman OLS regression do not to deviate significantly from zero, indicating that there is no observable sample selection bias. Models including all basic variables appear to fit better than those with a reduced number of variables, i.e. adjusted R^2 measures are higher. However, there seem to be problems with the Heckman model in these specifications. Correlation of the error terms ρ is very high for the specifications using all basic variables. The sign is also different from the reduced specification. No significant coefficients appear despite the overall significance of the model. As these observations indicate multicollinearity problems it is advisable to refer to sub-sample OLS or full information models, such as Tobit. Comparing Tobit and sub-sample OLS results for the same variables however, reveals differences. Results should therefore be interpreted very cautiously.

Looking at the sub-sample OLS and Tobit results in detail, the most important determinants of cellular phone use are the size of the enterprise and the sector it belongs to. Expenditure of cellular phones is positively related to the size of the enterprise. Sub-sample OLS shows a significantly positive relation with age of the enterprise and intensity. Belonging to sectors 30,31 or 34 or 35 decreases the intensity of using cellular phones. In contrast to fax usage, the intensity of cellular use depends, as proposed, on the age of the CEO. This phenomenon is significant in the Tobit regression and misses acceptable significance level in the sub-sample OLS regressions only closely. The younger the interviewed CEO the higher is the expenditure on cellular phones. This trend is reversed at an age of about 40 (in OLS) or about 45 (Tobit) which may be due the fact that the younger generation is then entering the enterprise. In the market environment only the number of business contacts is positively related to the expenditure of cellular phone use. Location of business partners and the perceived importance of certain issues for competitiveness have no influence. Perceived importance of cellular phones' characteristics itself also have no influence on expenditure. Only the argument that it is expected by customers and suppliers is positively related to expenditure. This is reasonable since in India the calling party pays principle is not yet introduced (see section 3.1.2.2). If business partners urge the CEO to adopt a cellular phone and also call him later, this will add to his bill. The perception of cellular phones' benefits on competitiveness do not influence the intensity of use.

Table 4-15: Regression results for intensity of fax use (including fax office users)

Dependent variable	FR_FAX (FAX_USE)		
Method:	Sub-sample OLS		Tobit
N	1174	166	225
R²	0,409	0,497	
adjusted / pseudo R²	0,349	0,403	0,625
F-test value / Chi²-test value	6,80	5,28	152,26
Degrees of freedom	16 / 157	26 / 139	16
Significance level	0,0000	0,0000	0,0000
Independent variables	*Coeff.* *t-ratio*	*Coeff.* *t-ratio*	*Mar.eff.* *t-ratio*
CONST	-39,353 -1,295	-31,846 -0,950	-27,332 -1,265
Age_CEO²	-0,0082 -0,716	-0,0017 -0,138	-0,0007 -0,090
Age_CEO	0,8687 0,851	0,3604 0,325	0,1285 0,173
Edu_year	-0,0755 -0,079	0,2599 0,269	-0,2483 -0,364
Adv_tech	2,4808 0,780	4,0700 1,223	4,1549 1,780 *
Sec_3031	-4,8160 -0,932	-6,9627 -1,324	-1,0547 -0,286
Sec_33	0,3493 0,065	0,2939 0,054	4,1682 1,114
sec_34	1,0768 0,245	0,6859 0,151	2,4588 0,800
sec_35	4,9311 1,086	3,3381 0,736	5,8264 1,829 *
Age_ent	-0,1722 -0,972	-0,2488 -1,370	-0,1307 -1,031
Ln_size	7,5791 4,273 ***	7,4201 4,019 ***	7,6374 6,120 ***
Contact	0,1622 4,349 ***	0,1742 4,501 ***	0,1373 4,976 ***
Nat_busi	0,1738 3,115 ***	0,1817 3,212 ***	0,1568 3,886 ***
Int_busi	0,0922 0,563	-0,0951 -0,551	0,1390 1,148
Im_flex	-3,5528 -1,211	-2,9383 -0,954	-0,2550 -0,123
Im_pric	4,7885 1,545	6,2538 2,027 **	5,2240 2,465 **
Im_qual	1,4667 0,459	1,2102 0,369	-1,4984 -0,651
Ye_fax			
Im_f_spe		2,3982 1,390	
Im _f_bin		-2,0904 -1,229	
Im_f_eas		-3,4894 -1,894 *	
Im_f_cos		0,0885 0,083	
Im_f_com		0,9625 0,830	
Im_f_exp		0,8339 0,823	
Ef_f_sig		7,3355 1,672 *	
Ef_f_sli		4,4332 1,199	
Co_f_sig		4,3649 1,057	
Co_f_sli		-1,2563 -0,359	
LAMBDA			
RHO			

* significant at 10% level; ** significant at 5% level; *** significant at 1% level;

Table 4-15 continued

Dependent variable	FR_FAX (FAX_USE)				
Method:	Heckman two-step				
	Probit	OLS			
N	225	174	174	166	166
R^2		0,409	0,378	0,497	0,459
adjusted / pseudo R^2	0,525	0,345	0,356	0,398	0,401
F-test value / Chi^2-test value	95,14	6,36	16,95	5,05	7,91
Degrees of freedom	16	17 / 156	6 / 167	27 / 138	16 / 149
Significance level	0,0000	0,0000	0,0000	0,0000	0,0000
Independent variables	*Mar.eff. t-ratio*	*Coeff. t-ratio*	*Coeff. t-ratio*	*Coeff. t-ratio*	*Coeff. t-ratio*
CONST	0,6199 1,317	-38,980 -1,347	-15,061 -2,257 **	-31,746 -1,033	-13,078 -1,171
Age_CEO^2	0,0004 2,011 **	-0,0087 -0,783		-0,0018 -0,158	
Age_CEO	-0,0375 -2,065 **	0,9171 0,922		0,3722 0,357	
Edu_year	-0,0119 -0,881	-0,0661 -0,073		0,2612 0,295	
Adv_tech	0,1414 2,228 **	2,2055 0,675		4,0099 1,225	
Sec_3031	0,0913 1,194	-5,0185 -1,004		-7,0078 -1,431	
Sec_33	0,1768 2,363 **	-0,0289 -0,005		0,2026 0,038	
sec_34	0,0940 1,586	0,8962 0,210		0,6416 0,151	
sec_35	0,0921 1,367	4,7026 1,060		3,2883 0,770	
Age_ent	-0,0020 -0,759	-0,1696 -1,005	-0,1240 -0,785	-0,2481 -1,487	-0,1512 -0,973
Ln_size	0,1226 3,729 ***	7,3416 3,674 ***	7,8697 4,416 ***	7,3655 3,658 ***	7,6022 4,186 ***
Contact	0,0016 2,136 **	0,1592 4,207 ***	0,1662 4,705 ***	0,1735 4,562 ***	0,1707 4,790 ***
Nat_busi	0,0025 2,494 **	0,1700 3,051 ***	0,1605 2,982 ***	0,1808 3,306 ***	0,1568 2,985 ***
Int_busi	0,0062 1,604	0,0837 0,523	0,0048 0,033	-0,0971 -0,596	-0,2056 -1,359
Im_flex	0,1161 2,615 ***	-3,7720 -1,274		-2,9878 -0,999	
Im_pric	0,1198 2,657 ***	4,5431 1,443		6,1968 2,034 **	
Im_qual	-0,1189 -2,279 **	1,7342 0,531		1,2623 0,397	
Ye_fax					
Im_f_spe				2,3935 1,514	2,4815 1,525
Im _f_bin				-2,0820 -1,330	-1,6507 -1,090
Im_f_eas				-3,4945 -2,069 **	-3,2423 -1,874 *
Im_f_cos				0,0853 0,087	0,1314 0,136
Im_f_com				0,9717 0,902	0,6995 0,651
Im_f_exp				0,8311 0,895	0,9789 1,028
Ef_f_sig				7,3300 1,825 *	6,5307 1,631
Ef_f_sli				4,4426 1,312	4,6959 1,384
Co_f_sig				4,3614 1,154	4,8556 1,316
Co_f_sli				-1,2963 -0,392	-1,8616 -0,569
LAMBDA		-1,6318 -0,222	-0,0489 -0,008	-0,3691 -0,050	-1,8989 -0,326
RHO		-0,1018	-0,0030	-0,0247	-0,1225

* significant at 10% level; ** significant at 5% level; *** significant at 1% level;

Table 4-16: Regression results for intensity of fax use (fax owners only)

Dependent variables	FR_FAX (FAX_OWN)		
Method:	Sub-sample OLS		Tobit
N	138	128	225
R²	0,438	0,523	
adjusted / pseudo R²	0,363	0,394	0,540
F-test value / Chi²-test value	5,88	4,06	134,11
Degrees of freedom	16 / 121	27 / 100	16
Significance level	0,0000	0,0000	0,0000
Independent variables	*Coeff. t-ratio*	*Coeff. t-ratio*	*Mar.eff. t-ratio*
CONST	-24,662 -0,712	-21,448 -0,514	-29,183 -1,306
Age_CEO²	-0,0052 -0,407	-0,0051 -0,344	0,0019 0,227
Age_CEO	0,6021 0,535	0,6109 0,469	-0,1624 -0,214
Edu_year	-0,5821 -0,512	-0,5310 -0,429	0,1556 0,216
Adv_tech	0,6434 0,174	1,5965 0,398	2,7114 1,115
Sec_3031	-0,6044 -0,104	-3,0583 -0,507	-1,4618 -0,388
Sec_33	-1,8552 -0,304	-0,1227 -0,019	3,0479 0,786
sec_34	2,8861 0,588	2,7961 0,526	0,3711 0,117
sec_35	6,3810 1,260	4,8628 0,919	4,0443 1,239
Age_ent	-0,2970 -1,487	-0,4702 -2,106 **	-0,1135 -0,870
Ln_size	7,1005 3,494 ***	7,8461 3,483 ***	7,9080 6,100 ***
Contact	0,2193 4,788 ***	0,2272 4,673 ***	0,1031 3,593 ***
Nat_busi	0,1382 2,142 **	0,1195 1,730 *	0,1696 4,070 ***
Int_busi	0,0316 0,174	-0,1495 -0,756	0,1312 1,069
Im_flex	-2,6667 -0,769	-3,9338 -1,027	-1,3547 -0,623
Im_pric	5,8654 1,619	7,4103 1,931 *	3,4529 1,558
Im_qual	2,9053 0,743	2,4434 0,608	0,4480 0,184
Ye_fax		0,2045 0,415	
Im_f_spe		1,9355 0,928	
Im _f_bin		-1,3338 -0,581	
Im_f_eas		-4,4398 -1,884 *	
Im_f_cos		0,3528 0,269	
Im_f_com		1,2739 0,844	
Im_f_exp		0,8110 0,644	
Ef_f_sig		3,7879 0,732	
Ef_f_sli		4,9640 1,050	
Co_f_sig		8,9966 1,726 *	
Co_f_sli		0,7444 0,177	
LAMBDA			
RHO			

* significant at 10% level; ** significant at 5% level; *** significant at 1% level.
Coefficients for Probit and Tobit regressions are reported in Table A-8-3 in Annex 8.

Table 4-16 continued

Dependent variables	FR_FAX (FAX_OWN)									
Method:	Heckman two-step									
	Probit		OLS							
N	225		138		138		128		128	
R²			0,438		0,405		0,526		0,489	
adjusted / pseudo R²	0,423		0,359		0,377		0,392		0,410	
F-test value / Chi²-test value	84,63		5,51		14,84		3,92		6,20	
Degrees of freedom	16		17 / 120		6 /131		28 / 99		17 / 110	
Significance level	0,0000		0,0000		0,0000		0,0000		0,0000	
Independent variables	*Mar.eff.*	*t-ratio*	*Coeff.*	*t-ratio*	*Coeff.*	*t-ratio*	*Coeff.*	*t-ratio*	*Coeff.*	*t-ratio*
CONST	0,2047	0,222	-19,377	-0,550	-13,507	-0,988	-5,5778	-0,131	-4,1854	-0,222
Age_CEO²	0,0006	1,459	-0,0070	-0,546			-0,0081	-0,573		
Age_CEO	-0,0535	-1,551	0,7893	0,680			0,9188	0,728		
Edu_year	0,0117	0,425	-0,7035	-0,631			-0,8137	-0,686		
Adv_tech	0,1675	1,647 *	-0,0403	-0,010			0,1246	0,030		
Sec_3031	-0,0447	-0,305	-0,2976	-0,054			-2,6427	-0,469		
Sec_33	0,1778	1,232	-2,9262	-0,462			-2,6591	-0,393		
sec_34	-0,0520	-0,421	3,1696	0,675			3,1626	0,641		
sec_35	0,0167	0,126	6,0292	1,238			3,9445	0,783		
Age_ent	-0,0002	-0,034	-0,2964	-1,568	-0,2567	-1,444	-0,4813	-2,330 **	-0,4176	-2,209 **
Ln_size	0,2690	5,119 ***	5,7484	1,504	7,6349	2,657 ***	4,8667	1,202	6,9151	2,251 **
Contact	0,0000	0,008	0,2192	5,062 ***	0,2246	5,537 ***	0,2284	5,080 ***	0,2239	5,431 ***
Nat_busi	0,0059	3,381 ***	0,1101	1,200	0,1577	2,040 **	0,0565	0,581	0,1001	1,233
Int_busi	0,0066	1,138	0,0030	0,016	-0,0540	-0,324	-0,2100	-1,062	-0,2922	-1,690 *
Im_flex	0,0509	0,619	-2,6250	-0,800			-3,8398	-1,091		
Im_pric	0,1066	1,300	5,4265	1,514			6,5146	1,774 *		
Im_qual	-0,0678	-0,746	3,1896	0,848			3,1586	0,831		
Ye_fax							0,2652	0,595	0,1856	0,444
Im_f_spe							1,6785	0,897	1,9643	1,041
Im _f_bin							-1,2841	-0,637	-0,6998	-0,354
Im_f_eas							-4,5411	-2,186 **	-4,2391	-1,995 **
Im_f_cos							0,4390	0,377	0,9130	0,794
Im_f_com							1,2325	0,930	0,4957	0,375
Im_f_exp							0,7328	0,657	1,1639	1,032
Ef_f_sig							3,9019	0,856	3,0655	0,670
Ef_f_sli							5,0609	1,228	5,8638	1,437
Co_f_sig							8,8950	1,922 *	10,163	2,324 **
Co_f_sli							0,4860	0,131	0,9376	0,256
LAMBDA			-4,9886	-0,411	1,8491	0,225	-10,889	-0,875	-4,4290	-0,492
RHO			-0,2989		0,1094		-0,6513		-0,2757	

* significant at 10% level; ** significant at 5% level; *** significant at 1% level.
Coefficients for Probit and Tobit regressions are reported in Table A-8-3 in Annex 8.

Table 4-17: Regression results for intensity of cellular phone use

Dependent variable:	EX_CEL_B		
Method:	**Sub-sample OLS**		**Tobit**
N	77	66	217
R^2	0,361	0,533	
adjusted / pseudo R^2	0,191	0,259	0,357
F-test value / Chi^2-test value	2,12	1,95	53,67
Degrees of freedom	16 / 60	24 / 41	16
Significance level	0,0190	0,0296	0,0000
Independent variables	*Coeff.* *t-ratio*	*Coeff.* *t-ratio*	*Mar.eff.* *t-ratio*
CONST	-10981 -1,286	-12053 -1,082	-4630,4 -2,294 **
Age_CEO^2	-4,8 -1,487	-5,6 -1,498	-1,7 -2,168 **
Age_CEO	382,9 1,297	457,5 1,337	137,0 1,941 *
Edu_year	-30,2 -0,133	-232,5 -0,742	-3,4 -0,055
Adv_tech	124,4 0,141	-412,6 -0,397	207,3 0,995
Sec_3031	-3484,9 -2,679 ***	-3215,4 -2,127 **	-536,9 -1,656 *
Sec_33	-912,9 -0,709	-1255,7 -0,835	166,9 0,533
sec_34	-2272,0 -2,047 **	-2154,9 -1,625	-479,4 -1,767 *
sec_35	-2082,0 -1,929 *	-2307,7 -1,737 *	-233,4 -0,851
Age_ent	117,0 2,358 **	152,9 2,576 **	-2,7 -0,239
Ln_size	1525,1 3,467 ***	1513,5 2,838 ***	515,8 4,514 ***
Contact	11,8 1,233	23,2 1,898 *	4,2 1,703 *
Nat_busi	-9,3 -0,659	-11,2 -0,576	0,5 0,147
Int_busi	-31,1 -0,922	-60,0 -1,381	11,4 1,114
Im_flex	136,5 0,176	608,1 0,592	-253,7 -1,344
Im_pric	614,6 0,780	-330,0 -0,312	276,4 1,434
Im_qual	1083,1 1,265	816,0 0,808	107,3 0,507
Ye_cell		265,6 0,581	
Im_c_emp		101,6 0,275	
Im_c_eas		-326,9 -0,785	
Im_c_sta		301,8 0,751	
Im_c_com		-102,7 -0,289	
Im_c_exp		788,7 2,271 **	
Co_c_sig		581,9 0,520	
Co_c_cli		-1350,4 -1,367	
LAMBDA			
RHO			

* significant at 10% level; ** significant at 5% level; *** significant at 1% level
Coefficients for Probit and Tobit regressions are reported in Table A-8-3 in Annex 8.

Table 4-17 continued

Dependent variable:		EX_CEL_B				
Method:		Heckman two-step				
	Probit	OLS				
N	220	72	72	66	66	
R^2		0,384	0,214	0,571	0,381	
adjusted / pseudo R^2	0,378	0,190	0,141	0,303	0,211	
F-test value / Chi²-test value	55,54	1,98	2,95	2,13	2,24	
Degrees of freedom	16	17 / 54	6 / 65	25 / 40	14 / 51	
Significance level	0,0000	0,0300	0,0132	0,0160	0,0185	
Independent variables	*Mar.eff. t-ratio*	*Coeff. t-ratio*	*Coeff. t-ratio*	*Coeff. t-ratio*	*Coeff. t-ratio*	
CONST	-1,3930 -1,692 *	-43227 -0,865	-885,5 -0,324	-59177 -0,740	-6110,5 -1,755 *	
Age_CEO²	-0,0005 -1,668 *	-15,0 -0,934		-19,8 -0,799		
Age_CEO	0,0427 1,472	1172,7 0,905		1532,0 0,772		
Edu_year	-0,0007 -0,026	-121,9 -0,189		-244,8 -0,230		
Adv_tech	0,0469 0,510	766,3 0,298		690,7 0,177		
Sec_3031	-0,1117 -0,796	-4883,7 -1,229		-5017,2 -0,849		
Sec_33	0,1836 1,358	2547,4 0,444		3895,2 0,423		
sec_34	-0,0478 -0,419	-2691,2 -0,859		-3022,6 -0,635		
sec_35	0,0259 0,217	-1053,4 -0,334		-889,0 -0,177		
Age_ent	-0,0082 -1,685 *	-41,7 -0,170	109,3 1,924 *	-65,0 -0,172	131,1 2,409 **	
Ln_size	0,1756 3,651 ***	4512,9 1,029	897,9 1,606	5971,3 0,861	1224,9 2,288 **	
Contact	0,0012 1,101	32,5 0,845	4,3 0,426	55,8 0,886	18,0 1,697 *	
Nat_busi	0,0015 0,934	23,2 0,417	-6,5 -0,441	28,1 0,333	-18,0 -1,135	
Int_busi	0,0126 2,297 **	159,7 0,579	-69,1 -1,717 *	210,2 0,487	-81,0 -2,064 **	
Im_flex	-0,1299 -1,944 *	-2607,3 -0,589		-3256,7 -0,489		
Im_pric	0,1163 1,391	2318,7 0,725		1863,0 0,381		
Im_qual	-0,0251 -0,277	896,0 0,392		277,6 0,079		
Ye_cell				435,9 0,357	375,7 1,004	
Im_c_emp				228,5 0,231	31,0 0,098	
Im_c_eas				-415,6 -0,373	-132,2 -0,414	
Im_c_sta				343,7 0,341	158,0 0,477	
Im_c_com				46,1 0,050	-52,0 -0,177	
Im_c_exp				722,4 0,790	775,0 2,626 ***	
Co_c_sig				136,8 0,044	368,5 0,411	
Co_c_cli				-1926,8 -0,712	-1609,6 -1,958 *	
LAMBDA		10110 0,744	-1586,4 -1,036	14628 0,684	-772,3 -0,507	
RHO		1,0000	-0,5316	1,0000	-0,3004	

* significant at 10% level; ** significant at 5% level; *** significant at 1% level
Coefficients for Probit and Tobit regressions are reported in Table A-8-3 in Annex 8.

Table 4-18: Regression results for intensity of e-mail use

Dependent variable:	EX_CEL_B		
Method:	Sub-sample OLS		Tobit
N	77	66	217
R²	0,361	0,533	
adjusted / pseudo R²	0,191	0,259	0,357
F-test value / Chi²-test value	2,12	1,95	53,67
Degrees of freedom	16 / 60	24 / 41	16
Significance level	0,0190	0,0296	0,0000
Independent variables	*Coeff.* *t-ratio*	*Coeff.* *t-ratio*	*Mar.eff.* *t-ratio*
CONST	-10981 -1,286	-12053 -1,082	-4630,4 -2,294 **
Age_CEO²	-4,8 -1,487	-5,6 -1,498	-1,7 -2,168 **
Age_CEO	382,9 1,297	457,5 1,337	137,0 1,941 *
Edu_year	-30,2 -0,133	-232,5 -0,742	-3,4 -0,055
Adv_tech	124,4 0,141	-412,6 -0,397	207,3 0,995
Sec_3031	-3484,9 -2,679 ***	-3215,4 -2,127 **	-536,9 -1,656 *
Sec_33	-912,9 -0,709	-1255,7 -0,835	166,9 0,533
sec_34	-2272,0 -2,047 **	-2154,9 -1,625	-479,4 -1,767 *
sec_35	-2082,0 -1,929 *	-2307,7 -1,737 *	-233,4 -0,851
Age_ent	117,0 2,358 **	152,9 2,576 **	-2,7 -0,239
Ln_size	1525,1 3,467 ***	1513,5 2,838 ***	515,8 4,514 ***
Contact	11,8 1,233	23,2 1,898 *	4,2 1,703 *
Nat_busi	-9,3 -0,659	-11,2 -0,576	0,5 0,147
Int_busi	-31,1 -0,922	-60,0 -1,381	11,4 1,114
Im_flex	136,5 0,176	608,1 0,592	-253,7 -1,344
Im_pric	614,6 0,780	-330,0 -0,312	276,4 1,434
Im_qual	1083,1 1,265	816,0 0,808	107,3 0,507
Ye_cell		265,6 0,581	
Im_c_emp		101,6 0,275	
Im_c_eas		-326,9 -0,785	
Im_c_sta		301,8 0,751	
Im_c_com		-102,7 -0,289	
Im_c_exp		788,7 2,271 **	
Co_c_sig		581,9 0,520	
Co_c_cli		-1350,4 -1,367	
LAMBDA			
RHO			

* significant at 10% level; ** significant at 5% level; *** significant at 1% level.
Coefficients for Probit and Tobit regressions are reported in Table A-8-3 in Annex 8.

Table 4-18 continued

Dependent variable:		EX_CEL_B				
Method:		Heckman two-step				
	Probit		OLS			
N	220	72	72	66	66
R^2		0,384	0,214	0,571	0,381
adjusted / pseudo R^2	0,378	0,190	0,141	0,303	0,211
F-test value / Chi^2-test value	55,54	1,98	2,95	2,13	2,24
Degrees of freedom	16	17 / 54	23894	25 / 40	14 / 51
Significance level	0,0000	0,0300	0,0132	0,0160	0,0185
Independent variables	*Mar.eff. t-ratio*	*Coeff. t-ratio*	*Coeff. t-ratio*	*Coeff. t-ratio*	*Coeff. t-ratio*
CONST	-1,3930 -1,692 *	-43227 -0,865	-885,5 -0,324	-59177 -0,740	-6110,5 -1,755 *
Age_CEO^2	-0,0005 -1,668 *	-15,0 -0,934		-19,8 -0,799	
Age_CEO	0,0427 1,472	1172,7 0,905		1532,0 0,772	
Edu_year	-0,0007 -0,026	-121,9 -0,189		-244,8 -0,230	
Adv_tech	0,0469 0,510	766,3 0,298		690,7 0,177	
Sec_3031	-0,1117 -0,796	-4883,7 -1,229		-5017,2 -0,849	
Sec_33	0,1836 1,358	2547,4 0,444		3895,2 0,423	
sec_34	-0,0478 -0,419	-2691,2 -0,859		-3022,6 -0,635	
sec_35	0,0259 0,217	-1053,4 -0,334		-889,0 -0,177	
Age_ent	-0,0082 -1,685 *	-41,7 -0,170	109,3 1,924 *	-65,0 -0,172	131,1 2,409 **
Ln_size	0,1756 3,651 ***	4512,9 1,029	897,9 1,606	5971,3 0,861	1224,9 2,288 **
Contact	0,0012 1,101	32,5 0,845	4,3 0,426	55,8 0,886	18,0 1,697 *
Nat_busi	0,0015 0,934	23,2 0,417	-6,5 -0,441	28,1 0,333	-18,0 -1,135
Int_busi	0,0126 2,297 **	159,7 0,579	-69,1 -1,717 *	210,2 0,487	-81,0 -2,064 **
Im_flex	-0,1299 -1,944 *	-2607,3 -0,589		-3256,7 -0,489	
Im_pric	0,1163 1,391	2318,7 0,725		1863,0 0,381	
Im_qual	-0,0251 -0,277	896,0 0,392		277,6 0,079	
Ye_cell				435,9 0,357	375,7 1,004
Im_c_emp				228,5 0,231	31,0 0,098
Im_c_eas				-415,6 -0,373	-132,2 -0,414
Im_c_sta				343,7 0,341	158,0 0,477
Im_c_com				46,1 0,050	-52,0 -0,177
Im_c_exp				722,4 0,790	775,0 2,626 ***
Co_c_sig				136,8 0,044	368,5 0,411
Co_c_cli				-1926,8 -0,712	-1609,6 -1,958 *
LAMBDA		10110 0,744	-1586,4 -1,036	14628 0,684	-772,3 -0,507
RHO		1,0000	-0,5316	1,0000	-0,3004

* significant at 10% level; ** significant at 5% level; *** significant at 1% level.
Coefficients for Probit and Tobit regressions are reported in Table A-8-3 in Annex 8.

The proposed model of intensity of technology use seems not be applicable for the **intensity of e-mail usage for business purposes** (see Table 4-18). F-tests for appropriateness of OLS models are not significant, i.e. the models do not have any explanatory power. There also appear no significant dependent variables in these models. Only the Tobit model and the selection equation of the Heckman model show significant variables (size, number of contacts, national and international business share). However, the fact that these effects occur only in adoption equations and not in pure intensity equations (neither in sub-sample OLS nor in the OLS equations of the Heckman model) indicates that these variables derive their significance from the adoption process and not from the usage of the technology. The proposed models therefore fail to identify determinants of the intensity of e-mail usage, a detailed discussion of results is not possible. The only remarkable effect can be discovered when private mails are included.[198] In this case the experience with the technology, displayed by the length of time it has already been used, has a statistically significant effect on the frequency of use both in sub-sample OLS and in the Heckman model. Adding one year of experience, the number of mails sent and received weekly increases by about six. This result indicates, on the one hand, that with the use of e-mail new usage opportunities occur but on the other, it could indicate that nowadays heavy users adopt the technology early because they had reasons to use it.

4.5.4.4. Conclusion

Although facing some shortcomings in the model determination the results from analysing several ICT's determinants of usage intensity lead to the following conclusions:

1. Determinants of fax and cellular phone usage are easier to identify than for e-mail usage. This indicates that for the former two technologies specific usage patterns exist that could be captured by the models used. In the case of e-mail usage still seems unstructured, depending on factors not accounted for by the chosen models. Usage patterns, depending on enterprise and market characteristics as observed in the decision to adopt the technology, still have to emerge. This probably will happen over time, as the result (including private use) that usage increases with the length of time the technology is used shows.

2. For fax and cellular phones, intensity of use depends mainly on characteristics of the enterprise, e.g. size and age, and on market factors, such as the location of business partners. Personal characteristics of the CEO have no significant influence on fax use. Cellular use seems to be more intense with younger CEOs, who might be more open to new communication patterns. Perception of the technologies' characteristics do not have a general influence on the intensity of use in these two technologies. Perception of benefits also does not significantly influence the decision how much to use fax and mobile phones. Only for the impact of fax on competitiveness, a positive relation can be observed. This means that low volume users see the technologies to be as beneficial as high volume users do.

---

[198] This result also should be treated cautiously because the overall model fit for models including private e-mail use indicates that these models have no significant explanatory power.

3. Since the model, which has been basically derived to analyse adoption decisions, does not fit very well for modelling intensity of usage, other model specifications, comprising for example particular usage patterns and business relations in more detail, should be employed in further analysis.

4.6. Discussion of results

The aim of this chapter was to explore the determinants of ICT adoption in small-scale enterprises. Derived from a review of literature on technology adoption, a model was constructed that accounted for different determining dimensions. These are the personal, organisational, environmental and technological dimension. The model was specified and applied to a data-set of urban Indian SSI enterprises.

In a first exercise, adoption determinants at the time of the survey have been examined with Probit regression models. Subsequently, the determinants for the time of adoption were analysed using Tobit censored regression models. In a third stage an attempt was made to use the same model structure to identify determinants of the intensity of ICT use, applying sub-sample OLS, Tobit and Heckman sample selection models. For the first two exercises the models performed reasonably well with problems only arising for the case of adoption of pagers. Identifying determinants for intensity of technology was possible for the use of fax and cellular phones, but failed for the use of e-mail.

The personal dimension, i.e. personal characteristics of the CEO, proved, in general, to be no determinant of technology adoption and use. This might be for various reasons. Firstly, most interviewed enterprises are run by families. In a number of enterprises more than one generation is in charge of business. In these cases it is difficult to assign technology use to one generation, and it was determined by chance which generation was interviewed.[199] Secondly, the entrepreneurs' educational background may be too similar to let differences appear.[200] More than 50 percent are graduates in engineering or science and only about 20 percent have no college education. Thirdly, using attributes of the entrepreneur as proxies, as proposed by Baumol (1995), might be too imprecise. Studies that use more complicated methods to explore the entrepreneur's attitude towards innovation managed to find significant influences (e.g. Thong 1999, Harrison et al. 1997).

The organisational dimension proved to be a determinant for ICT adoption. Size turned out to be the most significant single determining factor for all technologies. This was expected since almost all studies on technology adoption report similar results (see sections 4.3.3 and 4.3.4). The importance of size results from some economies of scale in ICTs, generated by indivisibilities in acquiring and applying the technologies. It also reflects the increasing relative advantage of using ICTs with increasing enterprise size, triggered by the potential to lower co-ordination costs. The other performance related factor, age of the enterprise, proved to be not significant at all. Structure related variables, the use of advanced production technologies and enterprise sector performed differently depending on the technology in question. Enterprises are

---

[199] The measurable (but in most cases not significant) "children effects" point to this explanation.

[200] Lal (1999), however, reports a positive influence of education on the intensity of technology use for Indian electronics enterprises.

probably too similar for significant differences to occur.[201] Studies that covered a wider range of sectors, for example, service, manufacturing and trade, could prove differences in ICT use (e.g. Duncombe 1999).

The importance of relative advantages for ICT adoption are clearly shown by the results in the environmental dimension, i.e. by market specific factors. In the case of fax, pager and e-mail the probability of ICT adoption rises with the number of business contacts. The insignificance of the effect in respect to computers points to the fact that they are mainly used in office automation rather than in communication. The influence of markets' location also reflects relative advantages. Operating in national and international markets will increase adoption of fax, computer and e-mail.[202] For pagers the reverse holds true, indicating that it is basically a local communication tool. Cellular phone adoption is determined by international market participation. Explanations might be "cosmopoliteness" of the users and demonstration effects through international partners. For the influence of specific competition parameters' importance on ICT adoption no clear picture emerges. The only remarkable result indicates that if flexibility is of prime importance it is more likely that fax machines are used. The results within the market dimension show that location of markets is a stronger determinant for ICT adoption in small enterprises than other market specific characteristics. ICTs are adopted because of their relative advantage of reducing costs and increasing speed of communication. Strategic deliberations do not seem to play an important role.

The technological dimension was not measured directly. However, as it has been discussed for the other dimensions, it appears, that the advantage of using an ICT over conventional technologies is one of the main trigger of adoption. Less obviously is the importance of availability. The fast growth of e-mail, especially within exporting enterprises, indicates that there had been a potential demand for this technology even before it became available in 1995. The intersection between relative advantage and availability is quality of service. As long as quality is low, especially for cellular phones and Internet, some options do not become available or remain expensive. The role of other technological factors, such as observability, trialability, compatibility and complexity is difficult to extract from the results.

The model applied to analyse the adoption of ICTs in small enterprises has some limitations. First, it is based only on cross-sectional data, which makes it difficult to capture dynamic processes such as technology adoption. However, sophisticated and reliable time-series are very difficult to obtain from small-scale enterprises. Time series data would also make it easier to identify the technological influences of ICTs as properties and prices change rapidly. Secondly, the influence of the general business environment and infrastructure is difficult to capture because only enterprises from one location have been examined. Nevertheless, the results gained provide a good impression of the determining factor of ICT adoption and use in small-scale enterprises.

---

[201] Only the "basic metal and alloy" sector stands out for some ICTs. This might be a reflection of the on average large size of enterprises in this sector.

[202] This is in line with the results by Lal (1999a) who shows that exporting companies are more likely to use advanced technologies.

5. THE IMPACT OF ICTS ON SMALL-SCALE ENTERPRISES' PERFORMANCE

5.1. Measuring the impact of ICTs on small-scale enterprises – issues and problems

The possible impact of ICTs on business development has been briefly discussed in chapter 2. The mechanisms through which ICTs affect productivity, flexibility and scale were described and a few results presented. It was shown that, despite the failure to measure it in macro-statistics, investments in ICTs generate significant productivity effects, in particular when combined with changes in enterprises' organisation. In addition ICTs will also enhance enterprises' flexibility because they can speed up information processing. The possible impact of ICTs on optimal scale were identified to occur in both directions, with slightly more evidence pointing to a decrease.

In this chapter we will review the methods of analysis that can be applied to small-scale enterprises. It will be shown that this is rather difficult, restricting empirical verification of ICTs' impacts.

5.1.1. ICTs and productivity

The most common way to analyse productivity effects of investments is via a Cobb-Douglas production function. Based on a basic production function in the form

$$Q = F(C, K, S, L, j, t), \tag{5.1}$$

with quantity of output (Q), computer capital (C), non-computer capital (K), IT staff labour (S) and other labour and expenses (L) and allowing to control for business sector (j) and time (t) (Brynjolfsson / Hitt 1996:545). The Cobb-Douglas specification of this model is in turn:

$$Q = e^{\beta_0} C^{\beta_1} K^{\beta_2} S^{\beta_3} L^{\beta_4}, \tag{5.2}$$

with coefficients β_0 to β_4 summing up to one. The model can be estimated by taking logarithms and adding an error term ε. The production function then becomes

$$\ln Q_{it} = \beta_t + \beta_j + \beta_1 \ln C_{it} + \beta_2 \ln K_{it} + \beta_3 \ln S_{it} + \beta_4 \ln L_{it} + \varepsilon_t, \tag{5.3}$$

with i being the index of the individual firm.

Applying this model to a data set of 367 large U.S. firms for the years 1987 to 1991 Brynjolfsson and Hitt (1996) managed to show strong evidence of positive returns to IT spending and claimed to have solved the productivity paradox. So far, attempts such as this one have only been undertaken for large enterprises. They are practically not feasible for small-scale enterprises for a number of reasons:

Firstly, data requirements for analysing productivity effects are very high. For their data set Brynjolfsson and Hitt (1996) rely on two different sources. One source provides financial information of large, mostly publicly listed companies. Owing to strict publication requirements for listed enterprises, this information is to a large extent standardised. The second source is an annual survey of IS managers from 1000 large enterprises (Fortune 500 manufacturing and Fortune 500 service). To a large extent Brynjolsson and Hitt account the success of their survey, i.e. proving the returns to IT investment, for the detailed data. For small-scale enterprises, especially in developing countries, data sets such as the one described, do not exist. Data might be with the enterprises themselves but reliability and comparability of self reported data is questionable.[203] The smaller the enterprises in question is, the smaller is the probability that written records exist at all, or if they exist, that they cover a long time span.

Secondly, in small-scale enterprises investments in IT are not continuous. As has been shown in chapter 3, expenses for IT equipment are not trivial for developing country small-scale enterprises. Therefore, investment, for example in a PC, may only occur every couple of years. For a long time series data set, this problem is manageable, but these probably do not exist for small-scale enterprises (the Brynjolfsson and Hitt data set covers five years).

Thirdly, it is difficult, to assign a specific share of labour to IT services in small-scale enterprises. In chapter 2 it was shown that one of the decisive factors defining a small-scale enterprise is the lack of specialised functions within the enterprise. Therefore, one cannot expect to find IT professionals, or an IT department, in small-scale enterprises. This function will be covered, either by the CEO himself, or by any other employee, or partially by a couple of persons in the enterprise. Assigning a quantifiable share of their work to handle IT will prove difficult leaving a high uncertainty in the valuation.

As it is stressed by Brynjolfsson and Hitt, who are the most experienced researchers in this field,[204] quality of data (together with time span of data) is decisive for valid results, one cannot expect to derive good results on productivity effects of ICTs from developing country small-scale enterprises. One will have to rely on more simple methods, with less data requirements, but also with less certain results.

5.1.2. ICTs and qualitative characteristics – the example of "flexibility"

Avgerou (2000:570) stresses, that impact of ICTs in organisations will be of "a non-straightforward economic nature", i.e. covering issues of organisational structure, strategic gains and losses etc. Other authors claim that the potential benefits of ICTs can only be realised, when their adoption goes hand in hand with organisational adaptations (e.g. Brynjolfsson / Hitt 2000; Dos Santos / Sussman 2000; Hitt / Brynjolfsson 1997; Porter / Millar 1985). These qualitative changes are, however, difficult to quantify and to structure in a general manner.

This can be illustrated for the issue of flexibility, which has been identified in Chapter 2 as one business characteristic that is positively affected by the use of ICTs. Flexibility was defined as the capacity to adapt to changes in the business' environment (Golden / Powell 2000). Golden and Powell (2000) report on the difficulties in

---

[203] Even in their survey, Brynjolfsson and Hitt (1996) report difficulties with the reliability of the data obtained from interviews with IT managers.

[204] See Brynjolfsson and Hitt (1995, 1996, 2000), Brynjolfsson and Yang (1996), Hitt and Brynjolfsson (1995) or Hitt (1999) as examples cited in this work.

measuring flexibility and in quantifying the "value of flexibility". Flexibility is a multi-dimensional concept and a meaningful measurement has to reflect these dimensions. Golden and Powell identify four different metrics: firstly, efficiency, i.e. the ability to accommodate changes with a minimal amount of degradation in performance, secondly, responsiveness, i.e. the ability to respond within an appropriate time frame, thirdly, versatility, i.e. the extent to which it is possible or planned to respond to changes, and fourthly, robustness, i.e. the ability to respond successfully to unforeseen changes. This list of dimensions indicates the complexity of measuring qualitative changes in an organisation. Golden and Powell point out that operationalising the metrics is rather complex, depending on the specific issue that is to be measured, i.e. it can only be achieved in a situation-specific context. This notion calls for case studies rather than quantitative surveys, and for focusing on specific aspects of technology use rather than a more general exploration of a group of technologies.[205]

5.1.3. Measuring business performance by observable outcome indicators

5.1.3.1. Basic argument

Some of the most important presumed impacts of ICTs on business performance are very difficult to measure. Especially qualitative measure, such as flexibility or competitiveness, are hardly possible to capture in a formalised framework. Another option to explore the impact of ICTs on business performance would be not to look at the consequences of performance indicators, rather than the indicators themselves. These consequences can be observed in market behaviour or changes in enterprise characteristics, such as size, profitability etc.

Bedi (1999) showed in detail how ICTs enhance the functioning of markets through reduction of transaction costs. Enterprises applying ICTs in a way to capture these benefits will perform differently, i.e. they can obtain more favourable prices and they can expand the reach of factor as well as product markets. If enterprises manage to adopt ICTs faster, or more effectively, than their competitors they can, at least for some time, generate better margins than their peers. Alternatively they can expand their market share and reach. Thus, improved business performance through ICTs may be represented by overall growth, profitability, and growth in new markets. Additionally, if ICTs enhance labour productivity this should leave scope for higher wages (if the assumption holds that labour is rewarded by its marginal product). Employees that operate information technologies gain new skills, or if this is not possible, enterprises will employ higher skilled labour. Higher skills will lead to higher wages. Thus, one can expect higher wages to be an indicator for technologically more advanced enterprises.

A further method to explore the impact of ICTs on enterprises would be to ask the CEOs about their perception of the technologies' impact. Roger (1995) stresses the importance of perceived technological characteristics for technology adoption. Furthermore, decision making in small-scale enterprises is, in many cases, intuitive instead of being based on formalised procedures and evaluations (Blili / Raymond 1993;

---

[205] Levy and Powell (1998), for example, just investigate in depth four British SMEs to arrive at conclusions about the role of information systems to enhance of hinder flexibility.

Pleitner 1995). Therefore, the "subjective" estimation of the CEO might be more important than the "objective", measurable effects.

5.1.3.2. Some evidence

Profitability

Hitt and Brynjolfsson examine the relationship between profitability parameters, such as return of assets, return of equity and total shareholder return. Applying a simple regression model in the form

$$profitability\ ratio = \beta_0 + \beta_1\ (IT\ stock) + control\ variables + \varepsilon, \quad (5.4)$$

they find no results when only single years are accounted for. When pooling the data over more years, even negative effects for return on asset and total return arise. All in all the impact of IT on profitability is very small. Hitt and Brynjolfsson suggest that their results indicate that enterprises use the correct amount of IT, i.e. no improvements can be reached by lowering or raising IT investment. From this they conclude that IT investments are necessary to maintain competitive position, but do not generate competitive advantages.

A similar result is derived for enterprises in Hong Kong, Singapore, Malaysia and Taiwan by Tam (1998). Tam tests the effect of computer capital on return of equity, return on assets, total shareholder return and return on sales. Evidence is mixed, even for lagged specifications there is no positive significant impact on total shareholder return and return on sales. The only positive effects occur for return on equity in Hong Kong enterprises and return on assets in Singapore enterprises. Effects for both measures are not significant for Malaysia and even negative for Taiwan. Tam concludes that the relationship between IT investments and these accounting ratios is affected by institutional and cultural factors. Furthermore, he accounts the failure of the model to produce significant results to the simplicity of the applied models.

Stoneman and Kwon (1996), on the other hand, use a more complex model and find significant impact of technology adoption on profitability. Based on an adoption model similar to the Karshenas and Stoneman (1993) model (presented in section 4.2.2.2) and an empirical test on the diffusion of CNC machines, computers, microprocessors and carbide tools in British manufacturing enterprises, they conclude, that for non adopting enterprises profit is underperforming, firm specific characteristics play a role (rank effects) and that the early adopters gain more (stock effects).

Labour and wages

The issue of wage and employment effects of computers has been widely discussed since the 1990s. Bedi (1999:28) reports Kruger's (1993) comprehensive research on wage effects of computer use in U.S. enterprises. The results indicate that in the 1980s workers earned about 10 to 15 percent more as a result of their computer skills. However, a number of other studies question whether the wage differentials reflect other attributes that lead to higher computer usage. After reviewing these studies Bedi (1999:31) concludes that "the results are consistent with the conclusion that firms with more highly skilled workers are more likely to adopt new technologies. However, subsequent to adoption, these technologies do not have much impact on wages." Other studies conclude that the demand for skilled workers is rising with the increasing diffusion of computers. Lal (2000:27) reviews evidence in this direction from enterprises in developing countries. However, how the diffusion of ICTs will in the end influence wages and wage inequality seems to depend very much on the institutional framework within different countries. While effects in the U.S. are clearly positive, for European countries, such as France, these are less clear or even negative.

In his own survey Lal (1996) examined the relation between a number of conduct and performance parameters and IT use in 59 Indian electronics and electrical goods enterprises. He found that IT using enterprises employ more skilled manpower and have a better qualified management. Wage rate was, however, not significant.

Export performance

There is ample evidence that export performance is related to IT adoption. Lal (1999a) shows in a survey of Indian garment manufacturers that the degree of IT adoption is positively related to the export intensity of these enterprises. For Italian small manufacturing enterprises Nassimbeni (2001) examines the relation between exports and technology. Just as the results in other areas, such as productivity and flexibility, he concludes that it is not technology alone but the application of other intangible resources and competencies that make technologies work, that decide on the success of the business. Furthermore, Nassimbeni sees causality between enterprise characteristics and export performance not just in one direction but in both. The notion of simultaneity is stressed by many studies on effects of technologies (e.g. Brynjolfsson and Hitt (2000) for productivity effects of IT investment).

Perceptions of technology use

Exploring CEOs perceptions of impact of the technologies they have adopted or they plan to adopt is a subjective but valid method to explore the impact of technologies. TechnConsult (2000), for example, which surveys e-business and the Internet in German SMEs, asked CEOs about their perception of these technologies. The interviewed managers see the information sharing property of the Internet as most important, followed by the marketing possibilities and the enabling of new business relationships. Innovative applications, such as tele-learning or introduction of virtual organisations, are only of minor importance. Expected effects of the Internet are foremost better service, increased market transparency and larger selection of products and services. As a consequence, knowledge and information will become a more and more important factor of production.

These results indicate, that exploring perceptions will generate in general no quanitfiable results but give a good idea about directions and thrust of impacts. Perceived impacts will as well give a hint of future developments since future adoption decisions will be partially based on the present (perceived) situation.

5.2. Analysis of survey data

5.2.1. Introductory remarks

The rather short and certainly incomplete review presented a couple of proxies and directly observable measures that indicate the underlying impact of ICTs on business performance. In the following section the impact of ICTs on the surveyed small-scale enterprises in Ambattur Industrial Estate are examined. First, it is shown that the impact of ICTs is generally perceived in a positive light by the using enterprises. Additionally, anecdotal evidence is available for successful Internet use. In a second step it is explored whether these perceptions manifest themselves in improved performance of user enterprises.

The latter analysis is constrained by the cross-sectional nature of the available data. It was not possible to obtain comprehensive performance data for past periods, aside from basic financial data, which is available for three years. A number of enterprises were only able or willing to give information on the actual business year. It is questionable whether three years are sufficient to identify impacts of ICT adoption. Brynjolfsson and Hitt (1996), for example, managed to identify effects of ICT investments only by using data over a period of six years.

5.2.2. Perceived effects and anecdotal evidence

The entrepreneurs' perception of the impact of used ICTs has already been briefly presented technology by technology in section 3.4. In this section they are put into context. Moreover, anecdotes of successful Internet use are presented in more detail.

Enterprises were asked whether they think, specific ICTs improve the competitiveness of their enterprise. The perception of effects is generally positive (see Table 5-1). In all cases, with the exception of pagers, more than 50 percent of users felt an improvement. Especially well perceived are computers and e-mail with about one third of users seeing a significant improvement in competitiveness.

Table 5-1: Improvement of the enterprise's competitiveness through the use of ICTs (percentages)

	Fax	Pager	Cellular phone	Computer	E-mail	WWW
Yes, significantly	24.0	14.1	20.0	37.2	31.3	19.6
Yes, slightly	28.0	27.3	30.5	26.1	33.3	39.2
No, no effect	38.9	50.5	40.0	25.0	24.0	31.4
No, even negative	0.0	0.0	0.0	1.1	0.0	0.0
Don't Know	9.1	8.1	9.5	10.6	11.5	9.8
Number of observations	*175*	*99*	*105*	*188*	*96*	*51*

For office automation technologies, such as fax, computers and as well e-mail the perception of impact on efficiency of administration was explored. Results are even more positive than for competitiveness as a whole (see Table 5-2). Only a minority of users identify no effects. For computers over 70 percent see a significant improvement.

Table 5-2: Improvement of administration's efficiency through the use of ICTs (percentage)

	Fax	Computer	E-mail
Yes, significantly	42.9	71.8	38.5
Yes, slightly	36.0	23.4	33.3
No, no effect	16.0	4.3	19.8
No, even negative	0.6	0.0	0.0
Don't Know	4.6	0.5	8.3
Number of observations	*175*	*188*	*96*

The perception of basic ICTs' impact on efficiency and competitiveness is positive. Although the Internet is considered to have the largest potential to improve operations, the enterprises' perception of the impact of the WWW still lags behind other technologies. Firstly, this may be due to the low quality of Internet access and secondly, due to the lack of experience most enterprises have with these new technologies and their potential. However, a few Internet users could provide some anecdotal evidence of how the Internet has been used in a beneficial way:

1. The CEO of an engineering company that develops and produces metal cutting tools stated that he managed to find a second hand machine in an Internet based exchange.

2. Another light engineering company, producing automobile components, managed to locate the supply source for spare parts of an old machine. Without identifying this source the machine would have been scrapped.

3. A company that produces cooling systems reported, that the Internet is used to collect patent information. The company was also one of the few that already had their own web-page at the time of the survey.

4. The managing director and owner of a rubber-parts company reported that he exchanges spreadsheet files by e-mail with the co-owner of the company who resides in another city. Since data can be manipulated directly and sent back immediately planning becomes easier and more flexible. Moreover the Internet enables this entrepreneur to get direct access to specialist technical literature.

These anecdotes show that the Internet is beginning to show some impact. This impact was, however, still small and limited to a few cases at the time of the survey.

5.2.3. Linking performance indicators and ICT use

5.2.3.1. Selection of adequate performance indicators

There are only a few easy to obtain and relatively reliable measures that can be used as proxies for enterprise performance. Some of these have been discussed in previous sections. In the case of small scale enterprises in Ambattur Industrial Estate the following aspects were possible to cover:

Productivity

Productivity effects of ICTs are difficult to measure in small-scale enterprises. In addition to the general problems described above, it was difficult to obtain values for the employed capital from the surveyed enterprises. Thus, measuring total factor productivity did not prove possible. The only productivity measure available with a reasonable degree of reliability is labour productivity. It could be obtained for 1997/98 and 1998/99, i.e. it is also possible to research labour productivity growth at least for one year (see Table 5-3).[206]

Table 5-3: Basic statistics for labour productivity and growth of labour productivity

		Labour productivity for 1998/99 (in Rs.)	Growth of labour productivity between 1997/98 and 1998/99 (in percent)
N	Valid	251	231
	Missing	44	64
Mean		369,657	9.16
Median		250,000	3.90
Std. Deviation		417,713	36.66
Minimum		14,911	-60
Maximum		3,428,571	213

Table 5-4: Basic statistics for net profit and profit growth

		Net profit / loss 1998/99 (in percentage of turnover)	Change in profit margin between 1996/97 and 1998/99 (in percentage points)
N	Valid	244	204
	Missing	51	91
Mean		6.9	-2.2
Median		7.3	.0
Std. Deviation		15.5	14.7
Minimum		-166.7	-173.3
Maximum		40.0	30.0

Profitability

Another performance indicator discussed was profit margins. If ICTs have a positive impact on competitive advantage, there might be a positive impact on profits. Profit margins are available as returns to sales for 1996/97 to 1998/99, i.e. it is possible to

---

[206] Basic results for labour productivity have already been presented in section 3.3.2.

analyse margin and margin growth (see Table 5-4).[207] However, only about two thirds of the enterprises were willing to provide full information for all three years.

Wages and employment

It has also been discussed, that ICT use induces higher wages. This can also be expected in the Indian SSI context since the entrepreneurs are indicating a wage surcharge. When being asked about the importance of computer skills for new administrative staff, more than three quarters state that these are essential or very important (see Table 5-5). Moreover, more than 50 percent indicate that there is a considerable wage surcharge of more than 10 percent for computer skills (see Table 5-6). Thus, more heavily computerised enterprises should have an upward biased wage structure. In the survey wage measures were obtained for employees in management and administration. These are the potential ICT users within the enterprise. Literature on employment effects states as well that with increasing use of IT the demand for higher skilled labour is rising. Whether ICT-using enterprises in the sample are using higher skilled labour is tested by examining the share of employees in administration and management that have a college degree and above (see Table 5-7).

Table 5-5: Importance of computer skills for new administrative staff

	Frequency	Percent
Essential	91	47.9
Very important	58	30.5
Of some importance	31	16.3
Not important	9	4.7
Don't know	1	0.5
Total	190	100.0

Table 5-6: Average wage surcharge for employees with computer skills

	Frequency	Percent
No higher wages	69	36.5
Less than 10%	20	10.6
10% to 25%	72	38.1
25% to 50%	21	11.1
More than 50%	2	1.1
Don't know	5	2.6
Total	189	100.0

---

[207] Basic results for development of profit margins have already been presented in section 3.3.2.

Table 5-7: Basis statistics for wage and skills in administration and management

		Average monthly wage for employees in administration and management (in Rs.)	Percentage of graduates in management and administration
N	Valid	259	249
	Missing	36	46
Mean		3,822	68.6
Median		3,500	80.0
Std. Deviation		1,542	36.3
Minimum		1,350	0
Maximum		10,000	100

Growth

The last issue to examine is the expansion of markets through ICT use. The analysis in chapter 4 on adoption of ICTs has shown, that operating in foreign markets is a deter-minant of cellular phone, computer and e-mail use. Thus, a relation between those two measures exists. Whether the causality is also in direction of ICTs causing exports and imports to rise, is difficult to assess (Nassimbeni 2001). Due to changes in exchange rates, for example, exports and imports normally change with larger amplitude than domestic sales. It would be difficult therefore to identify the impact of ICTs. Thus, turnover growth will be applied as a proxy for expanding market reach. Turnover fig-ures are available for 1996/97, 1997/98 and 1998/99, therefore growth rates can be traced over two periods (see Table 5-8).[208]

Table 5-8: Basic statistics for enterprise growth

		Turnover growth 1996/97 to 1998/99 (in percent)
N	Valid	229
	Missing	66
Mean		13.4
Median		5.0
Std. Deviation		83.7
Minimum		-93.7
Maximum		1,100.0

5.2.3.2. ICT use indicators

There are different ways to account for ICT use. The most simple method is to check for differences between the samples of current users and non-users for single tech-

---

[208] Basic results for turnover growth have already been presented in section 3.3.2.

nologies. For this purpose, the same categories as for the dependent variables from the regression in section 4.5.2 are used (see Table 4-4 for details). This method is, however, very simple and does not account for lagged effects, i.e. effects in early adopting enterprises are stronger, and for the overall technological level of the enterprise.

As Brynjolfsson and Hitt (1996 and 2000) and others (e.g. Lefebvre / Lefebvre 1996) have pointed out, there might be a considerable lag before the adoption of ICTs will lead to measurable effects. In their equilibrium diffusion models Karshenas and Stoneman (1995 and 1993) account for order effects, i.e. the returns for enterprises from adopting a technology depend on their order in the adoption order. Rogers (1995) identifies different adopter categories, depending on the order of adoption. He divides entrepreneurs into "innovators", "early adopters", "early majority", "late majority" and "laggards". Assuming adoption to be normally distributed over time, the groups are positioned in a defined way on the diffusion curve (see Figure 5-1).

Since the observed adoption patterns in the sample (displayed in Figure 3-4) follow the proposed shape, this quantification can be used to divide the adopters into different groups according to their time of adoption. Taking Rogers' categorisation as a rough guidance, the enterprises can be split up in the following way according the time of ICT adoption (see Table 5-9):[209]

Figure 5-1: Adopter categorisation by Rogers

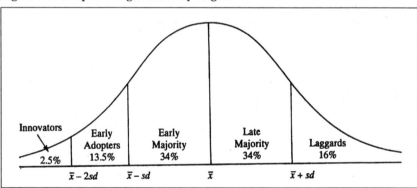

Source: Rogers (1995), p. 262.

---

[209] In the case of fax and pagers the growth rate of adoption is already declining. Peak growth years were 1995 to 1997 for fax and 1997 for pagers. Assuming that the middle of this period shows 50 percent of final adopters, one arrives at final user numbers of about 200 for fax and 125 for pagers. Category borders are set according to these numbers. For cellular phones and e-mail no slowdown in growth was observable. A final user rate of 100 percent is assumed to set borders.

Enterprises that adopted a technology but discontinued its use are included in the sample. Enterprises that adopted a technology in the same year as they were founded are excluded. This is the same procedure as applied in section 4.5.3.

Table 5-9: Categorising ICT users by adoption time

	Fax		Pager		Cellular phone		E-mail	
	Year	Number	Year	Number	Year	Number	Year	Number
Innovators					1995-1996	26	1995-1996	13
Early adopters	until 1992	31	1994-1995	21	1997	29	1997	21
Early majority	1993-1996	81	1996-1997	59	1998-1999	56	1998-1999	61
Late majority	1997-1999	45	1998-1999	27	-	-	-	-
Non adopters	-	133	-	181	-	179	-	196

Looking at single technologies might be not sufficient since their impact depends on the general technological level of the enterprise as well. When usage patterns for different office automation technologies are examined, an interesting "technology ladder" emerges (see Table 5-10). The five shaded categories, reflecting different levels of ICT use, from "only telephone used" to "telephone, fax machine, computer and e-mail used", account for 84 percent of all cases. We can assume that there is a step-by-step adoption of technologies, starting with using public fax offices, then buying a fax machine, later a computer, and at last getting access to e-mail.

Table 5-10: Categorising levels of ICT use

		Computer used			
		no		yes	
		E-mail used		E-mail used	
		no	yes	no	yes
Fax	No fax used	52	1	14	9
usage	Fax office	22		15	5
	Fax machine owned	25	3	67	82

5.2.3.3. Results

The three proposed ICT use measures are tested for their relation to the presented performance indicators. In a first step it is explored whether there are significant differences in performance indicators between users and non-users of specific ICTs. Means are calculated for the two samples (user / non-user). A t-test is used to test whether these two samples can be considered independent, i.e. estimated distribution of the values around the mean is as such that both distributions can be considered significantly different.[210] The results of the calculations are presented in Table 5-11 to 5-15.

---

[210] Equal variance is assumed for both samples. For some variables the test for this assumption fails. Applying the T-test allowing for different variances in the sample leads, however, does hardly influence the results. Therefore, for simplicity of presentation, only the results for the test assuming equal variance are displayed.

Table 5-11: Performance variables for fax owners and non-owners

	t-test for Equality of Means			
	t	df	Sig. (2-tailed)	Mean Difference
Labour productivity	-2.466	249	.014	-130137
Growth of labour productivity	.889	229	.375	4.35
Net profit/loss	-1.060	242	.290	-2.134
Change in profit margin	-1.000	202	.318	-2.09
Average monthly wage	-1.231	257	.219	-241.12
Percentage of graduates	-1.277	247	.203	-5.98
Turnover growth	-1.931	227	.055	-21.60

Table 5-12: Performance variables for pager users and non-users

	t-test for Equality of Means			
	t	df	Sig. (2-tailed)	Mean Difference
Labour productivity	-2.886	249	.004	-159,938
Growth of labour productivity	1.215	229	.226	6.21
Net profit/loss	-.008	242	.993	-1.751E-02
Change in profit margin	-1.038	202	.300	-2.23
Average monthly wage	-.847	257	.398	-169.99
Percentage of graduates	-.470	247	.638	-2.28
Turnover growth	-1.285	227	.200	-15.02

Table 5-13: Performance variables for cellular phone users and non-users

	t-test for Equality of Means			
	t	df	Sig. (2-tailed)	Mean Difference
Labour productivity	-4.472	249	.000	-239,522
Growth of labour productivity	1.482	229	.140	7.51
Net profit/loss	-.633	242	.527	-1.308
Change in profit margin	-.466	202	.642	-1.01
Average monthly wage	-1.990	257	.048	-390.88
Percentage of graduates	-2.007	247	.046	-9.61
Turnover growth	-3.018	227	.003	-34.38

Table 5-14: Performance variables for computer users and non-users

	t-test for Equality of Means			
	t	df	Sig. (2-tailed)	Mean Difference
Labour productivity	-2.935	249	.004	-159,351
Growth of labour productivity	.531	229	.596	2.68
Net profit/loss	.161	242	.872	.337
Change in profit margin	.083	202	.934	.18
Average monthly wage	-1.062	257	.289	-214.15
Percentage of graduates	-1.716	247	.087	-8.33
Turnover growth	-1.585	227	.114	-18.32

Table 5-15: Performance variables for e-mail users and non-users

	t-test for Equality of Means			
	t	df	Sig. (2-tailed)	Mean Difference
Labour productivity	-2.881	249	.004	-157,768
Growth of labour productivity	-1.022	229	.308	-5.23
Net profit/loss	-.297	242	.767	-.621
Change in profit margin	-.426	202	.671	-.91
Average monthly wage	-1.959	257	.051	-394.11
Percentage of graduates	-.257	247	.798	-1.25
Turnover growth	-.348	227	.728	-4.05

In general most mean differences show the expected sign, i.e. users perform better than non-users. Only for growth in labour productivity between 1997/98 and 1998/99 non-users for all examined technologies except e-mail appear to have performed better on average, but these differences are not significant.[211] This is unexpected because the level of labour productivity in 1998/99 is significantly higher for all ICT users. The mean differences extend from about Rs. 130,000 for fax owning to about Rs. 240,000 for cellular phone using enterprises. This difference may be due to the wide range of this variable (Rs. 15,000 to Rs. 3,000,000). Applying non-parametric, tests that compare the ranks of cases, generate significant results as well.[212] Thus, labour productivity is higher in enterprises that use ICTs (although it appear to grow slower).

Other significant differences (at the five percent level) appear for cellular phone users and non-users. Employees in cellular phone using enterprises' management and administration earn on average Rs. 390 more per month (about ten percent of overall average), and the percentage of graduates is on average 9.6 percentage points higher (overall mean is 68 percent).[213] Cellular phone using enterprises also enjoyed a higher turnover growth between 1996/97 and 1998/99. The difference is nearly 35 percent

---

[211] The wrong sign, as well not significant, was as well found for computer users' profit margin and profit margin growth.

[212] Non-parametric test values that account for differences in rank distribution of the samples are significant at least at the five percent level for all technologies (see Table A-9-1 in Annex 9). Mean rank differences indicate that labour productivity is lower in non-using enterprises (see Tables A-9-2 to A-9-6 in Annex 9)

[213] Non-parametric tests fail to identify a significant difference between users and non-users for for the share of graduates for wage measures significance is low. This indicates that the significance may be generated by outliers (see Table A-9-1 in Annex 9).

(the mean growth was 13.4 percent). Non-parametric tests, that test for differences in the cases' rank identify significant differences in turnover growth between 1996/97 and 1998/99 for all other technologies, aside e-mail (see Table A-9-1- in Annex 9). In all cases the average rank of non-users is lower, i.e. they have on average grown slowed than users (see Table A-9-2 to Table A-9-6 in Annex 9).

Other significant non-parametric test results are for profit growth between 1996/97 and 1998/99. On average pager-using and cellular phone-using enterprises managed to increase their profit margins stronger than non-users (see Table A-9-3 and Table A-9-4 in Annex 9). The last significant results, identified by non-parametric tests is that e-mail-using enterprises pay their employees in management and administration higher wages on average, than the non-using enterprises (see Table A-9-6 in Annex 9). Comparing the means shows significant results at the ten percent level, quantifying the difference to nearly Rs. 400 per month (see Table 5-15).

Table 5-16: Kruskal Wallis Test for independence adoption categories

		Labour productivity for 1998/99 (in Rs.)	Growth of labour productivity between 1997/98 and 1998/99 (in percent)	Net profit/loss (1998/99) in percentage of turnover	Change in profit margin between 1996/97 and 1998/99 (in percentage points)	Average monthly wage for employees in administration and management (in Rs.)	Percentage of graduates in management and administration	Turnover growth 1996/97 to 1998/99 (in percent)
Fax	Chi^2	0,927	2,088	4,850	4,311	0,705	2,657	2,087
	df	2	2	2	2	2	2	2
	Significance	0,629	0,352	0.088*	0,116	0,703	0,265	0,352
Pager	Chi^2	3,823	3,586	3,127	1,505	0,663	1,131	0,048
	df	2	2	2	2	2	2	2
	Significance	0,148	0,166	0,209	0,471	0,718	0,568	0,976
Cellular phone	Chi^2	0,373	0,983	0,320	2,802	4,488	0,948	1,002
	df	2	2	2	2	2	2	2
	Significance	0,830	0,612	0,852	0,246	0,106	0,622	0,606
E-mail	Chi^2	10,675	0,211	0,024	0,076	0,360	4,273	1,418
	df	2	2	2	2	2	2	2
	Significance	0.005***	0,900	0,988	0,963	0,835	0,118	0,492

* significant at 10% level; *** significant at 1% level

The next level of analysis aims to explore whether there are, besides the differences between the groups, also differences within the group of users. The users are grouped according to the time of adoption. The non-parametric Kruskal Wallis test is applied to test for differences in the user groups. Test values are displayed in Table 5-16.[214]

The applied test fails to show any significant results aside the difference in labour productivity for the e-mail adopter categories and for profit margin for fax owners. Looking at the mean rank of these two cases shows that the rank of labour productivity is on average lower for the adopters after 1997.[215] The profit margin in the case of fax-owning enterprises derives its significance from the strong position of the adopters post 1997, i.e. it is counter to the expected effect. In general time of adoption play no role in enterprise performance as measured in this case.

So far, the technologies have been considered individually. Fax, computers and e-mail may be joined into categories that constitute a kind of index of technology use. Testing for independence of these categories, i.e. for significant differences between the categories, leads to the results presented in Table 5-17.[216]

Table 5-17: Kruskal Wallis Test for independence of ICT use categories

	Labour productivity for 1998/99 (in Rs.)	Growth of labour productivity between 1997/98 and 1998/99 (in percent)	Net profit/loss (1998/99) in percentage of turnover	Change in profit margin between 1996/97 and 1998/99 (in percentage points)	Average monthly wage for employees in administration and management (in Rs.)	Percentage of graduates in management and administration	Turnover growth 1996/97 to 1998/99 (in percent)
Chi²	16,265	6,701	4,994	3,871	5,337	6,236	7,901
df	4	4	4	4	4	4	4
Significance	0.003***	0,153	0,288	0,424	0,254	0,182	0.095***

*** significant at 1% level

Turnover growth also differs significant over the different categories, but looking at the mean ranks, however, reveals two groupings with fairly similar average ranks. The two lower groups were on average growing less than the groups that own a fax machine. For the other performance indicators there is no significant effect in the level of ICT use. For net profit, change in profit margin and wages appears an upward trend when more technologies are used. These trends are, however, not significant.

---

[214] The mean ranks of the categories can be found in Tables A-9-7 to Table A-9-10 in Annex 9.

[215] The mean value for adopters between 1995 and 1997 is about Rs. 600,000 and for adopters after 1997 about Rs. 425,000.

[216] The mean ranks of the categories are presented in Table A-9-11 in Annex 9.

Labour productivity is significantly related to the degree of technology use. The average rank of the lowest category (only telephone use) is lower than the next category, which is lower than the next and so forth. Comparing the means of the different categories as well shows a number of significant differences.[217]

5.2.3.4. Discussion

The analysis of relation between enterprise performance and ICT use revealed some interesting results. It appears, that ICT use and labour productivity are positively related in the sample. Labour in ICT using enterprises is on average more productive. With an increasing level of ICT use productivity is rising as well. However, no direct effect is observed for labour productivity growth. Productivity and productivity growth also appear not to depend on the time of adoption. Thus, there is a lack of evidence for causality from ICT use to productivity.

As is has been shown extensively in chapter 4, ICT adoption is strongly related to enterprise size. The evidence in this chapter shows that there is also a relation between ICT use and enterprise growth. ICT-using enterprises grow on average faster than theirs non-using peers. This holds for almost all technologies. Again, the time of adoption does not matter in this respect, but the level of adoption. The threshold of owning a fax machine constitutes also a growth threshold. In the case of growth, causality is as well a question although there is more evidence for causality in direction from ICT use. However, it is still imaginable that the enterprises that performed better during the recession in the years covered by the survey had more resources to invest in new technologies.

The other performance indicators are in general not related to ICT use. Profit margins are not significantly related to ICT use, although enterprises that use pager and cellular phones appear to have on average higher margin growth than their peers. In general one can expect, that profit margin depends first of all on market characteristics and the specific structure of relations with customers and suppliers.

A wage surcharge was only observed for e-mail as well as for cellular phone-using enterprises. Surprisingly no significant surcharge was observed for computer using enterprises, although a majority of entrepreneurs had stated that computer skills would be remunerated higher. However, there is, as expected, a tendency for computer-using enterprises to employ more graduates.

Shortcomings of these findings are for the significant relations the lack of evidence about causality. Unfortunately, the cross-sectional nature of the data set and the short time span that could be covered with information from the entrepreneurs, makes it impossible to include appropriate lags to the data. For the performance indicators that showed no effect, specifications need to be refined. Data on wages and qualifications, for example, may be still too imprecise to generate appropriate results. Refinement to account for technology users in an enterprise and their characteristics could lead to improved results.

---

[217] Labour in enterprises using all technologies is on average significantly more productive than labour in enterprises only using telephone, telephone and fax office, or telephone and their own fax machine.

5.3. Conclusion

The aim of this chapter was to explore the impact of ICTs in small enterprises. First, problems to identify these effects in a quantitative manner in small-scale enterprises were discussed. Although there seems to be considerable evidence on productivity effects, researching these effects poses strong requirements on the data used. Other effects assigned to ICTs are of qualitative nature and therefore difficult to capture. This has been shown for the case of flexibility, one of the core characteristics of small-scale enterprises. It was therefore proposed to concentrate on easy observable measures, such as labour profitability, wages and exports, that can be used a proxies for more general performance indicators. Moreover, it was proposed to examine the entrepreneurs' perceptions of technology effects as a means to identify the impact on technology performance.

These proposed measures were extracted from the sample of Indian SSI enterprises. It was shown, that the majority of ICT users see a positive impact of use on competitiveness and administrative efficiency. Additionally some anecdotal information was gathered on the benefits of Internet use, that was, however, still in its infancy at the time of the survey.

The positive perception is only partly mirrored by hard data. Analysing enterprise performance data revealed no general positive effect on productivity, productivity growth, wages and employment. However, a significant relation between technology use and labour productivity as well as turnover growth was observed. It is unfortunately not clear in which direction causality points for these measures. As most other authors that discuss on this problem we suspect causality to work in both directions.

The failure to show a better performance of early users over late adopters might be a problem of wrongly selected categories. However, it is more probable that these effects do not exist nor are very strong. Karshenas and Stoneman (1993), for example, found in their data set no evidence that early adoption will be more beneficial *per se*. It has been shown in the previous chapter that adoption depends very much on the relative advantages and potential benefits in terms of lowering costs and speeding up information flows. Rather than just being early, these properties will have a much stronger impact on the actual benefits of ICT use.

6. SUMMARY AND CONCLUSIONS

6.1. Summary

The aim of this work was to explore the use and impact of information and communication technologies (ICTs) in small-scale enterprises.

It was shown in chapter 2 that ICTs have the potential to enhance market activities and business development by stimulating economic activity. ICTs, when used in enterprises, have the ability to increase productivity and flexibility, and to influence efficient scale of operation. These potentials also exist for small-scale enterprises in developing countries, but are in many cases hindered by a deficient ICT infrastructure and institutional weaknesses.

Chapter 3 explored the actual use of ICTs in 295 enterprises from the Indian Small Scale Industry (SSI) sector. These enterprises are located at Ambattur Industrial Estate in Chennai. A majority of the interviewed enterprises is engaged in engineering. Average employment was about five times higher than the official average for this sector. The Indian SSI sector in general is characterised by strong regulations, and its enterprises complain about problems with finance and infrastructure. Indian ICT markets are characterised by a messy regulation that has led to low penetration rates in most technologies. Nevertheless, due to advanced liberalisation growth in fixed lines, cellular phones and Internet access has significantly increased over the last years.

The survey on the use of ICTs was undertaken in Spring 1999. It covered telephone, fax, pager, cellular phones, computers and the Internet, revealing a high ICT penetration. The majority of enterprises used fax machines and computers. Cellular phones, pagers and e-mail were used by one third of the enterprises surveyed. The number of e-mail subscribers observed was surprisingly high since at the time of the survey total Indian Internet subscriber base was around 300,000. Although the examined enterprises spent a significant amount of money on ICTs, information technologies (IT), such as personal computers (PCs) and the World Wide Web (WWW) these technologies still appear to be under-utilised. PCs are used mostly for simple tasks such as word processing, and the WWW is hardly used at all.

Determinants of the observed adoption were explored in Chapter 4. After reviewing theoretical approaches and empirical studies on technology and ICT adoption a model was derived that grouped determinants into personal, organisational, environmental and technological dimensions. A number of variables representing these dimensions were defined and subsequently tested (a) for their influence on the adoption of ICTs at the time of the survey, (b) on the adoption time and (c) on the intensity of use after adoption. The model performed well for ICT adoption and time of adoption but exhibited shortcomings in analysing intensity of use. Variables of the personal dimension, i.e. age and education of the CEO, appeared in general not to have any effect. On the organisational level, size appeared to be the most important determinant indicating the existence of economies of scale in ICTs. Other variables such as the use of advanced production technologies and the enterprise sector showed different results. For environmental variables, i.e. market characteristics, results were mixed. The number of business contacts proved to be a determinant in fax, pager and e-mail adoption. Operating on national or international markets positively influences fax, computer and e-mail adoption. In total, location of markets appeared to be a stronger determinant for ICT adoption than other market specific characteristics. The differences in results for different technologies were, however, expected since it was assumed that each technology has its own characteristics that mediate the impact of other determining factors. The described results suggest that the main technological determinants are availability and relative advantage. ICTs have a relative advantage, derived from lower communication cost and faster communication, especially in areas where only costly or slow communication channels existed before.

Effects of ICTs usage on business performance were finally explored in Chapter 5. Since it proved difficult to quantify performance indicators such as total factor productivity and flexibility for small-scale enterprises it was proposed to concentrate on the one hand on easy observable measures, such as labour productivity, profitability, wages and turnover growth, and on the other on perceptions of technology effects. The majority of CEOs perceived ICTs to positively influence efficiency of administration and the competitiveness of their enterprises. This was partly reflected by performance data. Significant relations between ICT use and labour productivity as well as ICT use and turnover growth were revealed.[218] Effects on wages and employment were in general not measurable. With the current data set no clear statement about causality of the observed relations was possible. However, evidence from other surveys and some indications in the results suggest that causality is in both directions.

6.2. Conclusions and recommendations

To sum up, ICTs are rapidly adopted by small-scale enterprises if these technologies are available and provide an advantage over other technologies, i.e. if they are available at reasonable price and quality. The relative advantage of ICTs over conventional methods to gather, store, process and distribute information is as well influenced by the markets served and by size of the enterprise, i.e. ICTs incur some economies of scale, generated by indivisibilities in acquiring and applying the technologies. The application of ICTs goes hand in hand with rising labour productivity and enhanced growth. Although the causality of this relation is not totally clear one can conclude that ICTs have the potential to be an important tool to improve performance and competitiveness of small-scale businesses.

The potential of advanced ICTs is, however, not yet fully realised since their use is in general superficial (PCs) or still in its infancy (Internet). The reviewed literature suggest that these information technologies can unleash their full benefits only when enterprises incorporate them across their operations and incorporate them into their competitive strategies (e.g. Alcorta 1994; Brynjolfsson / Hitt 2000; Levy / Powell 1998; Lybaert 1998; Porter / Millar 1985).

These conclusions call for specific action in developing countries. Firstly, the regulatory framework should be designed in a way that (a) does not constrain the development of networks, (b) makes it possible to provide ICTs at internationally competitive

---

[218] Results from chapter three and four show as well relations between ICT use and size and ICT use and exports.

costs and (c) enables universal access to ICTs. Infrastructure development is therefore of prime importance to provide favourable cost-benefit ratios for the adoption of ICTs. Businesses in remote areas and small local markets could gain substantially from the distance reducing and market enhancing properties of ICTs (Barten / Bear 1999). In addition, since ICTs incur some economies of scale, smaller enterprises will on average lag behind larger competitors. This does not constitute a problem *per se* if it reflects different cost and organisational structures. Cost-benefit ratios can, however, change significantly in favour of small enterprises when applications adapted to their structure and situation are provided. To enhance the speed of adoption in the case of changes in technological cost-benefit ratios in favour of small enterprises, awareness of these technologies' properties should be enhanced. This holds especially for information technologies that are still under-utilised in many small-scale enterprises.

Developing and offering appropriate ICT application, especially in the areas of information technology could be a task fulfilled by collective, self-organising bodies such as business associations. These organisations can, on the one hand, help to diffuse knowledge about new technologies (Swan / Newell 1995) and on the other, provide applications that incur network effects or economies of scale, i.e. hosting of enterprise web pages or provision of data bases.

6.3. Limitations and further research needs

This research is based on a cross-sectional data set, which made it difficult to capture dynamic developments and effects. However, it was pointed out that many of the effects of ICTs emerge only with a certain time lag. In order to account for these effects it would be necessary to observe enterprises over a longer period. In the case of small-scale enterprises this is a difficult task since it is not possible to rely on accurate aggregate statistics. Moreover, many of the impacts of ICTs are of qualitative nature, calling for different methods of analysis.

ICTs are pervasive technologies that have the potential to change enterprises' operations profoundly. Real competitive advantage from ICTs can only be expected when strategies and operations are changed to accommodate the benefits they offer. However, it was shown that the impact on small-scale enterprises' structures has so far been small and basically restricted to transaction costs savings. Thus, there is a need to explore how operations and organisation in small-scale enterprises might be best adapted to new strategic opportunities.

The intensive use of the Internet by exporting enterprises indicates that a major thrust for adoption emerges from global business relations. It is therefore necessary to explore how ICTs change not only internal operations but also how they influence organisation and the composition of values chains in which small enterprises participate. This would be especially worthwhile on the global level since it is expected that ICTs enable developing countries to participate increasingly in global value chains (Forge 1995). Whether developing countries' small-scale enterprises will in the long-run be net-beneficiaries of these ICT-induced developments still has to be researched.

REFERENCES

Acs, Zoltan J, / Audretsch, David B. (1991): Innovation and Size at the Firm Level, in: The Southern Economic Journal, Vol. 57, pp. 739-744.

Acs, Zoltan J. / Audretsch, David B. (1990): Small Firms in the 1990s, in: Acs, Zoltan J. / Audretsch, David B. (eds.) (1990), The Economics of Small Firms: A European Challenge, pp. 1-22.

AIEMA (Ambattur Industrial Estate Manufacturers' Association) (1998): Buyers Guide '98, Chennai.

Alagh, Yoginder K. (1998): Technological Change in Indian Industry, in: Economic and Political Weekly, Vol. 33, pp. 181-184.

Alcorta, Ludovico (1994): The Impact of New Technologies on Scale in Manufacturing Industries: Issues and Evidence, in: World Development, Vol. 22, pp. 755-769.

All Indian Association of Industries (1995): Small-Scale Sector in India: Prospects and Challenges, Mumbai.

Antonelli, Cristiano (1992): The Economic Theory of Information Networks, in: Antonelli, Cristiano (ed.) (1992): The Economics of Information Networks, Amsterdam et al., pp. 5-27.

Avgerou, Chrisanthi (2000): Information Systems: What Sort of Science is it?, in: OMEGA International Journal of Management Science, Vol. 28, pp. 567-579.

Avgerou, Chrisanthi (1998): How can IT Enable Economic Growth in Developing Countries, in: Information Technology for Development, Vol. 8, pp. 15-28.

Bala Subrahmanya, M.H. (1998): Shifts in India's Small Industry Policy, in: Small Enterprise Development, Vol. 9, pp. 35-45.

Bamberger, Ingolf (1989): Developing Competitive Advantage in Small and Medium-Sized Firms, in: Long Range Planning, Vol. 5, pp. 80-88.

Barton, Clifton / Bear, Marshall (1999): Information and Communications Technologies: Are They the Key to Viable Business Development Services for Micro and Small Enterprises?, Bethesda.

Batz, F.-J. / Peters, K. J. / Jannsen, W. (1999): The Influence of Technology Characteristics on the Rate and Speed of Adoption, in: Agricultural Economics, Vol. 21, pp. 121-130.

Baumol, William J. (1995): Formal Entrepreneurship Theory in Economics: Existence and Bounds, in: Bull, Ivan / Thomas, Howard / Willard, Gary (eds.) (1995), pp. 17-38.

Bayes, Abdul / von Braun, Joachim / Akhter, Rasheda (1999): Village Pay Phones and Poverty Reduction: Insights from a Grameen Bank Initiative in Bangladesh (ZEF-Discussion Papers on Development Policy, No. 8), Bonn.

Bedi, Arjun S. (1999): The Role of Information and Communication Technologies in Economic Development – A Partial Survey (ZEF-Discussion Papers on Development Policy, No. 7), Bonn.

Beck, A. / Köppen, R. (1999): Internet in kleinen und mittleren Unternehmen: eine empirische Erhebung zu Problemen und Erwartungen im Handwerk, Karlsruhe.

Besant Raj International Ltd. (1999): Gearing Up for Global Competition – Strategies for Small Scale Industries (Report prepared for AIEMA - Ambattur Industrial Estate Manufacturers' Association), Chennai.

Bhasin, Sanjay / Srinivasan, Prasanna (1999): Policy and Regulatory Framework, in: Debroy, Bibek (ed.) (1999): Agenda for Change - Communications, Broadcasting and Information Technology: Working for the Common Man, New Delhi et al.

Blili, Samir / Raymond, Louis (1993): Information Technology: Threats and Opportunities for Small and Medium-Sized Enterprises, in: International Journal of Information Management, Vol. 13, pp. 439-448.

Brouwer, Jan (1999): Modern and Indigenous Perceptions in Small Enterprises, in: Economic and Political Weekly, Vol. 34, No. 48.

Brouwer, Maria (2000): Entrepreneurship and Uncertainty: Innovation and Competition Among the Many, in: Small Business Economics, Vol. 15, pp. 149-160.

Brouwer, Maria (1998): Firm Size and Efficiency in Innovation: Comment on van Dijk et al., in: Small Business Economics, Vol. 11, pp. 391-393.

Brunetti, Aymo / Kisunko, Gregory / Weder, Beatrice (1998): How Businesses See Government: Responses from Private Sector Surveys in 69 Countries (IFC Discussion Paper Number 33), Washington D.C.

Brynjolfsson, Erik / Hitt, Lorin M. (2000): Beyond Computation: Information Technology, Organizational Transformation and Business Performance, in: Journal of Economic Perspectives, Vol. 14(4), pp. 23-48.

Brynjolfsson, Erik / Hitt, Lorin M. (1996): Paradox Lost? Firm-level Evidence on the Returns to Information Systems Spending, in: Management Science, Vol. 42, pp. 541-558.

Brynjolfsson, Erik / Hitt, Lorin M. (1995): Information Technology as a Factor of Production: The Role of Difference Among Firms, in: Economics of Innovation and New Technology, Vol. 3, pp. 183-200.

Brynjolfsson, Erik / Yang, Shinkyu (1996): Information Technology and Productivity: A Review of the Literature, in: Advances in Computers, Vol. 43, pp. 179-214.

Bull, Ivan / Thomas, Howard / Willard, Gary (eds.) (1995): Entrepreneurship: Perspectives in Theory Building, Oxford.

Bull, Ivan / Willard, Gary (1995): Towards a Theory of Entrepreneurship, in: Bull, Ivan / Thomas, Howard / Willard, Gary (eds) (1995), pp. 1-16.

Cane, Alan (1992): Information Technology and Competitive Advantage: Lessons from the Developed Countries, in: World Development, Vol. 20, pp. 1721-1736.

Canning, David (1999): Internet Use and Telecommunications Infrastructure (CAER II Discussion Paper 54), Cambridge.

Casson, Marc (1999): The Economics of the Family Firm, in: Scandinavian Economic History Review, Vol. 47, pp. 10-23.

Casson, Marc (1997): Information and Organization: A New Perspective on the Theory of the Firm, Oxford.

Casson, Marc (1982): The Entrepreneur: An Economic Theory, Oxford.

Chowdary, T.H. (1998): Politics and Economics of Telecom Liberalization in India, in: Telecommunications Policy, Vol. 22, pp. 9-22.

Chowdary, T.H. (1995): Reforming Telecoms the Indian Way, in: Telecommunications, Vol. 29, pp. 111-114.

CII (Confederation of Indian Industry) (1998): 13th Business Outlook of Small Industry, New Delhi.

CII (Confederation of Indian Industry) (1994): 9th Business Outlook of Small Industry, New Delhi.

CIT Publications Ltd. (1999): Datafile of Asia-Pacific Telecommunications, December 1999, (www.citpubs.com/apta/january.htm).

CIT Publications Ltd. (2000): CIT Publications Update, 7.8.2000, Singtel to make Indian Investment (www.citpubs.com/).

CIT Publications Ltd. (2000a): Datafile of Asia-Pacific Telecommunications, December 2000, (www.citpubs.com/apta/dec2000.htm).

COAI – Cellular Operators' Association of India (2001): Cellular Statistics (http://www.coai.com/index.html).

Coase, Ronald (1937): The Nature of the Firm, in: Economica, Vol. 4, pp. 386-405.

Cyber Times (2000): India fastest growing market in APAC, Cyber Times Today, 3.8.2000 (www.ciol.com).

Cyber Times (2000a): Chennai on Top in Net Access, Cyber Times Today, 3.7.2000 (www.ciol.com).

Das, Pinaki / Srinivasan, P.V. (1999): Demand for Telephone Usage in India, in: Information Economics and Policy, Vol. 11, pp. 177-194.

Dasgupta, Subhasish / Agarwal, Devraj / Ioannidis, Anthony / Gopalakrishnan, Shanthi (1999): Determinants of Information Technology Adoption: An Extension of Existing Models to Firms in a Developing Country, in: Journal of Global Information Management, Vol. 7, No. 3, pp. 30-40.

Dataquest (2000): Demystifying the SME market, Part II, 15.03.2000 (www.dataquest.com).

Davidson, Russell / MacKinnon, James G. (1993): Estimation and Inference in Econometrics, New York, Oxford.

De Soto, Hernando (1989): The Other Path: The Invisible Revolution in the Third World, New York.

Dedrick, Jason / Kraemer, Kenneth L. (1993): Information Technology in India – The Quest for Self-Reliance, in: Asian Survey, Vol. 33, pp. 463-492.

Dewees, Christopher M. / Hawkes, Glenn R. (1988): Technical Innovation in the Pacific Coast Trawl Fishery: The Effects of Fishermen's Characteristics and Perceptions on Adoption Behavior, in: Human Organization, Vol. 47, pp. 224-234.

Dhrymes, Phoebus J. (1986): Limited Dependent Variables, in: Griliches, Zvi / Intriligator, M.D. (ed.) (1986): Handbook of Econometrics, Vol. III, Amsterdam, pp. 1567-1631.

van Dijk, Bob / den Hertog, René / Menkveld, Bert / Thurik, Roy (1997): Some New Evidence on the Determinants of Large- and Small-Firm Innovation, in: Small Business Economics, Vol. 9, pp. 335-343.

Dokeniya, Anupama (1999): Re-forming the State: Telecom Liberalization in India, in: Telecommunications Policy, Vol. 23, pp. 105-128.

Dos Santos, Brian / Sussman, Lyle (2000): Improving the Return on IT Investment, in: International Journal of Information Management, Vol. 20, pp. 429-440.

Dosi, Giovanni (1988): Sources, Procedures, and Microeconomic Effects of Innovation, in: Journal of Economic Literature, Vol. 26, pp. 1120-1171.

Downs, George W. / Mohr, Lawrence B. (1976): Conceptual Issues in the Study of Innovation, in: Administrative Science Quarterly, Vol. 21, pp. 700-714.

Duncombe, Richard (1999): Information and Communication Technology for Small Medium and Micro Enterprise Development in Botswana (Interim Report), mimeo.

Duncombe, Richard / Heeks, Richard (2001): ICTs and Small Enterprises in Africa: Lessons from Botswana, Manchester.

Duncombe, Richard / Heeks, Richard (1999): Information, ICTs and Small Enterprise: Findings from Botswana (Development Informatics Working Paper Series, No. 7), Manchester.

Economic Times (2001): Southside Story: Not by North West, 07.01.2001.

Economic Times (2000): Trai's Powers Redefined, Telecom gets New Referee, 19.1.2000.

Economic Times (2000a): Hutchison Max Surrenders Paging Licence, 14.4.2000.

Economic Times (2000b): Tamil Nadu is New IT Star: Harvard Study, 16.5.2000.

Elliot, Stephen R. (1995): Strategies for Improving the Competitiveness of Business in Developing Countries Through the Use of Information Systems, in: UNCTAD (ed.) (1995): Information Technology for Development (Advanced Technology Assessment System, Issue 10), New York, Geneva, pp. 355-365.

European Commission (1996): Guidebook for European Investors in India, Brussels.

Fink, Dieter (1998): Guidelines for the Successful Adoption of Information Technology in Small and Medium Enterprises, in: International Journal of Information Management, Vol. 18, pp. 243-253.

Forge, Simon (1995): The Consequences of Current Telecommunications Trends for the Competitiveness of Developing Countries, Washington D.C.

G8 – (Group of Eight) (2000): Okinawa Charter on Global Information Society (http://www.dotforce.org/reports/it1.html).

Gagnon, Yves-C. / Toulouse, Jean-Marie (1996): The Behavior of Business Managers When Adopting New Technologies, in: Technological Forecasting and Social Change, Vol. 52, pp. 59-74.

Ganapati, Priya (1999): Where Have All the Cowboys Gone?, in: Rediff on the Net, 21.8.1999 (www.rediff.com/computer/1999/aug/21isp.htm).

Gaur, K.D. / Reddy, Pratap (1995): Government and Small Scale Industries in India, in: Gaur, K.D. (ed.) (1995): Development and Planning, Vol. 2: Dynamics of Economic Development in India, New Delhi.

Geroski, Paul A. (2000): Models of Technology Diffusion, in: Research Policy, Vol. 29, pp. 603-625.

Goedhuys, Micheline (2000): Wages and Firm Profitability in the Manufacturing Sector in Côte d'Ivoire, in: Tijdschrift voor Economie en Management, Vol. 45, pp. 233-251.

Goedhuys, Micheline / Sleuwaegen, Leo (2000): Entrepreneurship and Growth of Entrepreneurial Firms in Côte d'Ivoire, in: The Journal of Development Economics, Vol. 36, pp. 122-145.

Goedhuys, Micheline / Sleuwaegen, Leo (1999): Barriers to Growth of Firms in Developing Countries: Evidence from Burundi, in: Audretsch, David B. / Thurik A.R. / Thurik, Roy (eds.) (1999): Innovation, Industry Evolution, and Employment, Cambridge, pp. 297-314.

Golden, William / Powell, Philip (2000): Towards a Definition of Flexibility: In Search of the Holy Grail?, in: OMEGA International Journal of Management Science, Vol. 28, pp. 373-384.

Government of India (2001): Economic Survey 2000/2001, New Delhi.

Government of India (2000): Economic Survey 1999/2000, New Delhi.

Government of India (2000a): Ministry of Small Scale Industries & Agro and Rural Industries Annual Report 1999/2000, New Delhi (http://ssi.nic.in/ar1999-2000.html).

Government of India (1999): New Telecom Policy 1999 (NTP 1999), New Delhi (http://www.nic.in:80/got/ntp-pol.html).

Government of India (1999a): Economic Survey 1998/1999, New Delhi.

Government of India (1998): Guidelines and General Information for Internet Service Providers (ISP) No.845-51/97-VAS, New Delhi (http://wwwdel.vsnl.net.in/tec/guidline.html).

Government of India (1995): Small Scale Industries – Incentives and Facilities for Development, New Delhi.

Government of India (1991): Small Sector Industrial Policy 1991, reprinted in: Kapila, Uma (ed.) (1994): Recent Developments in Indian Economy, Part II, New Delhi.

Government of Tamil Nadu (2000): Small Industries – Incentives Available to Small Scale Industrial Units (G.O.Ms. No. 37, 20.07.2000) (http://www.tn.gov.in/gorders/sind37%2De.htm).

Government of Tamil Nadu (1998): Statistical Handbook of Tamil Nadu 1998, Chennai (http://alpha.tn.nic.in/stathandbook/default.htm).

Greene, William H. (1998): LIMDEP Version 7.0, User's Manual, Plainview.

Griliches, Zvi (1957): Hybrid Corn: An Exploration in the Economics of Technological Change, in: Econometrica, Vol. 25, pp. 501-522.

Hair, Joseph F. / Anderson, Rolph E. / Tatham, Ronald L. / Black, William C. (1998): Multivariate Data Analysis, 5th edition, Upper Saddle River.

Hallberg, Kristin (2000): A Market-Oriented Strategy for Small and Medium-Scale Enterprise (IFC Discussion Paper No. 40), Washington D.C.

Hamelink, Cees J. (1997): New Information and Communication Technologies, Social Development and Cultural Change (UNRISD Discussion Paper No. 86), Geneva.

Hanna, Nagy (1994): Exploiting Information Technology for Development: A Case of India (World Bank Discussion Papers, No. 246), Washington D.C.

Hanna, Nagy / Boyson, Sandor / Gunaratne, Shakuntala (1996): The East Asian Miracle and Information Technology: Strategic Management of Technological Learning (World Bank Discussion Papers, No .326), Washington D.C.

Harrison, David A. / Mykytyn, Peter P. / Riemenschneider, Cynthia K. (1997): Executive Decisions About Adoption of Information Technology in Small Business: Theory and Empirical Tests, in: Information Systems Research, Vol. 8, pp. 171-195.

Hart, Keith (1973): Informal Income Opportunities and Urban Employment in Ghana, in: The Journal of Modern African Studies, Vol. 11, pp. 61-89.

Heckman, James J. (1976): The Common Structure of Statistical Models of Truncation, Sample Selection and Limited Dependent Variables and a Simple Estimator for Such Models, in: Annals of Economic Social Measurement, Vol. 5, pp. 475-492.

Heeks, Richard (1999): Information and Communication Technologies, Poverty and Development (Development Informatics Working Paper Series, No. 5), Manchester.

Heeks, Richard (1996): India's Software Industry – State Policy, Liberalisation, and Industrial Development, New Delhi.

Hitt, Lorin H. (1999): Information Technology and Firm Boundaries: Evidence from Panel Data, in: Information Systems Research, Vol. 10, pp. 134-149.

Hitt, Lorin / Brynjolfsson, Erik (1997): Information Technology and Internal Firm Organization: An Exploratory Analysis, in: Journal of Management Information Systems, Vol. 14, pp. 81-101.

Hitt, Lorin H. / Brynjolfsson, Erik (1996): Productivity, Profit and Consumer Welfare: Three Different Measures of Information Technology's Value, MIS Quarterly, June 1996.

Iacovou, Charalambos L. / Benbasat, Izak / Dexter, Albert S. (1995): Electronic Data Interchange and Small Organizations: Adoption and Impact of Technology, in: MIS Quarterly, December 1995, pp. 465-485.

IDC India (International Data Corporation India) (1999): Internet subscribers in India to Reach 530,000 by March 2000, says IDC (www.idcindia.com/Pressrel/19Nov99.html).

ILO (International Labour Office) (1972): Employment, Incomes and Equality: A Strategy for Increasing Productive Employment in Kenya, Geneva.

India Abroad News Service (2000): Who's Going to Win the Cellphone Sweepstakes?, 30.7.2000.

ITU (International Telecommunications Union) (2001): World Telecommunication Indicators 2000/2001, Geneva.

ITU (International Telecommunications Union) (2001a): ITU Telecommunication Indicators Update, January - February - March 2001, Geneva.

ITU (International Telecommunications Union) (1999): World Telecommunications Indicators '99, Geneva.

ITU (International Telecommunications Union) (1999a): World Telecommunication Development Report 1999 – Mobile Cellular, Geneva.

Julien, Pierre-André (1995): New Technologies and Technological Information in Small Businesses, in: Journal of Business Venturing, Vol. 10, pp. 459-475.

Julien, Pierre-André / Raymond, Louis / Réal, Jacob / Ramangalahy, Charles (1999): Types of Technological Scanning in Manufacturing SMEs: An Empirical Analysis of Patterns and Determinants, in: Entrepreneurship & Regional Development, Vol. 11, pp. 281-300.

Karshenas, Massoud / Stoneman, Paul (1995): Technological Diffusion, in: Stoneman (ed.) (1995), pp. 265-297.

Karshenas, Massoud / Stoneman, Paul (1993): Rank, Stock, Order, and Epidemic Effects in the Diffusion of New Process Technologies: An Empirical Model, in: Rand Journal of Economics, Vol. 24, pp. 503-528.

Katrak, Homi (1999): Small-scale Enterprise Policy in Developing Countries: An Analysis of India's Reservation Policy, in: Journal of International Development, Vol. 11, pp. 701-715.

Khan, Wasif M. (1998): Technological Innovation in SMEs in Pakistan, in: Kanungo, Rabindra N. (ed.) (1998): Entrepreneurship & Innovation: Models for Development, New Delhi et al., pp. 287-309.

König, Wolfgang / Billand, Klaus (1992): Techniques and Criteria for Classifying Small and Medium-Scale Industries by Size (International Small Business Series, No. 10); Goettingen.

Krueger, Alan B. (1993): How Computers Have Changed the Wage Structure: Evidence from Microdata, 1984-1989, in: Quarterly Journal of Economics, Vol. 108, pp. 33-60.

Kumar, Neerja (2000): Beep! The Paging Industry Gets a Fresh Lease of Life, in: Financial Express, 10.08.2000.

Kumar, N. (1998): Indian Small Industry – the Technology Dimension, in: Tech Monitor, Jan-Feb 1998, pp. 49-52.

Lagos, Ricardo L. (1994): Formalizing the Informal Sector: Barriers and Costs, in: Development and Change, Vol. 26, pp. 111-131.

Lal, Kaushalesh (2000): Adoption of Information Technology and its Consequences in a Development Context: A Study of the Indian Electrical & Electronic Goods and Garments Sectors in Two Industrial Clusters, Amsterdam.

Lal, Kaushalesh (1999): Determinants of the Adoption of Information Technology: A Case Study of Electrical and Electronic Goods Manufacturing Firms in India, in: Research Policy, Vol. 28, pp. 667-680.

Lal, Kaushalesh (1999a): Information Technology and Exports: A Case Study of Indian Garments Manufacturing Enterprises (ZEF – Discussion Papers on Development Policy, No. 15), Bonn.

Lal, Kaushalesh (1998): The Adoption of Information Technology and its Consequences: A Case Study of Indian TV Manufacturing Firms, in: Science, Technology & Development, Vol. 16, pp. 81-100.

Lal, Kaushalesh (1996): Information Technology, International Orientation and Performance: A Case Study of Electrical and Electronic Goods Manufacturing Firms in India, in: Information Economics and Policy, Vol. 8, pp. 269-280.

Lefebvre, Élisabeth / Lefebvre, Louis A. (1996): Information and Telecommunication Technologies: The Impact of Their Adoption on Small and Medium-sized Enterprises, Ottawa.

Lefebvre, Élisabeth / Lefebvre, Louis A. / Roy, Marie-Josée (1995): Technological Penetration and Organizational Learning in SMEs: The Cumulative Effect, in: Technovation, Vol. 15, pp. 511-522.

Leibenstein, Harvey (1968): Entrepreneurship and Development, in: American Economic Review, Vol. 58, pp. 72-83.

Levy, Margi / Powell, Philip (1998): SME Flexibility and the Role of Information Systems, in: Small Business Economics, Vol. 11, pp. 183-196.

Little, Ian M.D. (1987): Small Manufacturing Enterprises in Developing Countries, in: The World Bank Economic Review, Vol. 1, pp. 203-235.

Little, Ian M.D. / Mazumdar, Dipak / Page, John M. (1987): Small Manufacturing Enterprises - A Comparative Analysis of India and Other Countries, New York et al.

Lybaert, Nadine (1998): The Information Use in a SME: Its Importance and Some Elements of Influence, in: Small Business Economics, Vol. 10, pp. 171-191.

Maddala, G.S. (1992): Introduction to Econometrics, 2nd edition, Englewood Cliffs.

Maddala, G.S. (1983): Limited-dependent and Qualitative Variables in Econometrics, Cambridge.

MAIT (Manufacturers Association of Information Technology) (2000): IT Industry Performance: Annual Review 1999-2000, New Delhi (http://www.mait.com/indusstats.htm).

Mansell, Robin (1999): Information and Communication Technologies for Development: Assessing the Potential and the Risk, in: Telecommunications Policy, Vol. 23, pp. 35-50.

Mansfield, Edwin (1963): The Speed of Response of Firms to New Techniques, in: Quarterly Journal of Economics, Vol. 77, pp. 290-311.

Mathur, Ashok (1994): Upgradation and Diffusion of Technology in Small Scale and Cottage Industries: A Review Article, in: Indian Economic Review, Vol. 29, pp. 79-89.

Maußner, Alfred / Klump, Rainer (1996): Wachstumstheorie, Berlin et al.

McKelvey, Richard D. / Zavoina, William (1975): A Statistical Model for the Analysis of Ordinal Level Dependent Variables, in: Journal of Mathematical Sociology, Vol. 4, pp. 103-120.

Mead, Donald / Liedholm, Carl (1998): The Dynamics of Micro and Small Enterprises in Developing Countries, in: World Development, Vol. 26, pp. 61-74.

Mead, Donald / Morrisson, Christian (1996): The Informal Sector Elephant, in: World Development, Vol. 24, pp. 1611-1619.

Meier, Ralf (1997): Kammern und Verbände in der Dritten Welt – Funktionsfähigkeit und Entwicklungspotential für Handwerk und Kleinunternehmen, Goettingen.

Meeus, Marius T.H. / Oerlemans, Leon A.G. (2000): Firm Behaviour and Innovative Performance - An Empirical Exploration of the Selection-adaptation Debate, in: Research Policy, Vol. 29, pp. 41-58.

Mehta, Arun, (2000): Telecom, in: Alternative Survey Group (ed.) (2000): Alternative Economic Survey, New Delhi, pp. 106-111.

Metcalfe, J. Stan (1995): The Economic Conditions of Technology Policy: Equilibrium and Evolutionary Perspectives, in: Stoneman (ed.) (1995), pp. 409-512.

Metcalfe, J. Stan (1981): Impulse and Diffusion in the Study of Technological Change, in: Futures, Vol.13, pp. 396-408.

Morrisson, Christian / Solignac Lecomte, Henri-Bernard / Oudin, Xavier (1994): Micro-enterprises and the Institutional Framework in Developing Countries (OECD Development Centre Studies), Paris.

Moser, Caroline O. N. (1994): The Informal Sector Debate, Part 1: 1970 – 1983, in: Rakowski, Cathy A. (ed.) (1994): Contrapunto: The Informal Sector Debate in Latin America, Albany.

Müller-Falcke, Dietrich (1997): Informal Sector Enterprises in the Light of New Institutional Economics (International Small Business Series, No. 24), Goettingen.

Mugler, Josef (1993): Betriebswirtschaftslehre der Klein- und Mittelbetriebe, Wien , New York.

NASSCOM (National Association of IT Software and Service Industry) (2001): Internet & E-commerce Scenario in India (http://www.nasscom.org/template/inetec.htm).

NASSCOM (National Association of IT Software and Service Industry) (2000): Indian IT Software and Services Industry (http://www.nasscom.org/template/itinindia.htm).

Nassimbeni, Guido (2001): Technology, Innovation Capacity, and the Export Attitude of Small Manufacturing Firms: A Logit/Tobit Model, in: Research Policy, Vol. 30, pp. 245-262.

Nawata, Kazumitsu (1994): Estimation of Sample Selection Bias Models by Maximum Likelihood Estimator and Heckman's Two-step Estimator, in: Economics Letters, Vol. 45, pp. 33-40.

NCAER (National Council of Applied Economic Research) / FNF (Friedrich-Naumann- Stiftung) (1993): Structure and Promotion of Small Scale Industries in India - Lessons for Future Development, New Delhi.

Negatu, W. / Parikh, A. (1999): The Impact of Perception and Other Factors on the Adoption of Agricultural Technology in the Moret and Jiru Woreda (District) of Ethiopia, in: Agricultural Economics, Vol. 21, pp. 205-216.

Nelson, Richard R. / Winter, Sidney G. (1974): Neoclassical vs. Evolutionary Theories of Economic Growth: Critique and Prospectus, in: Economic Journal, Vol. 78, pp. 886-905.

Nooteboom, Bart (1994): Innovation and Diffusion in Small Firms: Theory and Evidence, in: Small Business Economics, Vol. 6, pp. 327-347.

Norton, Seth W. (1992): Transaction Costs, Telecommunications, and the Microeconomics of Macroeconomic Growth, in: Economic Development and Cultural Change, Vol. 41, pp. 175-196.

Paltridge, Sam (2000): Mobile Communications Update, in: Telecommunications Policy, Vol. 24, pp. 453-456.

Pavitt, Keith (1984): Sectoral Patterns of Technological Change: Towards a Taxonomy and a Theory, in: Research Policy, Vol. 13, pp. 343-373.

Pedersen, Jorgen Dige (2000): Explaining Economic Liberalization in India: State and Society Perspectives, in: World Development, Vol. 28, pp. 265 – 282.

Pedersen, Poul Ove (1994): Clusters of Enterprises Within Systems of Production and Distribution: Collective Efficiency, Transaction Costs and the Economics of Agglomeration (CDR Working Paper 94.14), Copenhagen.

Pleitner, Hans Jobst (1995): Kleinunternehmen und das Informationsproblem, in: Mugler, Joseph / Schmidt, Karl-Heinz (eds.) (1995): Klein- und Mittelunternehmen in einer dynamischen Wirtschaft, Berlin, et al., pp. 177-194.

Porter, Michael E. / Millar, Victor E. (1985): How Information Gives You Competitive Advantage, in: Havard Business Review, July-August 1985, pp. 149-160.

Puhani, Patrick, A. (2000): The Heckman Correction For Sample Selection and Its Critique, in: Journal of Economic Surveys, Vol. 14, pp. 53-68.

Rakowski, Cathy A. (1994): Convergence and Divergence in the Informal Sector Debate: A Focus on Latin America, 1984 – 92, in: World Development, Vol. 22, pp. 501 – 516.

Ramaswamy, K.V. (1994): Small-scale Manufacturing Industries in India: Some Aspects of Size, Growth and Structure (Indira Gandhi Institute of Development Research, Discussion Paper No. 105), Mumbai.

Ramaswamy, K.V. (1994a): Technical Efficiency in Modern Small-scale Firms in Indian Industry: Applications of Stochastic Production Frontiers, in: Journal of Quantitative Economics, Vol. 10, pp. 309-324.

Rao, Madanmohan (1999): Internet Content in India: Local Challenges, Global Aspirations, in: IICD E-journal, 29.09.1999
(http://www.iicd.org/base/show_article?url=/base/show_ article-cle&section=ejournal&PARAGRAPH_LIST_NUMBER=ALL&show_info_cont ent=t&backpage=&bgcolor=FFFFFF&subcat_id=6&article_id=191).

Rautenstrauch, Thomas (1997): Der Einsatz wissensbasierter Systeme in Handwerksbetrieben zum Ausgleich betriebsgrößenbedingter Nachteile (Göttinger Wirtschaftsinformatik, Band 24), Goettingen.

Rice, George H. / Hamilton, Richard E. (1979): Decision Theory and the Small Businessman, in: American Journal of Small Business, Vol. 4, pp. 1-9.

Richter, Rudolf / Furubotn, Eirik (1996): Neue Institutionenökonomik – ein Einführung und kritische Würdigung, Tuebingen.

Rogers, Everett M. (1995): Diffusion of Innovations, 4th edition, New York.

la Rovere, Renata Lèbre (1998): Diffusion of Information Technologies and Changes in the Telecommunications Sector: The Case of Brazilian Small- and Medium-sized Enterprises, in: Information Technology and People, Vol. 11, pp. 194-206.

Rudy, I.A. (1996): A Critical Review of Research on Electronic Mail, in: European Journal of Information Systems, Vol. 4, pp. 198-213.

Schmidt, Klaus-Dieter (1996): Small and Medium Sized Enterprises (SMEs) in International Business: A Survey of Recent Literature (Kiel Working Paper No. 721), Kiel.

Schmitz, Hubert (1995): Collective Efficiency: Growth Path for Small-Scale Industry, in The Journal of Development Studies, Vol. 31, pp. 529 - 566.

Schneider-Barthold, Wolfgang (1998): Kleingewerbe in Entwicklungsländern: Bedeutung, Beschränkungen, Förderansätze, in: ifo Schnelldienst, No. 34-35, 1998, Munich, pp. 56-62.

Schoder, Detlef (2000): Forecasting the Success of Telecommunication Services in the Presence of Network Effects, in: Information Economics and Politics, Vol. 12, pp. 181-200.

Seibel, Sabine / Müller-Falcke, Dietrich / Bertolini, Romeo (1999): Informations- und Kommunikationstechnologien in Entwicklungsländern – Trends und Potentiale (ZEF-Discussion Papers on Development Policy, No. 4), Bonn.

Senthil Nathan, C.S. (1999): Laudable Lingual mission Launched, in: The Hindu, 21.6.1999.

Seyal, Afzaal H. / Rahim, Md. Mahbubur / Rahman, Mohd. Noah A. (2000): An Empirical Investigation of Use of Information Technology Among Small and Medium Business Organisations: A Brunei Scenario, in: The Electronic Journal on Information Systems in Developing Countries, Vol. 2 (http://www.is.cityu.edu.hk/ejisdc/ejisdc.htm).

Sillince, John A.A. / MacDonald, Stuart / Lefang, Bernard / Frost, Brian (1998): Email Adoption, Diffusion, Use and Impact Within Small Firms: A Survey of UK Companies, in: International Journal of Information Management, Vol. 18, pp. 231-242.

Silverberg, Gerald / Dosi, Giovanni / Orsenigo, Luigi (1988): Innovation, Diversity and Diffusion: A Self-organization Model, in: The Economic Journal, Vol. 98, pp. 1032-1054.

Simon, Herbert A. (1987): Bounded Rationality, in: Eatwell, John / Milgate, Murray / Newman, Peter (eds.) (1987): The New Palgrave – A Dictionary of Economics, Vol. 1, London, pp. 226-268.

Singh, J.P. (2000): The Institutional Environment and Effects of Telecommunication Privatization and Market Liberalization in Asia, in: Telecommunications Policy, Vol. 24, pp. 885-906.

Singh, J.P. (1999): Leapfrogging Development? The Political Economy of Telecommunications Restructuring, Albany.

Singhal, Amitabh (2000): Private ISPs: One Year of Internet Privatization, in: Voice & Data 27.01.2000.

Srivastara, Lara / Sinha, Sidharth (2001): TP Case Study: Fixed-mobile Interconnection in India, in: Telecommunications Policy, Vol. 25, pp. 21-38.

Stiglitz, Joseph E. (1988): Economic Organization, Information, and Development, in: Chenery, H. / Srinivasan T.N. (eds.) (1988): Handbook of Development Economics, Vol. 1, Amsterdem et al.,pp. 93-160.

Stoneman, Paul (ed.) (1995): Handbook of the Economics of Innovation and Technological Change, Oxford, Cambridge.

Stoneman, Paul / Battisti, Giuliana (1997): Intra-firm Diffusion of New Technologies – The Neglected Part of Technology Transfer (Paper presented at the VII International Conference on Economics and Policies of Innovation, in Cremona, 11.-13.6.1997), mimeo.

Stoneman, Paul / Kwon, Myong Joong (1996): Technology Adoption and Firm Profitability, in: The Economic Journal, Vol. 106, pp. 952-962.

Swan, Jacky A. / Newell, Sue (1995): The Role of Professional Associations in Technology Diffusion, in: Organization Studies, Vol. 16, pp. 847-874.

Tam, Kar Yan (1998): The Impact of Information Technology Investments on Firm Performance and Evaluation: Evidence from Newly Industrialized Economies, in: Information Systems Research, Vol. 9, pp. 85-98.

TechConsult GmbH (2000): Internet- and E-Business-Einsatz im bundesdeutschen Mittelstand, Kassel.

Thong, James Y.L. (1999): An Integrated Model of Information Systems Adoption in Small Businesses, in: Journal of Management Information Systems, Vol. 15, pp. 187-214.

Thong, James Y.L. / Yap, Chee-Sing (1995): CEO Characteristics, Organizational Characteristics and Information Technology Adoption in Small Business, in: OMEGA International Journal of Management Science, Vol. 23, pp. 429-442.

Tybout, James (1998): Manufacturing Firms in Developing Countries: How Well Do They Do and Why? (World Bank Policy Research Paper 1965), Washington D.C.

Varma, Yograj (2000):The ISP Scene: Innovate and Survive, in: Dataquest, 31.1.00 (www.dqindia.com/jan3100/coverstory.html).

Varma, Yograj (2000a): The Five Million Mark: Outgrowing the Little League, in: Cyber Times Today, 7.12.2000 (www.ciol.com).

Veall, Michael R. / Zimmermann, Klaus F. (1994): Goodness of Fit Measures in the Tobit Model, in: Oxford Bulletin of Economics and Statistics, Vol. 56, pp. 485-499.

Voice & Data (2000): Paging Services, 07.07.2000 (http://voicendata.ciol.com).

Voice & Data (1999): Paging, 01.07.1999 (http://voicendata.ciol.com).

Voice & Data (1998): Paging – The Industry Fell Short of Expectations, July 1998 (www.voicendata.com/jul98/seg_paging.html).

Wang, Eunice Hsiao-hui (1999): ICT and Economic Development in Taiwan: Analysis of the Evidence, in: Telecommunications Policy, Vol. 23, pp. 235-243.

Wang, F.K. / Du, T.C.T. (2000): Using Principal Component Analysis in Process Performance for Multivariate Data, in: OMEGA International Journal of Management Science, Vol. 28, pp. 185-194.

Weiber, Rolf (1992): Diffusion von Telekommunikation: Problem der kritischen Masse, Wiesbaden.

Wellenius, Björn / Braga, C.A. Primo / Qiang, Christine Z. (2000): Investment and Growth of the Information Infrastructure: Summary Results of a Global Survey, in: Telecommunications Policy, Vol. 24, pp. 639-643.

Welsh, John A. / White Jerry F. (1981): A Small Business is not a Little Big Business, in: Harvard Business Review, Vol. 59(4), pp. 18-32.

Wernerfelt, Birger (1984): A Resource-based View of the Firm, in: Strategic Management Journal, Vol. 5, pp. 171-180.

Williamson, Oliver E. (1985): The Economic Institutions of Capitalism – Firms, Markets, Relational Contracting, New York, London.

Wittstock, Matthias (1990): Neue Informations- und Kommunikationstechnologien in Kleinbetrieben, in: Berger, Johannes / Domeyer, Volker / Fender, Maria (eds.) (1990): Kleinbetriebe im wirtschaftlichen Wandel, Frankfurt, New York, pp. 181-191.

World Bank (2000): World Development Report 2000/01 – Attacking Poverty, Washington D.C.

World Bank (1998): World Development Report 1998/99 – Knowledge for Development, Washington D.C.

World Bank (1997): World Development Report 1997 – The State in a Changing World, Washington D.C.

World Bank Global Information and Communication Technologies Department (2000): The Networking Revolution: Opportunities and Challenges for Developing Countries (infoDev Working Paper), Washington D.C.

Yap, Chee-Sing / Soh, C.P.P. / Raman, K.S. (1992): Information Systems Success Factors in Small Business, in: OMEGA International Journal of Management Science, Vol. 20, pp. 597-609.

You, Yong-Il (1995): Small Firms in Economic Theory, in: Cambridge Journal of Economics, Vol. 19, pp. 441-462.

ANNEX

Annex 1: Indian Basic Telecommunications, Information Technology and Media Indicators (1960 - 2000)

	1960	1965	1970	1975	1980	1985	1990	1991	1992	1993	1994	1995	1996	1997	1998**	1999**	2000***
Public call offices ('000)											137	161			463**	570**	740***
Main telephone lines in operation ('000)	332	623	981	1.465	2.149	3.165	5.075	5.810	6.797	8.026	9.795	11.978	14.543	17.802	21.594	26.511	32.436
Main lines per 100 inhabitants	0,07	0,12	0,17	0,23	0,31	0,41	0,59	0,67	0,77	0,89	1,06	1,29	1,54	1,86	2,19	2,66	3,20
Estimated facsimile machines ('000)						0	5	10	35	45	50	70	100	150			
Cellular mobile telephone subscribers ('000)												77	328	882	1.195	1.599	3.107
Radio-paging subscribers ('000)												167	480	762	670*	600*	
Telex subscribers ('000)		1	5	12	19	30	47	49	49	49	47	44	32	25			
Number of internet hosts							0	0	79	138	359	788	3.138	7.175	13.253	23.445	35.810
Number of internet subscribers ('000)												50*	90*	140*	280*	961*	1.800
Number of internet users ('000)												250*	450*	700*	1.400*	2.800*	5.500
Number of personal computers ('000)							270	350	410	560	800	1.200	1.500	2.000	2.700	3.300	5.000
Telecom. service revenue (Mio. US$)		142	189	377	837	1.057	2.541	2.184	2.392	2.691	3.253	3.860	4.369	5.051		3.650	
Telecom investment (Mio. US$)		50	74	209	330	688	1.584	1.495	1.777	1.830	2.172	2.533	2.375	2.405		2.911	
Radio receivers ('000)	17.000		21.000	21.000	26.000	50.000	67.000	80.000	85.000	90.000	95.000	111.000	113.500	116.000			
Television receivers ('000)		1	28	515	1.750	3.955	27.000	30.000	34.858	45.000	50.000	57.000	60.000	66.000	70.000	75.000	
Cable television subscribers ('000)										7.250	10.000	16.000	17.000	18.000	37.000		

* end of fiscal year (ends at 31.3. of following year) ** 30.09.; ***31.10.
Sources: ITU (1999; 2001); COAI (2001); Government of India (2001; 2000; 1999a); NASSCOM (2001); Voice & Data (2000 and 1999).

Annex 2: Execution of interviews

The interviews at Ambattur Industrial Estate were conducted by ten second year MBA students from Velammal College of Management and Computer Studies, Chennai, and by the author in the period between 21st May and 11th June 1999.

The interviewers were given a number of company names and addresses. They either fixed appointments with the entrepreneurs by phone or went directly to the enterprises' sites. In many cases it was rather difficult to fix an appointment for the interview which made it necessary to visit most companies a couple of times before the interview was completed.

Ideally interviews should have been conducted in a way that both entrepreneur and interviewer had a copy of the questionnaire, giving the entrepreneur the possibility to read questions and answers read out to him by the interviewer. Filling in of the questionnaire had to be done by the interviewer himself. This procedure was followed in 87 percent of cases. In the other 13 percent the interviewed person insisted on filling in the questionnaire himself, in the presence of the interviewer.

The questionnaire was designed in English, and English was supposed to be the language of the interviews since the vast majority of entrepreneurs were expected to be fluent in that language. 85 percent of all interviews were done in English, 6 percent were mixed with English and a regional language (i.e. Tamil or Malayalam) and 9 percent were conducted in a regional language only.

Average duration of the interviews was 43 minutes, with time ranging from 20 to 145 minutes (Three quarters of the interviews took between 30 and 45 minutes). On average each interviewer managed to conduct 2.1 interviews per day which underlines the difficulties of getting in contact with the entrepreneurs and finding the time to do the interview. Nevertheless, when the interviews took place, the willingness of the interviewed person to answer was high. Problems were reported in only eleven percent of interviews. Where this unwillingness clearly led to deficiencies in the answers the questionnaires were excluded from the analysis.

Annex 3: Comparing enterprises by position of the interviewed person

Table A-3-1: Mean of enterprise characteristics by position of the interviewed person (CEOs against subordinate managers)

		N	Mean	Std. Deviation	Std. Error Mean
Fax used	CEO	266	.75	.43	2.67E-02
	Manager	29	.69	.47	8.74E-02
Fax owned	CEO	266	.5977	.4913	3.012E-02
	Manager	29	.6207	.4938	9.170E-02
Pager used now	CEO	266	.34	.48	2.91E-02
	Manager	29	.41	.50	9.31E-02
Cellular phone used now	CEO	266	.37	.48	2.97E-02
	Manager	29	.38	.49	9.17E-02
Computer owned	CEO	266	.65	.48	2.94E-02
	Manager	29	.69	.47	8.74E-02
E-mail account	CEO	266	.35	.48	2.92E-02
	Manager	29	.28	.45	8.45E-02
Year enterprise was established	CEO	265	1981.37	8.01	.49
	Manager	29	1983.31	8.79	1.63
Employees at time of survey	CEO	260	26.80	29.14	1.81
	Manager	29	35.45	25.76	4.78
LN (Employees at time of survey)	CEO	260	2.8823	.8773	5.441E-02
	Manager	29	3.3098	.7481	.1389
Annual turnover (1998/99)	CEO	231	10.653.064	22.425.489	1.475.489
	Manager	29	12.119.900	13.970.327	2.594.225
LN (Annual turnover 1998/99)	CEO	231	15.3532	1.2688	8.348E-02
	Manager	29	15.7082	1.1664	.2166
Advanced production technology used	CEO	266	.1992	.4002	2.454E-02
	Manager	29	.2759	.4549	8.447E-02
export (yes/no)	CEO	255	.18	.38	2.39E-02
	Manager	27	.26	.45	8.59E-02
import (yes/no)	CEO	261	.12	.32	2.01E-02
	Manager	29	.14	.35	6.52E-02

Table A-3-2.: Testing for equality of means from Table A-3-1

		Levene's Test for Equality of Variances		t-test for Equality of Means		
		F	Sig.	t	df	Sig. (2-tailed)
Fax used	Equal variances assumed	1.517	.219	.682	293	.496
Fax owned	Equal variances assumed	.271	.603	-.239	293	.811
Pager used now	Equal variances assumed	1.519	.219	-.767	293	.444
Cellular phone used now	Equal variances assumed	.022	.883	-.075	293	.940
Computer owned	Equal variances assumed	1.049	.307	-.460	293	.646
Email account	Equal variances assumed	3.122	.078	.754	293	.451
Year enterprise was established	Equal variances assumed	.267	.606	-1.227	292	.221
Employees at time of survey	Equal variances assumed	.055	.815	-1.533	287	.126
Ln (Employees at time of survey)	Equal variances assumed	1.004	.317	-2.523	287	.012
Annual turnover (1998/99)	Equal variances assumed	.008	.929	-.344	258	.731
LN (Annual turnover	Equal variances assumed	.328	.567	-1.432	258	.153
Advanced production	Equal variances assumed	3.000	.084	-.966	293	.335
export (yes/no)	Equal variances assumed	3.569	.060	-1.053	280	.293
import (yes/no)	Equal variances assumed	.345	.558	-.299	288	.765

Annex 4: Principal Component Analysis for variables of the environmental dimension

In order to structure the information gathered on the enterprises' market environment Principal Component Analysis (PCA) is applied. PCA is one of the most common tools of factor analysis.[*] The objective of PCA is to reduce the information entailed in a large number of variables into a smaller set of variates, the so-called factors, with a minimum loss of information (Hair et al. 1998). The smaller number of variates is more operational for prediction purposes, i.e. for applying other statistical techniques.[**] PCA can also serve to identify the underlying structure of a large set of variables or to identify specific representative variables in a large set of variables (Hair et al. 1998:95). In this work PCA is used for the latter purpose, i.e. factors are identified and for each factor one appropriate variable is chosen to feed into the regression model.

Not the whole set of market related variables is used, and some variables are transformed in order to bring them into a form that can be used for PCA and regression analysis:[***] The variables that indicate the percentage of products sold and supplies bought on the local level were dropped. These two variables are closely correlated with the percentages of national sales and purchases (with correlation coefficients of – 0.927 for sales and –0,945 for purchases). It is obvious that local sales and purchases are nearly the inverse of national sales and purchases as only few enterprises export on a significant scale. All other variables are used for the analysis. In order to convert the variables representing the number of customers and suppliers into a metric form they are transformed into the median of the ranges offered as options to the interviewees.[****] The other ordinally scaled variables are transformed into dichotomous variables in order to use them as dummy variables in later analysis. The new variable for the importance of each attribute for competitiveness was given a "1" if its original value belongs to the highest category given by the interviewee and a "0" otherwise.[*****] Thus, the importance of attributes of competitiveness variables will represent whether the attribute is considered to be of prime importance for competitiveness by the interviewed CEO, or whether other attributes are considered more important. The

---

[*] See Negatu / Parikh (1999) and Thong (1999) for empirical application of PCA in a similar setting.

[**] Maddala (1992:284-289) is critical about the benefits of PCA in solving the multicollinearity problem. He argues - rightly - that if all principal components are used, it is exactly the original set of variables. If some principal components are omitted prior information on the relations of the variables is needed. Additionally it is not clear whether this information can be interpreted in a economically reasonable manner. However, despite this critique PCA can serve as a useful tool to clarify the structure of large variable sets and to make them easier to handle.

[***] In general only metric variables should be used for PCA, but the use of dummy variables is also possible. (Hair et al. (1998:98).

[****] The new values are 2.5 for "less than 5", 7.5 for "5-10", 15.5 for "11-20", 35.5 for "21 to 50" and 75 for "more than 50".

[*****] In general the highest valuation is also the highest category, i.e. 7, "very important", but in 22 cases it is 6 and in 4 cases just 5 on the scale from 1, "not important", to 7, "very important".

answers to the question on the intensity of competition are also transformed into a dichotomous variable so that the new variable has the value "1" if the interviewed CEO considers competition to be "fierce", i.e. she/he marked highest possible category. The number of cases in the following PCA analysis is 212, i.e. 54 observations are excluded due to missing data in some of the variables. Comparing the variable means of the PCA and the whole sample reveals only minor deviations for almost all variables.[*] Therefore the sub-sample can be considered representative for the whole sample. The validity of applying PCA can be tested with the Measure of Sampling Adequacy (MSA)-test and the Bartlett-Test of Sphericity (Hitt et al. 1998:99-100). The Bartlett-Test tests for the presence of correlation among the tested variable. For the tested sample the hypothesis of the presence of correlation is strongly supported (see table A.-4-1). The MSA-test measures the predictive power of the set of variables. Test values range from 0 to 1 with 1 being the perfect prediction without error for each variable by all other variables. The test value of 0.72 can be considered fairly good confirming the appropriateness of using PCA for this set of variables.[**]

Table A-4-1: Tests for the appropriateness of principle component analysis

KMO and Bartlett's Test		
Kaiser-Meyer-Olkin Measure of Sampling Adequacy.		.720
Bartlett's Test of Sphericity	Approx. Chi-Square	957.990
	df	153
	Sig.	.000

The next step in PCA is the decision on the number of factors to be extracted from the data set. Most common is the latent root criterion (Hitt et al. 1998:103-104). Only factors that have a latent root or eigenvalue greater than 1 are considered. The results presented in table A-4-2 suggest an extraction of six factors, which is supported by the fact that the explained variance of the six factors is reasonably high (64 percent) and the six factors will have economically meaningful explanations. For analysis the factors are rotated orthogonally with the Varimax-technique. Using orthogonal rotation will leave the factors independent. The rotated component matrix that provides the factor loadings, i.e. the correlation of each variable with the factor, is presented in table A-4-3. For a sample size of 200 only factor loadings of more than 0.40 are considered significant (Hair et al. 1998:112). For the ease of interpretation only significant variable loadings are displayed.

---

[*] The only larger deviation can be found for the amount of exports. The mean for all values (including enterprises excluded from the diffusion analysis) is 4.11 compared with 3.39 for the reduced sample, leaving an anti-export bias in the sub-sample.

[**] Individual MSA-values range from 0.82 to 0.47 for the variables leaving all but one variable ("importance of quality") above the acceptance threshold of 0.5.

Table A-4-2: Calculation and identification of factors

Total Variance Explained

Component	Initial Eigenvalues			Rotation Sums of Squared Loadings		
	Total	% of Variance	Cumulativ e %	Total	% of Variance	Cumulativ e %
1	4.126	22.924	22.924	2.635	14.636	14.636
2	1.917	10.651	33.576	2.235	12.416	27.052
3	1.660	9.220	42.796	2.166	12.031	39.083
4	1.273	7.073	49.869	1.573	8.740	47.824
5	1.200	6.668	56.537	1.326	7.367	55.190
6	1.076	5.977	62.514	1.318	7.323	62.514
7	.899	4.997	67.511			
8	.817	4.538	72.049			
9	.737	4.092	76.141			
10	.729	4.049	80.190			
11	.613	3.406	83.596			
12	.563	3.129	86.724			
13	.534	2.966	89.691			
14	.506	2.812	92.503			
15	.448	2.491	94.994			
16	.375	2.081	97.075			
17	.288	1.599	98.674			
18	.239	1.326	100.000			

Extraction Method: Principal Component Analysis.

All included variables have at least one significant loading on one of the factors. Only one variable is significant for more than one factor, but interpreting this is unproblematic. An examination of the six factors reveals that they can be interpreted in economically meaningful ways. Consequently, the interpretation suggests the labelling of the factors and a selection of variables representative for each factor in the following way:

Factor 1: *"Quantity of business contacts"*

This factor responds positively to the number of suppliers and customers. This is reflected by the positive relation to the number of customers and suppliers as well as by the negative relation to concentration of customers and suppliers. The positive relation to national sales indicates that the probability to sell outside the local area increases with the number of customers.

Factor 2: *"National market focus"*

This factor responds positively to the amount of business done on the national level.

Factor 3: *"International focus"*

This factor responds positively to the amount of business done at the international level.

Table A-4-3: Factor loadings for market environment factors

Rotated Component Matrix

	Component					
	1	2	3	4	5	6
Number of suppliers (mean of range)	.790					
Percentage share of the largest three suppliers	-.763					
Percentage of output sold to the three largest customers	-.713					
Number of customers (mean of ranges)	.631					
Percentage of supplies and raw materials bought nationally		.752				
Location of main competitors (Chennai and surrounding)		-.729				
Location of main competitors (India)		.667				
Percentage of sales (national)	.418	.602				
Location of main competitors (abroad)			.748			
Percentage of sales (export)			.702			
Percentage of supplies and raw materials imported			.656			
Importance of capacity				.800		
Importance of after sales services				.670		
Importance of flexibility				.499		
Importance of price					.751	
Intensity of competition					.721	
Importance of quality						.817
Importance of punctuality of delivery						.621

Extraction Method: Principal Component Analysis.
Rotation Method: Varimax with Kaiser Normalization.
a. Rotation converged in 7 iterations.

Factor 4: *"Customer orientation"*

This factor responds positively to increasing importance assigned to meeting customers needs (punctuality of delivery, flexibility, after sales services).

Factor 5: *"Price competition"*

This factor responds positively to increasing importance assigned to output prices. Considering the other competition parameters one can see that price is the toughest competition criterion, i.e. entrepreneurs that compete via price will perceive competition more intense.

Factor 6: *"Quality competition"*

This factor responds positively to increasing importance assigned to quality aspects (product quality and process quality).

Out of these factors representative variables are selected to move into the regression analyses.

Annex 5: Correlation coefficients of explanatory variables

Table A-5-1: Correlation matrix for explanatory variables for adoption and time of adoption

Correlations

	AGE_CEO	EDU_YEAR	ADV_TECH	SEC_3031	SEC_33	SEC_34	SEC_35	AGE_ENT	LN_SIZE	CONTACT	NAT_BUSI	INT_BUSI	IM_FLEX	IM_PRIC	IM_QUAL
AGE_CEO	1.000	-.129	-.093	-.111	.043	-.056	.054	.297	.007	.053	-.087	-.044	.067	-.136	-.046
N	265	262	265	265	265	265	265	264	259	258	251	251	246	259	259
EDU_YEAR		1.000	.136	.072	-.044	.020	-.064	.061	.112	-.028	-.022	.129	.011	.009	-.007
N		263	263	263	263	263	263	262	257	256	249	249	244	257	257
ADV_TECH			1.000	-.005	-.115	.005	.050	.015	.231	.087	.098	.106	.054	-.068	.029
N			266	266	266	266	266	265	260	259	252	252	247	260	260
SEC_3031				1.000	-.144	-.280	-.204	.023	-.028	.117	.126	.159	-.073	.143	-.024
N				266	266	266	266	265	260	259	252	252	247	260	260
SEC_33					1.000	-.305	-.223	-.136	-.095	-.077	-.181	-.031	.099	-.036	.033
N					266	266	266	265	260	259	252	252	247	260	260
SEC_34						1.000	-.433	-.067	-.076	-.315	-.201	-.181	-.105	-.030	.104
N						266	266	265	260	259	252	252	247	260	260
SEC_35							1.000	.152	.110	.295	.169	.017	.037	-.048	-.126
N							266	265	260	259	252	252	247	260	260
AGE_ENT								1.000	.145	.113	.111	-.055	-.094	-.015	-.079
N								265	259	258	251	251	246	259	259
LN_SIZE									1.000	.352	.374	.241	-.041	-.107	.049
N									260	253	246	246	242	254	254
CONTACT										1.000	.396	.308	-.019	-.119	-.143
N										259	250	250	241	253	253
NAT_BUSI											1.000	.178	-.032	.005	-.102
N											250	252	235	246	246
INT_BUSI												1.000	-.090	-.241	-.005
N												252	235	246	246
IM_FLEX													1.000	.076	.060
N													247	247	247
IM_PRIC														1.000	.081
N														247	260
IM_QUAL															1.000
N															260

Table A-5-2: Correlation matrix for reasons for using and owning fax

	IM_F_SPE	IM_F_BIN	IM_F_EAS	IM_F_EXP	IM_F_COM	IM_F_COS
IM_F_SPE	1.00000	.34119	.29454	.09621	.20271	.16540
IM_F_BIN		1.00000	.24509	.01184	.20100	-.02017
IM_F_EAS			1.00000	.27591	.18264	.06912
IM_F_EXP				1.00000	.39909	.21238
IM_F_COM					1.00000	.31292
IM_F_COS						1.00000

Table A-5-3: Correlation matrix for reasons of using cellular phone

	IM_C_EMP	IM_C_EAS	IM_C_STA	IM_C_COM	IM_C_EXP
IM_C_EMP	1.00000	.13362	.01975	.12998	.15962
IM_C_EAS		1.00000	-.00315	.29688	.33575
IM_C_STA			1.00000	.24031	-.14934
IM_C_COM				1.00000	.30584
IM_C_EXP					1.00000

Annex 6: Probit regression

A.6.1 Binominal Probit Regression

Binominal Probit regression is an appropriate technique to estimate models that re-gress on a dichotomous dependent variable.[*] The regression model is

$$y_i^* = \beta_0 + \sum_{j=1}^{k} \beta_j x_{ij} + u_i \tag{A.6.1}$$

with y_i^* being a not observable, so-called "latent" variable, x_j being the independent variables, b_j being the parameters of the independent variable x_j, and u_i being the dis-turbance term. Observed is a dummy variable y_i defined as:

$$y_i = \begin{cases} 1 & if \ y^* > 0 \\ 0 & otherwise \end{cases} \tag{A.6.2}$$

From these two relations we get:

$$P_i = Prob(y_i = 1) =$$

$$= Prob\left[u_i > -\left(\beta_0 + \sum_{j=1}^{k} \beta_j x_{ij} \right) \right] = 1 - F\left[-\left(\beta_0 + \sum_{j=1}^{k} \beta_j x_{ij} \right) \right] \tag{A.6.3}$$

with F being the cumulative distribution function of u, which is the Normal Distribu-tion in case of the Probit model.

In the case of symmetry of u, with $1-F(-Z)=F(Z)$, P_i can be written as such:

$$P_i = F\left(\beta_0 + \sum_{j=1}^{k} \beta_j x_{ij} \right). \tag{A.6.4}$$

Since the observed y_i are outcomes of a binominal process with the probabilities de-fined in equation A.6.4, the likelihood function can be written as:

$$L = \prod_{y_i=0} P_i \prod_{y_i=1} (1 - P_i) \tag{A.6.5}$$

For the Probit model P_i is specified as followed:

$$P_i = \int_{-\infty}^{\left(\beta_0 + \sum_{j=1}^{k} \beta_j x_{ij} \right)/\sigma} \left(\frac{1}{\sqrt{2\pi}} \right) \exp\left(-\frac{t^2}{2} \right) dt . \tag{A.6.6}$$

Denoting $\Phi(.)$ as the distribution function and $\phi(.)$ as the density function of standard normal the likelihood function for the Probit model becomes

---

[*] See Dhrymes (1986:1568-1579), Maddala (1992:327-329) and Maddala (1983:22-27), for the following derivation of the binominal Probit regression model.

$$L = \prod_{i=1}^{n} \left[\Phi \left(\beta_0 + \sum_{j=1}^{k} \beta_j x_{ij} \right) \right]^{y_i} \left[1 - \Phi \left(\beta_0 + \sum_{j=1}^{k} \beta_j x_{ij} \right) \right]^{1-y_i} \tag{A.6.7}$$

and the log-likelihood function

$$\log L = \sum_{i=1}^{n} y_i \log \Phi \left(\beta_0 + \sum_{j=1}^{k} \beta_j x_{ij} \right) + \sum_{i=1}^{n} (1 - y_i) \log \left[1 - \Phi \left(\beta_0 + \sum_{j=1}^{k} \beta_j x_{ij} \right) \right]. \tag{A.6.8}$$

If $S(\beta)^*$ is the differentiation of $\log L$ with respect to β, i.e.

$$S(\beta) = \frac{\partial \log L}{\partial \beta} =$$

$$= \sum_{i=1}^{n} \frac{y_i - \Phi \left(\beta_0 + \sum_{j=1}^{k} \beta_j x_{ij} \right)}{\Phi \left(\beta_0 + \sum_{j=1}^{k} \beta_j x_{ij} \right) \left[1 - \Phi \left(\beta_0 + \sum_{j=1}^{k} \beta_j x_{ij} \right) \right]} \phi \left(\beta_0 + \sum_{j=1}^{k} \beta_j x_{ij} \right) x_i, \tag{A.6.9}$$

maximum likelihood estimators $\hat{\beta}_{ML}$ for the parameters β can be obtained by finding solutions to $S(\beta) = 0$, which is done by an iterative process because the equations are non-linear in β.

A.6.2 Ordered Probit regression[**]

The regression model is similar to the binomial Probit model:

$$y_{ij}^* = \beta_0 + \sum_{k=1}^{l} \beta_k x_{ik} + u_i, \tag{A.6.10}$$

The latent variable y_{ij}^* belongs to the jth of m categories if $\alpha_{j-1} < y^* < \alpha_j$ ($j = 1,2,...,m$). So there is a set of ordinal variables:

$$y_{ij} = \begin{cases} 1 & if \ y_{ij}^* \in j \\ 0 & otherwise \end{cases} (with \ i=1,2,...,n, \ j=1,2,...,m) \tag{A.6.11}$$

From these two relations we get:

$$P_{ij} = \text{Prob} \ (y_{ij} = 1) =$$

$$= \Phi \left[\alpha_j - \left(\beta_0 + \sum_{k=1}^{l} \beta_k x_{ik} \right) \right] - \Phi \left[\alpha_{j-1} - \left(\beta_0 + \sum_{k=1}^{l} \beta_{kj} x_{ik} \right) \right]. \tag{A.6.12}$$

The likelihood function for this model is

---

[*]   With $\beta = \beta_0, \beta_1,... \beta_k$.

[**]   See Maddala (1983), pp. 46-49, for the following derivation of the ordered Probit regression model.

$$L = \prod_{i=1}^{n} \prod_{j=1}^{m} \left[\Phi\left[\alpha_j - \left(\beta_0 + \sum_{k=1}^{l} \beta_{kj} x_{ik} \right) \right] - \Phi\left[\alpha_{j-1} - \left(\beta_0 + \sum_{k=1}^{l} \beta_{kj} x_{ik} \right) \right] \right]^{y_{ij}}, \quad \text{(A.6.13)}$$

the log-likelihood function consequently is

$$\log L = \sum_{i=1}^{n} \sum_{j=1}^{m} y_{ij} \log\left[\Phi\left[\alpha_j - \left(\beta_0 + \sum_{k=1}^{l} \beta_{kj} x_{ik} \right) \right] - \Phi\left[\alpha_{j-1} - \left(\beta_0 + \sum_{k=1}^{l} \beta_{kj} x_{ik} \right) \right] \right].$$

$$\text{(A.6.14)}$$

To derive the parameters' maximum likelihood estimators equation A.6.14 has to be differentiate with respect to β and α_j and set to zero. The equations are solved by an iterative process.

Annex 7: Goodness of fit measures

A.7.1 Goodness of fit measures in Probit regressions

A.7.1.1 Chi-Squared statistic test

Examining the maximised log-likelihood values for the estimated model can test the validity of the used model. A Chi-Squared statistic test tests the hypothesis H_0 that the vector β (not including the constant) is zero. The test value is calculated by taking minus two times the difference between the log likelihood function (log L_Ω), which is maximised with respect to all parameters $\beta_0, \beta_1, ...\beta_n$, and the restricted log likelihood function (log L_ω), which is maximised only with respect to the constant β_0 (Greene 1998:446):

Chi-Squared test value: $\qquad \chi^2 = -2\left(\log L_\Omega - \log L_\omega\right) \qquad$ (A.7.1)

A.7.1.2 Pseudo-R^2 measures

Due to the non-linear nature of the Probit regression it is not possible to derive appropriate results by using the Ordinary Least Squares R^2. What can be done is to estimate a so-called pseudo-R^2 measures that display similar properties.[*] Two Pseudo-R^2 measures are displayed, the McFadden-Pseudo-R^2 and the Cragg and Uhler-Pseudo-R^2.

The McFadden-Pseudo-R^2 values are calculated from the maximised values of the log-likelihood function (logL$_\Omega$) and the restricted log-likelihood function (logL$_\omega$)[**]

McFadden-Pseudo-R^2: $\qquad R^2_{MF} = 1 - \left(\dfrac{\log L_\Omega}{\log L_\omega} \right) \qquad$ (A.7.2)

The Cragg and Uhler-Pseudo-R^2, as presented by Maddala (1983:40), also uses the maximised likelihood values:

Cragg and Uhler-Pseudo-R^2: $\qquad R^2_{CU} = \dfrac{1 - \left(L_\omega / L_\Omega\right)^{2/n}}{1 - \left(L_\omega / L_{max}\right)^{2/n}}, \qquad$ (A.7.3)

with $L_{max}=1$.

A.7.1.3 Prediction accuracy

Another goodness of fit measure is the prediction accuracy of the estimated Probit models. Considering the problems of interpreting R^2 measures, this is an important indicator for the validity of the tested model. Actual and predicted adoption and non-adoption is compared. All cases i with an estimated value $y_i{}^* \geq 0.5$ are predicted to be users, all cases i with an predicted value $y_i{}^* < 0.5$ are predicted to be non-users.

---

[*]   Pseudo-R^2 measures should assume values within the range between zero and one and have a higher value for better fit. However, the numerical value cannot be interpreted in the straightforward manner used in OLS estimation, i.e. share of variance explained, since the distribution of the estimated R^2 is not known (McKelvey / Zavoina 1975:112).

[**]   See Maddala (1983:40) and Dhrymes (1986:1585).

A.7.1.4 Comparing the results from 4.4.2

Comparing the goodness of measures for all six regressions reveals that the order is basically similar for all techniques (see table A-7-1). The exception is the ownership of fax where the prediction accuracy ranks relatively bad compared to other measures.

Table A-7-1 Comparison of goodness of fit measures

Dependent variable	Rank (from best to worst fit)			
	Chi-Squared test	McFadden-Pseudo-R2	Cragg/Uhler-Pseudo-R2	Prediction accuracy
FAX_OWN	2	3	3	5
FAX_USE	1	1	1	1
PAG_NOW	6	6	6	6
CEL_NOW	5	5	5	4
COMP_OWN	4	4	4	3
E_MAIL	3	2	2	2

A.7.2 Pseudo-R^2 measures in Tobit regressions

Calculation of R^2 measures is even more problematic for the Tobit model than for the Probit model. Veall and Zimmermann (1994) examine various R^2 measures for their appropriateness in the Tobit model. The easy to calculate McFadden-R^2, that was used for the Probit model, is not appropriate because it is only correctly used for discrete models. A well performing measure presented by Veall and Zimmermann is a modified measure based on a proposed R^2 measure by Aldrich and Nelson. The so-called Weighted Aldrich and Nelson-R^2 is defined as followed (Veall and Zimmermann 1994:490):

$$R_{ANW}^2 = \left(1 - \frac{N_1}{N} R_D^2\right) R_{AN*}^2 + \frac{N_1}{N} R_D^2 \qquad (A.7.4)$$

with N being the number of observations, N_1 the number of non-limit observations. R_D^2 is the simple correlation coefficient between the predicted and actual Y_i for the non-limit observations only (Dhrymes R^2, see Dhrymes (1986:1603)).

$$R_D^2 = \left[corr_{>0}\left(\hat{Y}_i^A, Y_i\right)\right]^2 \qquad (A.7.5)$$

R_{AN*}^2 is the normalised Aldrich and Nelson R2 measure with the log-likelihood and restricted log-likelihood values of the Probit part of the Tobit regression.

$$R_{AN*}^2 = \frac{2\left(\log L_\Omega^* - \log L_\omega^*\right)}{2\left(\log L_\Omega^* - \log L_\omega^*\right) + N} \bigg/ \frac{-2\log L_\omega^*}{-2\log L_\omega^* + N} \qquad (A.7.6)$$

Annex 8: Regression coefficients

Table A-8-1: Probit coefficients for Table 4-5

	FAX_OWN		FAX_USE		PAG_NOW		CEL_NOW		COMP_OWN		E_MAIL	
	Coeff.	t-ratio	Coeff.	t-ratio	Coeff.	t-ratio	Coeff.	t-ratio	Coeff.	t-ratio	Coeff.	t-ratio
Constant	0,5717	0,222	4,2597	1,301	-2,5722	-1,166	-3,8197	-1,684 *	0,5066	0,202	-4,9011	-2,041 **
AGE_CEO^2	0,0015	1,444	0,0027	1,992 **	-0,0001	-0,158	-0,0015	-1,663 *	0,0014	1,354	0,0003	0,347
AGE_CEO	-0,1493	-1,535	-0,2580	-2,041 **	-0,0059	-0,079	0,1171	1,469	-0,1200	-1,293	-0,0221	-0,271
EDU_YEAR	0,0328	0,425	-0,0814	-0,888	0,0968	1,303	-0,0019	-0,026	-0,0158	-0,207	0,1430	1,824 *
ADV_TECH	0,4679	1,638	0,9715	2,398 **	-0,0076	-0,032	0,1286	0,510	0,6569	2,118 **	0,0631	0,234
SEC_3031	-0,1249	-0,305	0,6271	1,206	0,3111	0,829	-0,3064	-0,796	0,2013	0,481	0,0427	0,095
SEC_33	0,4966	1,232	1,2153	2,472 **	0,7400	2,014 **	0,5035	1,357	1,1588	2,824 ***	0,4717	1,040
SEC_34	-0,1453	-0,421	0,6462	1,586	0,1094	0,355	-0,1310	-0,419	0,5606	1,599	0,5811	1,532
SEC_35	0,0466	0,126	0,6330	1,400	-0,0780	-0,238	0,0711	0,217	0,1496	0,408	0,2024	0,532
AGE_ENT	-0,0005	-0,034	-0,0137	-0,767	-0,0011	-0,084	-0,0224	-1,684 *	0,0074	0,484	0,0168	1,183
LN_SIZE	0,7512	4,969 ***	0,8427	4,386 ***	0,4208	3,276 ***	0,4815	3,635 ***	0,5625	3,769 ***	0,3894	2,817 ***
CONTACT	0,0000	0,008	0,0110	2,050 **	0,0073	2,566 **	0,0033	1,102	0,0002	0,045	0,0078	2,569 **
NAT_BUSI	0,0164	3,334 ***	0,0174	2,713 ***	-0,0021	-0,493	0,0040	0,932	0,0151	3,088 ***	0,0126	2,806 ***
INT_BUSI	0,0184	1,136	0,0429	1,531	-0,0251	-1,742 *	0,0344	2,313 **	0,0559	1,901 *	0,0462	2,643 ***
IM_FLEX	0,1422	0,618	0,7979	2,636 ***	0,1542	0,738	-0,4383	-1,936 *	0,0014	0,006	0,0793	0,336
IM_PRIC	0,2976	1,298	0,8235	2,942 ***	-0,2074	-0,986	0,3188	1,390	0,0125	0,054	0,0126	0,054
IM_QUAL	-0,1893	-0,745	-0,8173	-2,408 **	-0,2001	-0,849	-0,0689	-0,278	-0,0761	-0,305	-0,1395	-0,526

* significant at 10% level; ** significant at 5% level; *** significant at 1% level

Table A-8-2: Tobit coefficients for Table 4-8

	YE_FAX Coeff.	YE_FAX t-ratio	YEF_FAX Coeff.	YEF_FAX t-ratio	YE_PAG Coeff.	YE_PAG t-ratio	YEF_PAG Coeff.	YEF_PAG t-ratio	YE_CELL Coeff.	YE_CELL t-ratio	YEF_CELL Coeff.	YEF_CELL t-ratio
Constant	-13,040	-1,990 **	-15,568	-2,193 **	-4,0801	-0,820	-6,3649	-0,886	-2,7586	-0,759	-3,2721	-0,687
AGE_CEO^2	-0,0006	-0,224	-0,0017	-0,615	-0,0006	-0,326	-0,0006	-0,195	-0,0015	-1,074	-0,0017	-0,912
AGE_CEO	0,0862	0,380	0,1843	0,742	0,0093	0,053	-0,0177	-0,070	0,1098	0,851	0,1156	0,693
EDU_YEAR	0,2155	1,050	0,1290	0,590	0,0094	0,060	0,0525	0,230	-0,1518	-1,389	-0,1880	-1,282
ADV_TECH	-0,2570	-0,357	-0,1576	-0,203	-0,3236	-0,568	0,0431	0,053	0,1936	0,489	0,3469	0,668
SEC_3031	0,5211	0,482	1,1788	1,008	1,2710	1,421	1,3828	1,084	-0,0010	-0,002	-0,2142	-0,268
SEC_33	1,1184	1,005	1,3960	1,157	2,6467	2,913 ***	3,3591	2,644 ***	0,8767	1,425	0,9069	1,112
SEC_34	0,3101	0,338	0,5392	0,541	1,3026	1,712 *	1,4193	1,340	0,1182	0,236	0,2445	0,371
SEC_35	0,9788	1,041	1,3188	1,286	0,6907	0,880	0,7659	0,697	0,1596	0,309	-0,0573	-0,083
AGE_ENT	0,0501	1,286	0,0463	1,093	0,0318	1,068	0,0400	0,927	-0,0336	-1,547	-0,0553	-1,910 *
LN_SIZE	1,8291	4,677 ***	2,1831	5,191 ***	0,9017	2,962 ***	1,2932	2,993 ***	0,8204	3,879 ***	1,0763	3,910 ***
CONTACT	0,0056	0,674	0,0093	1,035	0,0199	3,125 ***	0,0308	3,361 ***	0,0042	0,920	0,0075	1,238
NAT_BUSI	0,0301	2,401 **	0,0363	2,686 ***	0,0016	0,165	-0,0029	-0,208	0,0083	1,232	0,0106	1,178
INT_BUSI	0,0324	0,898	0,0373	0,947	-0,0343	-1,086	-0,0692	-1,516	0,0479	2,585 ***	0,0612	2,418 **
IM_FLEX	0,8016	1,285	1,2040	1,798 *	0,5044	1,043	0,5741	0,833	-0,3234	-0,917	-0,6101	-1,336
IM_PRIC	0,5769	0,903	0,8133	1,184	-0,3088	-0,629	-0,5507	-0,790	0,5703	1,614	0,3556	0,781
IM_QUAL	-0,6295	-0,910	-1,2781	-1,723 *	-1,0599	-1,997 **	-1,6684	-2,195 **	0,0704	0,181	-0,1257	-0,250

* significant at 10% level; ** significant at 5% level; *** significant at 1% level

Table A-8-3: Regression coefficients for Probit and Tobit regressions in Table 4-15, Table 4-16, Table 4-17 and Table 4-18

	FR_FAX (FAX_USE)				FR_FAX (FAX_OWN)				EX_CEL_B				FR_EMA_B			
	Tobit		Probit		Tobit		Probit		Tobit		Probit		Tobit		Probit	
	Coeff.	t-ratio	Coeff.	t-ratio	Coeff.	t-ratio	Coeff.	t-ratio	Coeff.	t-ratio	Coeff.	t-ratio	Coeff.	t-ratio	Coeff.	t-ratio
Constant	-36,245	-1,263	4,2597	1,301	-46,809	-1,301	0,5717	0,222	-17611	-2,265 **	-3,8197	-1,684 *	-52,254	-1,297	-4,9011	-2,041 **
AGE_CEO^2	-0,0010	-0,090	0,0027	1,992 **	0,0031	0,227	0,0015	1,444	-6,5	-2,160 **	-0,0015	-1,663 *	0,0082	0,561	0,0003	0,347
AGE_CEO	0,1705	0,173	-0,2580	-2,041 **	-0,2605	-0,214	-0,1493	-1,535	521,1	1,938 *	0,1171	1,469	-0,6956	-0,523	-0,0221	-0,271
EDU_YEAR	-0,3294	-0,364	-0,0814	-0,888	0,2502	0,216	0,0328	0,425	-12,9	-0,056	-0,0019	-0,026	1,1812	0,945	0,1430	1,824 *
ADV_TECH	5,5119	1,777 *	0,9715	2,398 **	4,3490	1,114	0,4679	1,638	788,5	0,995	0,1286	0,510	1,3659	0,325	0,0631	0,234
SEC_3031	-1,3992	-0,286	0,6271	1,206	-2,3447	-0,388	-0,1249	-0,305	-2042,2	-1,660 *	-0,3064	-0,796	9,5438	1,403	0,0427	0,095
SEC_33	5,5296	1,113	1,2153	2,472 **	4,8887	0,785	0,4966	1,232	634,9	0,532	0,5035	1,357	9,8157	1,301	0,4717	1,040
SEC_34	3,2619	0,800	0,6462	1,586	0,5952	0,117	-0,1453	-0,421	-1823,2	-1,767 *	-0,1310	-0,419	6,3960	1,036	0,5811	1,532
SEC_35	7,7292	1,828 *	0,6330	1,400	6,4869	1,239	0,0466	0,126	-887,9	-0,854	0,0711	0,217	8,1302	1,315	0,2024	0,532
AGE_ENT	-0,1734	-1,031	-0,0137	-0,767	-0,1821	-0,870	-0,0005	-0,034	-10,3	-0,238	-0,0224	-1,684 *	-0,0092	-0,040	0,0168	1,183
LN_SIZE	10,132	6,124 ***	0,8427	4,386 ***	12,684	6,074 ***	0,7512	4,969 ***	1961,6	4,512 ***	0,4815	3,635 ***	6,8342	2,997 ***	0,3894	2,817 ***
CONTACT	0,1821	5,025 ***	0,0110	2,050 **	0,1654	3,647 ***	0,0000	0,008	15,9	1,718 *	0,0033	1,102	0,0991	2,090 **	0,0078	2,569 **
NAT_BUSI	0,2081	3,894 ***	0,0174	2,713 ***	0,2720	4,073 ***	0,0164	3,334 ***	2,1	0,147	0,0040	0,932	0,2284	3,087 ***	0,0126	2,806 ***
INT_BUSI	0,1845	1,148	0,0429	1,531	0,2105	1,069	0,0184	1,136	43,2	1,111	0,0344	2,313 **	0,5001	2,696 ***	0,0462	2,643 ***
IM_FLEX	-0,3383	-0,123	0,7979	2,636 ***	-2,1729	-0,623	0,1422	0,618	-965,0	-1,333	-0,4383	-1,936 *	0,3261	0,084	0,0793	0,336
IM_PRIC	6,9301	2,457 **	0,8235	2,942 ***	5,5384	1,555	0,2976	1,298	1051,3	1,429	0,3188	1,390	-1,0783	-0,286	0,0126	0,054
IM_QUAL	-1,9878	-0,651	-0,8173	-2,408 **	0,7185	0,184	-0,1893	-0,745	408,1	0,508	-0,0689	-0,278	-2,7800	-0,669	-0,1395	-0,526

* significant at 10% level; ** significant at 5% level; *** significant at 1% level

Annex 9: Tests for independence of samples

Table A-9-1: Non parametric test values for independence of user and non-user samples

		Labour productivity for 1998/99 (in Rs.)	Growth of labour productivity between 1997/98 and 1998/99 (in percent)	Net profit/loss (1998/99) in percentage of turnover	Change in profit margin between 1996/97 and 1998/99 (in percentage points)	Average monthly wage for employees in administration and management (in Rs.)	Percentage of graduates in management and administration	Turnover growth 1996/97 to 1998/99 (in percent)
Fax	Mann-Whitney U	5169	5934	5753	4409	7059	7052	5078
	Wilcoxon W	10947	14979	10031	7895	12312	12305	9449
	Z	-4.457	-1.128	-0.854	-1.487	-1.618	-0.842	-2.532
	Asymp. Sig. (2-tailed)	0.000***	0.259	0.393	0.137	0.106	0.400	0.011**
Pager	Mann-Whitney U	5811	5723	5691	3058	7190	6986	3989
	Wilcoxon W	20176	8726	16422	11836	21386	10727	15617
	Z	-2.072	-0.431	-0.318	-4.225	-0.793	-0.046	-3.936
	Asymp. Sig. (2-tailed)	0.038**	0.666	0.751	0.000***	0.428	0.963	0.000***
Cellular phone	Mann-Whitney U	4563	5479	5358	3612	6861	6306	4082
	Wilcoxon W	18258	8639	15369	12657	19902	19347	15257
	Z	-4.638	-1.091	-1.335	-2.706	-1.768	-1.514	-3.931
	Asymp. Sig. (2-tailed)	0.000***	0.275	0.182	0.007***	0.077*	0.130	0.000***
Computer	Mann-Whitney U	5668	5383	5214	3974	6812	6380	4886
	Wilcoxon W	9673	16558	7842	6252	10817	9950	8126
	Z	-2.801	-1.494	-0.722	-1.563	-1.322	-1.082	-2.249
	Asymp. Sig. (2-tailed)	0.005***	0.135	0.470	0.118	0.186	0.279	0.025**
E-mail	Mann-Whitney U	5323	5666	5613	4626	6252	7004	5367
	Wilcoxon W	19018	8669	8773	13272	20958	10745	16542
	Z	-3.246	-0.549	-0.414	-0.388	-2.239	-0.011	-1.241
	Asymp. Sig. (2-tailed)	0.001***	0.583	0.679	0.698	0.025**	0.991	0.215

* significant at 10% level; ** significant at 5% level; *** significant at 1% level

Table A-9-2: Mean ranks of fax ownership

	Fax owned by entrepreneur	N	Mean Rank
Labour productivity for 1998/99 (in Rs.)	no	107	102.31
	yes	144	143.60
	Total	251	
Growth of labour productivity between 1997/98 and 1998/99 (in percent)	no	97	121.83
	yes	134	111.78
	Total	231	
Net profit/loss (1997/98) in percentage of turnover	no	92	109.03
	yes	134	116.57
	Total	226	
Change in profit margin between 1996/97 and 1998/99 (in percentage points)	no	83	95.11
	yes	121	107.57
	Total	204	
Average monthly wage for employees in administration and management (in Rs.)	no	102	120.71
	yes	157	136.04
	Total	259	
Percentage of graduates in management and administration	no	102	120.63
	yes	147	128.03
	Total	249	
Turnover growth 1996/97 to 1998/99 (in percent)	no	93	101.60
	yes	136	124.16
	Total	229	

Table A-9-3: Mean ranks of pager use

	Pager used now	N	Mean Rank
Labour productivity for 1998/99 (in Rs.)	no	169	119.38
	yes	82	139.63
	Total	251	
Growth of labour productivity between 1997/98 and 1998/99 (in percent)	no	154	117.34
	yes	77	113.32
	Total	231	
Net profit/loss (1997/98) in percentage of turnover	no	146	112.48
	yes	80	115.36
	Total	226	
Change in profit margin between 1996/97 and 1998/99 (in percentage points)	no	132	89.66
	yes	72	126.03
	Total	204	
Average monthly wage for employees in administration and management (in Rs.)	no	168	127.30
	yes	91	134.99
	Total	259	
Percentage of graduates in management and administration	no	163	125.14
	yes	86	124.73
	Total	249	
Turnover growth 1996/97 to 1998/99 (in percent)	no	152	102.74
	yes	77	139.20
	Total	229	

Table A-9-4: Mean ranks of cellular phone use

	cellular phone used now	N	Mean Rank
Labour productivity for 1998/99 (in Rs.)	no	165	110.65
	yes	86	155.44
	Total	251	
Growth of labour productivity between 1997/98 and 1998/99 (in percent)	no	152	119.46
	yes	79	109.35
	Total	231	
Net profit/loss (1997/98) in percentage of turnover	no	141	109.00
	yes	85	120.96
	Total	226	
Change in profit margin between 1996/97 and 1998/99 (in percentage points)	no	134	94.46
	yes	70	117.90
	Total	204	
Average monthly wage for employees in administration and management (in Rs.)	no	161	123.61
	yes	98	140.49
	Total	259	
Percentage of graduates in management and administration	no	161	120.16
	yes	88	133.85
	Total	249	
Turnover growth 1996/97 to 1998/99 (in percent)	no	149	102.40
	yes	80	138.48
	Total	229	

Table A-9-5: Mean ranks of computer use

	computer used	N	Mean Rank
Labour productivity for 1998/99 (in Rs.)	no	89	108.69
	yes	162	135.51
	Total	251	
Growth of labour productivity between 1997/98 and 1998/99 (in percent)	no	82	124.85
	yes	149	111.13
	Total	231	
Net profit/loss (1997/98) in percentage of turnover	no	72	108.92
	yes	154	115.64
	Total	226	
Change in profit margin between 1996/97 and 1998/99 (in percentage points)	no	67	93.31
	yes	137	107.00
	Total	204	
Average monthly wage for employees in administration and management (in Rs.)	no	89	121.54
	yes	170	134.43
	Total	259	
Percentage of graduates in management and administration	no	84	118.45
	yes	165	128.33
	Total	249	
Turnover growth 1996/97 to 1998/99 (in percent)	no	80	101.57
	yes	149	122.21
	Total	229	

Table A-9-6: Mean ranks of e-mail use

	email used	N	Mean Rank
Labour productivity for 1998/99 (in Rs.)	no	165	115.26
	yes	86	146.60
	Total	251	
Growth of labour productivity between 1997/98 and 1998/99 (in percent)	no	154	117.71
	yes	77	112.58
	Total	231	
Net profit/loss (1997/98) in percentage of turnover	no	147	114.82
	yes	79	111.05
	Total	226	
Change in profit margin between 1996/97 and 1998/99 (in percentage points)	no	131	101.31
	yes	73	104.64
	Total	204	
Average monthly wage for employees in administration and management (in Rs.)	no	171	122.56
	yes	88	144.45
	Total	259	
Percentage of graduates in management and administration	no	163	125.03
	yes	86	124.94
	Total	249	
Turnover growth 1996/97 to 1998/99 (in percent)	no	149	111.02
	yes	80	122.41
	Total	229	

Table A-9-7 Mean ranks of adopter categories for fax ownership

	Adopter categories for fax	N	Mean Rank
Labour productivity for 1998/99 (in Rs.)	until 1992	24	64.27
	1993 - 1996	66	65.87
	1997 and after	36	58.64
	Total	126	
Growth of labour productivity between 1997/98 and 1998/99 (in percent)	until 1992	21	55.02
	1993 - 1996	62	56.49
	1997 and after	34	66.03
	Total	117	
Net profit/loss (1998/99) in percentage of turnover	until 1992	26	71.85
	1993 - 1996	67	57.22
	1997 and after	34	71.37
	Total	127	
Change in profit margin	until 1992	22	55.45
	1993 - 1996	58	49.93
	1997 and after	29	64.79
	Total	109	
Average monthly wage for employees in administration and management (in Rs.)	until 1992	27	71.98
	1993 - 1996	71	71.80
	1997 and after	41	65.59
	Total	139	
Percentage of graduates in management and administration	until 1992	25	56.18
	1993 - 1996	66	65.73
	1997 and after	39	71.09
	Total	130	
Turnover growth 1996/97 to 1998/99 (in percent)	until 1992	24	58.13
	1993 - 1996	64	58.82
	1997 and after	34	68.93
	Total	122	

Table A-9-8: Mean ranks of adopter categories for pagers

Adopter categories for pagers		N	Mean Rank
Labour productivity for 1998/99 (in Rs.)	1994 and 1995	16	53.88
	1996 and 1997	50	43.54
	1998 and after	21	37.57
	Total	87	
Growth of labour productivity between 1997/98 and 1998/99 (in percent)	1994 and 1995	16	46.91
	1996 and 1997	48	43.06
	1998 and after	18	32.53
	Total	82	
Net profit/loss (1998/99) in percentage of turnover	1994 and 1995	17	50.59
	1996 and 1997	51	44.78
	1998 and after	19	36.00
	Total	87	
Change in profit margin	1994 and 1995	16	43.22
	1996 and 1997	44	35.64
	1998 and after	15	39.37
	Total	75	
Average monthly wage for employees in administration and management (in Rs.)	1994 and 1995	17	43.56
	1996 and 1997	52	48.96
	1998 and after	24	45.19
	Total	93	
Percentage of graduates in management and administration	1994 and 1995	16	42.19
	1996 and 1997	53	45.28
	1998 and after	22	50.50
	Total	91	
Turnover growth 1996/97 to 1998/99 (in percent)	1994 and 1995	17	41.32
	1996 and 1997	49	41.87
	1998 and after	17	43.06
	Total	83	

Table A-9-9: Mean ranks of adopter categories for cellular phone

Adopter categories for cellular phones		N	Mean Rank
Labour productivity for 1998/99 (in Rs.)	1995	4	45.25
	1996 - 1997	39	46.85
	1998 and after	46	43.41
	Total	89	
Growth of labour productivity between 1997/98 and 1998/99 (in percent)	1995	3	45.33
	1996 - 1997	37	43.46
	1998 and after	41	38.46
	Total	81	
Net profit/loss (1998/99) in percentage of turnover	1995	4	51.13
	1996 - 1997	36	44.07
	1998 and after	50	46.08
	Total	90	
Change in profit margin	1995	4	36.88
	1996 - 1997	30	32.17
	1998 and after	39	40.73
	Total	73	
Average monthly wage for employees in administration and management (in Rs.)	1995	4	64.25
	1996 - 1997	44	43.89
	1998 and after	52	55.04
	Total	100	
Percentage of graduates in management and administration	1995	5	49.40
	1996 - 1997	40	48.42
	1998 and after	46	43.52
	Total	91	
Turnover growth 1996/97 to 1998/99 (in percent)	1995	3	50.00
	1996 - 1997	38	44.64
	1998 and after	43	40.08
	Total	84	

Table A-9-10: Mean ranks of adopter categories for e-mail use

	Adoption categories for mail	N	Mean Rank
Labour productivity for 1998/99 (in Rs.)	1995 - 1996	10	49.90
	1997	16	55.31
	1998 and after	55	35.22
	Total	81	
Growth of labour productivity between 1997/98 and 1998/99 (in percent)	1995 - 1996	8	33.31
	1997	14	36.64
	1998 and after	50	36.97
	Total	72	
Net profit/loss (1998/99) in percentage of turnover	1995 - 1996	10	42.00
	1997	19	41.13
	1998 and after	52	40.76
	Total	81	
Change in profit margin	1995 - 1996	7	34.43
	1997	16	34.59
	1998 and after	47	35.97
	Total	70	
Average monthly wage for employees in administration and management (in Rs.)	1995 - 1996	11	42.68
	1997	16	45.03
	1998 and after	56	41.00
	Total	83	
Percentage of graduates in management and administration	1995 - 1996	11	45.36
	1997	18	49.19
	1998 and after	52	37.24
	Total	81	
Turnover growth 1996/97 to 1998/99 (in percent)	1995 - 1996	8	34.44
	1997	15	43.80
	1998 and after	52	36.88
	Total	75	

Table A-9-11: Mean ranks of adopter categories for ICT use categories

	ICT use categories	N	Mean Rank
Labour productivity for 1998/99 (in Rs.)	telephone	45	78.51
	+ fax office	19	84.39
	+ fax machine	21	98.86
	+ computer	52	109.69
	+ e-mail	68	120.57
	Total	205	
Growth of labour productivity between 1997/98 and 1998/99 (in percent)	telephone	41	92.98
	+ fax office	19	124.50
	+ fax machine	18	102.28
	+ computer	50	95.35
	+ e-mail	63	88.10
	Total	191	
Net profit/loss (1998/99) in percentage of turnover	telephone	42	85.27
	+ fax office	19	103.47
	+ fax machine	19	118.58
	+ computer	53	102.05
	+ e-mail	67	102.85
	Total	200	
Change in profit margin between 1996/97 and 1998/99 (in percentage points)	telephone	32	71.83
	+ fax office	17	77.50
	+ fax machine	14	89.54
	+ computer	45	92.22
	+ e-mail	59	84.89
	Total	167	
Average monthly wage for employees in management & administration (in Rs.)	telephone	45	92.03
	+ fax office	18	111.89
	+ fax machine	23	108.48
	+ computer	59	108.65
	+ e-mail	72	119.33
	Total	217	
Percentage of graduates in management & administration	telephone	44	104.95
	+ fax office	18	73.03
	+ fax machine	20	112.93
	+ computer	55	108.07
	+ e-mail	70	105.61
	Total	207	
Turnover growth 1996/97 to 1998/99 (in percent)	telephone	41	78.87
	+ fax office	17	79.79
	+ fax machine	18	100.81
	+ computer	49	105.61
	+ e-mail	66	102.37
	Total	191	

Development Economics and Policy

Edited by Franz Heidhues and Joachim von Braun

Band 1 Andrea Fadani: Agricultural Price Policy and Export and Food Production in Cameroon. A Farming Systems Analysis of Pricing Policies. The Case of Coffee-Based Farming Systems. 1999.

Band 2 Heike Michelsen: Auswirkungen der Währungsunion auf den Strukturanpassungsprozeß der Länder der afrikanischen Franc-Zone. 1995.

Band 3 Stephan Bea: Direktinvestitionen in Entwicklungsländern. Auswirkungen von Stabilisierungsmaßnahmen und Strukturreformen in Mexiko. 1995.

Band 4 Franz Heidhues / François Kamajou: Agricultural Policy Analysis – Proceedings of an International Seminar, held at the University of Dschang, Cameroon on May 26 and 27 1994, funded by the European Union under the Science and Technology Program (STD). 1996.

Band 5 Elke M. Förster: Protection or Liberalization? A Policy Analysis of the Korean Beef Sector. 1996.

Band 6 Gertrud Schrieder: The Role of Rural Finance for Food Security of the Poor in Cameroon. 1996.

Band 7 Nestor R. Ahoyo Adjovi: Economie des Systèmes de Production intégrant la Culture de Riz au Sud du Bénin: Potentialités, Contraintes et Perspectives. 1996.

Band 8 Jenny Müller: Income Distribution in the Agricultural Sector of Thailand. Empirical Analysis and Policy Options. 1996.

Band 9 Michael Brüntrup: Agricultural Price Policy and its Impact on Production, Income, Employment and the Adoption of Innovations. A Farming Systems Based Analysis of Cotton Policy in Northern Benin. 1997.

Band 10 Justin Bomda: Déterminants de l'Epargne et du Crédit, et leurs Implications pour le Développement du Système Financier Rural au Cameroun. 1998.

Band 11 John M. Msuya: Nutrition Improvement Projects in Tanzania: Implementation, Determinants of Performance, and Policy Implications. 1998.

Band 12 Andreas Neef: Auswirkungen von Bodenrechtswandel auf Ressourcennutzung und wirtschaftliches Verhalten von Kleinbauern in Niger und Benin. 1999.

Band 13 Susanna Wolf (ed.): The Future of EU-ACP Relations. 1999.

Band 14 Franz Heidhues / Gertrud Schrieder (eds.): Romania – Rural Finance in Transition Economies. 2000.

Band 15 Katinka Weinberger: Women's Participation. An Economic Analysis in Rural Chad and Pakistan. 2000.

Band 16 Christof Batzlen: Migration and Economic Development. Remittances and Investments in South Asia: A Case Study of Pakistan. 2000.

Band 17 Matin Qaim: Potential Impacts of Crop Biotechnology in Developing Countries. 2000.

Band 18 Jean Senahoun: Programmes d'ajustement structurel, sécurité alimentaire et durabilité agricole. Une approche d'analyse intégrée, appliquée au Bénin. 2001.

Band 19 Torsten Feldbrügge: Economics of Emergency Relief Management in Developing Countries. With Case Studies on Food Relief in Angola and Mozambique. 2001.

Band 20 Claudia Ringler: Optimal Allocation and Use of Water Resources in the Mekong River Basin: Multi-Country and Intersectoral Analyses. 2001.

Band 21 Arnim Kuhn: Handelskosten und regionale (Des-)Integration. Russlands Agrarmärkte in der Transformation. 2001.

Band 22 Ortrun Anne Gronski: Stock Markets and Economic Growth. Evidence from South Africa. 2001.

Band 23 Patrick Webb / Katinka Weinberger (eds.): Women Farmers. Enhancing Rights, Recognition and Productivity. 2001.

Band 24 Mingzhi Sheng: Lebensmittelkonsum und -konsumtrends in China. Eine empirische Analyse auf der Basis ökonometrischer Nachfragemodelle. 2002.

Band 25 Maria Iskandarani: Economics of Household Water Security in Jordan. 2002.

Band 27 Dietrich Müller-Falcke: Use and Impact of Information and Communication Technologies in Developing Countries' Small Businesses. Evidence from Indian Small Scale Industry. 2002.

Hermann Sautter / Rolf Schinke (eds.)

Social Justice in a Market Economy

Frankfurt/M., Berlin, Bern, Bruxelles, New York, Oxford, Wien, 2001.
195 pp., num. fig. and tab.
Göttinger Studien zur Entwicklungsökonomik / Göttingen Studies in
Development Economics.
Herausgegeben von / Edited by Hermann Sautter. Bd./Vol. 9
ISBN 3-631-37773-8 · pb. DM 69.–*
US-ISBN 0-8204-5375-7

Latin American market-oriented reforms along the lines of the Washington
Consensus need to be supplemented by a number of social policies to
achieve a more equitable society. While there has been considerable progress
in enhancing the efficiency, much less has been made with regard to
improving the social situation. Germany has a long and successful tradition
of a social market economy. However, developments in recent years have
shown various pitfalls in the current economic and social security systems
and the need for appropriate adjustments. Therefore, Germany as well as
most Latin American countries have to look for new solutions to combine
social justice with economic efficiency. This volume address some of the
most pertinent problems in this respect.

Contents: "Social Justice" - its Meaning and its Implementation in a Market
Economy · Indicators of Social Justice in Latin America · The Institutional
Framework of a Social Market Economy · Harmonizing Equity with Growth:
The Role of Educational and Health Policy · Labor Market Problems · Old
Age Security

Frankfurt/M · Berlin · Bern · Bruxelles · New York · Oxford · Wien
Distribution: Verlag Peter Lang AG
Jupiterstr. 15, CH-3000 Bern 15
Telefax (004131) 9402131

*incl. value added tax, the current german tax rate is applied
Prices are subject to change without notice
Homepage http://www.peterlang.de